Who are the science fiction authors?
Are they as strange as the stories they write?
Do they live in the future?
Do they see beyond what the rest of us see?

In an effort to answer these questions, Charles Platt describes an amazing series of encounters with some of our most notable imaginative writers, from Asimov to Vonnegut. The journey from one author to the next takes us from New York City, through the Midwest, to Los Angeles, and then to England. And there are surprises and revelations all along the way.

In scope and ambition, liveliness and insight, it is comparable to Vasari's LIVES, Johnson's LIVES OF THE POETS, or the famous PARIS REVIEW interviews. And in the field of science fiction itself, there is nothing with which to compare it at all.

DREAM MAKERS

THE UNCOMMON PEOPLE
WHO WRITE SCIENCE FICTION

Interviews by Charles Platt

DREAM MAKERS

THE UNCOMMON PEOPLE WHO WRITE SCIENCE FICTION

INTERVIEWS BY
CHARLES PLATT

BERKLEY BOOKS, NEW YORK

DREAM MAKERS: THE UNCOMMON PEOPLE
WHO WRITE SCIENCE FICTION

A Berkley Book / published by arrangement with
the author

PRINTING HISTORY
Berkley edition / November 1980

ISBN: 0-425-04668-0

A BERKLEY BOOK ® TM 757,375
PRINTED IN THE UNITED STATES OF AMERICA

Acknowledgments

I am indebted to Tom Durwood and Armand Eisen, of Ariel Books, for unwittingly starting me on this project; to Harlan Ellison, Victoria Schochet, and Kirby McCauley, for helping me to obtain interviews which otherwise might have eluded me; and to *The Encyclopedia of Science Fiction* (edited by Peter Nicholls and John Clute), which I used in compiling the bibliographical material which is appended to each profile herein.

Most of all, I thank the writers who took the time to talk to me so willingly and openly about themselves and their work.

For my friends,

John, Judith, Marnie, and Simon

Contents

Introduction

WHAT KIND OF A NUT...?

It is natural for someone who reads science fiction to wonder who writes it. Pick a few books off the shelves in your local store, and what do you find? Most of the authors seem to be men. They have funny names (like Asimov, van Vogt, Budrys, and Moorcock). They invent a lot of obscure jargon, and they have far-fetched ideas which they seem to take very seriously. Do these people use drugs? Or are they, so to speak, normal, with wife-kids-mortgage and a Ford in the garage? Do they get rich? What are their intentions, as writers? How old are they? What do they *look* like?

I think this kind of curiosity is legitimate; after all, the relationship between reader and writer is in some ways quite intimate. But most critics and college professors usually feel that it is better practice, more "objective," to restrict their interest to the printed word and avoid speculating about the author who wrote that word. It is . . . not *proper* to ask questions like, what kind of a nut writes books like this, and can we pick up any clues about him by reading between the lines?

I confess I am bored by too much "objectivity" and by critics and academics who prefer to ignore the practical facts of how a novel is conceived, written, and published in the real world. I believe that if you really want to understand a book you cannot isolate it from its origins: the personality and motives of the writer, and the commercial constraints, financial pressures, and other influences poisoning or fertilizing the creative process. All these matters are relevant in the genesis of a work of fiction, and knowing about them will enhance the experience of reading the fiction itself.

BETWEEN CLIFF'S NOTES AND RONA BARRETT

Of course, it's a delicate business, intruding into a writer's life and compiling a profile based on a ninety-minute interview and some quick impressions of life-style and environment. When I conceived this project I immediately realized the embarrassing possibilities. Certainly it was a good idea to humanize the dull data in science-fiction bibliographies and study-guides. On the other hand it wouldn't do to become intrusively personal and end up like some mutant Rona Barrett, gleaning gossip and scouring scandal from the weird, wacky world of sci-fi-dom. Definitely not!

Also I feared that this project might create or contribute to any kind of personality cult. (Unlikely as it may seem, in the past ten years there have been embryonic cults developing around just a few science-fiction authors—mainly younger ones with connections in the media.) Any kind of cult strikes me as a distortion of reality, and even mild forms of hero-worship bother me.

But truth is a good antidote to cultism, and I think I am in a reasonable position to see where the truth lies regarding science-fiction people. I have known many of them for a long time, I've been a science-fiction writer myself, and I've held various editing jobs. At the same time, much of my other work has been outside the field. So perhaps I am sufficiently immersed in science fiction to understand it, but not so much a part of the scene that I have special loyalties.

In the profiles in this book, I have tried to be, as they say, balanced. Neither obsequious nor snide; not too inquisitive, but not too discreet. I never demanded information that an author was reluctant to give, and I only dwelled on topics that were relevant to an author's published work.

NO CENSORSHIP!

Purists may question to what extent the interviews in this book have been edited. It is true that some editing was done, to make the prose readable and coherent.

In each interview I taped between sixty and ninety minutes of conversation (about 5,000 spoken words). All of this was then transcribed from the recording, typed out verbatim. I preferred not to employ outside help to do the transcription, because I would have had no way of checking that the person who helped me was entirely accurate, and I regard accuracy as the first obligation of any writer of nonfiction. So I did the transcripts myself—about 150,000 words in all.

Next I surveyed and reshuffled this raw material in a cut-and-paste operation, to improve the flow of each interview without degrading its content or interfering with the characteristic speech patterns of the interviewee. For example, if someone referred to a particular subject, and came back to that topic later on, I would shift the two statements close together. Unnecessary hesitations and repetitions were excised, and I removed some passages which were simply dull. Occasionally I eliminated sentences which were mere preamble or lacking in real content. To a very minor extent I imposed grammatical structure (say, if a verb was missing from a sentence) but in no case did I add words that were not there, and in no case did I censor anything that seemed opinionated or controversial. Lastly, the authors themselves were given the chance of editing or amending their own profiles, but none of them made substantial changes.

THE GUEST LIST

Each chapter focuses on a different author. I tried to approach all of them as if I were a total stranger discovering everything for the first time. I visited the homes or workplaces of most of the people I talked to, and I include details about these environments because I think they are quite relevant to the author's persona and art, as well as being important to give my narrative a sense of place. The chapters are in geographical order, starting from the east coast of the USA.

Inevitably, there are omissions. Some famous names are not here because I was unable to meet and talk to them. Other names are not included because of my own personal bias. Compiling this book was like compiling a guest list for a party: I wanted to invite everyone, but there wasn't enough room, so I picked those who seemed to me to be most fun, most famous, or most friendly. I chose not to seek interviews with a few writers whose work I happen to hate (they probably wouldn't have wanted to talk to me anyway) and I chose not to interview any fantasy authors because I know very little about that genre.

In all other respects I have tried to show as little personal bias as possible.

SCIENCE FICTION AND HOME REPAIRS

The inspiration for this book dates back to my days as an instructor at The New School, a New York college specializing in adult-education evening classes. I taught science fiction and home repairs (in two separate courses) for several years. At first, there were serious problems in the science-fiction class. The credit students were taking it because it seemed an easy way to pick up three credits. The noncredit students were science-fiction fans who saw it as a social event, enabling them to meet other science-fiction fans. No one was very interested in working hard and studying the literature that I was supposed to be teaching. In fact what they most expected of me was entertainment.

My answer was to digress frequently into anecdotes about the science-fiction field, publishing, editors, and the various authors whose books we were reading. These anecdotes satisfied the demands of the class to be entertained; at the same time, the anecdotes were informative and naturally led into interesting questions, and answers, about the books in the course. Thus the class was saved from becoming so abstract and academic as to be boring, but at the same time it was not superficial.

I hope to strike the same kind of balance in this book.

ISAAC ASIMOV'S UNDERSHIRT

My first interview was with Isaac Asimov. It wasn't my idea; I was assigned to do it for *Ariel* magazine.

When I got home and started writing the piece I realized that I needed to do much more than merely transcribe the tape word-for-word. At the very least, it would help to know the manner in which answers had been given—hesitations, asides, and facial expressions—all the signals that would have been visible if a film had been made of the conversation. Moreover, it was foolish to pretend that I myself was not a part of it. Not only did Asimov's perception of my personality bias his responses to some small degree, but my own intelligence filtered the whole experience. And I had a few observations that seemed worthwile as additional commentary. Asimov's informality, for instance—during the interview his attire was very casual (old trousers, an undershirt), as if self-consciously denying any charismatic image. This was part of his personality, part of the whole picture. I included it, and other details—his fear of heights, favorite TV shows, obsession with days and dates, and so on. Out of all this I hoped would emerge a whole picture of the man. Anyone who experienced it would be closer to hearing Asimov's real voice when reading one of his stories.

I was reasonably pleased with the way it turned out (though *Ariel* required a rewrite, adding a bit more respect for the author and subtracting some of my lay-analyst inferences). I realized I could compile a whole series of profiles of science-fiction writers; no one else was doing it, and few other people happened to be able to reach such a diversity of writers (from van Vogt to Vonnegut, Budrys to Ballard). So I used the Asimov interview as a sample of what I had in mind, and added a description of what I planned to write in the rest of the book, and I submitted this to Harper & Row, a hardcover publisher that has done various academic works on science fiction in the past.

Harper & Row wasn't interested, so I tried Berkley, because I happened to know their new science-fiction editor. Publishing is a small world, and science-fiction publishing is a small nation in that world. Everyone knows everyone else, and what kinds of things each editor likes and doesn't like.

I received a positive response, amplified further by Berkley's sales department. It turned out that the book could be larger and more ambitious than I had originally imagined, and Berkley would be able to pay me correspondingly more.

Of course, thus far hardly anything had actually been written, and we were talking about a half-formed idea. Even now I still don't know how the book will be published—cover price, distribution, and so on. These details are important; they determine who will read the book. If it isn't widely distributed, or if it isn't reasonably priced, it will have a very short and limited life. And this in turn will affect what I next choose to write, or am forced to write by commercial pressures.

Thus everything depends on and influences everything else, and the process by which a book gets into print influences the nature of the book itself, and subsequent books. Even a collection of nonfiction essays is molded by the commercial world at the same time as its content is determined by the author.

(New York, April 1979)

DREAM MAKERS

Isaac Asimov

Twenty years ago most people outside the science-fiction field had never heard of his name. Today that name is on more than 200 books, plus so many short stories and articles that a complete listing of his work does not exist (despite valiant efforts by dedicated fans).

He went from science-fiction novels (*Foundation, The Caves of Steel*) to science-fact articles (more than 240 for *Fantasy and Science Fiction* magazine alone) to an endless proliferation of nonfiction books demystifying microcosm and macrocosm for the masses. He has authored exhaustive reference tomes, little pieces in *TV Guide*, quixotic items such as three volumes of "lecherous limericks," *The Sensuous Dirty Old Man*, a new annotated *Don Juan*, and now a 640,000-word autobiography (this work alone is as long as a dozen science fiction novels put together; longer than Nixon's memoirs).

He is one of the most prolific writers in history; so prolific that some reviewers decided his name must be just a pseudonym used by a whole consortium of authors pooling their collective energies. But in truth there is only one of him, and he works entirely unaided, typing the first and the final draft of each manuscript himself, handling his own mail, answering his own phone. He does it all with a very modest little reference library, a cheap pocket calculator, and a remarkable memory. His name, of course, is Isaac Asimov.

He lives in an expensive but characterless New York high-rise—one of those modular towers with little fountains out in front and plastic chandeliers in the lobby. The sprawling penthouse apartment that he shares with his wife, Janet, is on the 33rd floor, overlooking Central Park.

There is a comfortable, contemporary living room, but no time for more than a glimpse of it. With vague, awkward gestures (he is not a graceful man) Asimov ushers me quickly down a hallway to a door with his name on a plastic plate beside it, like an M.D.'s office. "In these two rooms is where I work," he tells me. "Even my wife must knock on this door, to come in. I always do say 'come in,' but she has to knock anyway."

This private Asimov zone is less fulsomely furnished. His writing room is almost primitive. A cheap gray metal desk stands in the middle, facing a blank white wall. There are stacks of neatly labeled metal drawers. Very tidy, very bare. The shades are down over the windows, obscuring what must be a fabulous view of the Manhattan skyline. "I prefer working by artificial light," he tells me.

In truth, this guide to distant galaxies, this seer of stars and spaceflight, doesn't like heights, won't ever fly in airplanes, and generally keeps as close to Planet Earth as possible. It's no deprivation, because he isn't interested in travel anyway. "In my mind I have gone all over the universe, which may make it less important for me to make piddling little trips. I did visit England, by ship, in 1974. I did enjoy seeing Stonehenge. It looked exactly the way I thought it would look." He shrugs.

We sit in his "library" (which contains fewer books than the living rooms of most authors I know). He makes himself comfortable in a wrinkled undershirt, as if deliberately wanting to seem unimpressive, uncharismatic. Still he has a conscious Presence, an obvious pleasure in being Isaac Asimov. He's blunt ("I hate giving interviews," he says, as I turn on my tape recorder), but in the forgivable manner of a crusty middle-aged eccentric. He makes me feel an intruder in his precisely scheduled working life, but at the same time he obviously likes to be available (his name is openly listed in the phone book) and even gregarious in a forced style, to the extent that work permits:

"I work every day from the time I wake up to the time I go

to sleep—with plenty of interruptions. For biological functions: eating, eliminating, sex." He counts them off on his fingers. "For social interruptions: well, you have to go out and see your friends." I say he makes that sound less entertaining than staying home typing. "If that's how it sounds, maybe that's what I mean. Then there are business interruptions, like business lunches." He looks at me. "*You* count as an interruption."

His social ambivalence and self-imposed work ethic go back a long way. "I had in many ways a deprived childhood . . . I had to work in my father's candy store, I didn't play with the other kids much, I wasn't accepted by them. But what I chiefly wanted to do was read, anyway. So it didn't bother me much."

Perhaps to compensate for the alienation that he never recognized or admitted, the teenage Asimov started a meticulous diary. At first it was purely to keep track of baseball—"A whole series of double-entry bookkeeping devices"—but when he sold his first science-fiction story at age eighteen, the diary—"Filled with microscopic writing"—started logging his career instead, still with the same obsessive attention to facts and dates and figures, a private reality where everything was neatly organized and itemized.

His first sale was to John W. Campbell, Jr., editor of *Astounding Science Fiction* magazine. "I fell under his spell . . . he filled me with enthusiasm. He made science fiction the most exciting thing in the world. I celebrate my fortieth anniversary of my first sale on June 21." And now, as we talk, he suddenly realizes: "Oh my goodness!" His voice rises in pitch. He slaps his cheek. "Is *today* June 21? Oh my goodness! Today is the fortieth anniversary of the first day on which I walked into a science-fiction magazine—*Astounding*—and met John Campbell! Oh my goodness." He sits back in his chair, looking stunned. "Oh that's frightening— I might have—I only have four hours more to remember it in!" (During our whole conversation this was the only time he showed any emotional reaction or loss of equilibrium.) He shakes his head and pulls himself together, with some effort. "Well, anyway, June 21, 1938 was the day I first walked into John Campbell's office, and this is June 21, 1978. Well, gee." *That* is the importance of facts, dates (and John Campbell) in Isaac Asimov's life.

Writing mainly for Campbell, he quickly gained a reputation among science-fiction readers. Many early stories were about robots; paradoxically he admits he knows nothing about engineering, couldn't fix his own typewriter if it went wrong, and was never good at laboratory work. "I'm strictly an ivory-tower person. I can explain things but I can't do things."

His ability to explain things was what finally made him well-known outside of science fiction; but it didn't happen quickly. "It wasn't until I was past forty that it was at all clear I was going to be, quote, successful, unquote." And he says he was never aiming for success anyway. "I was, if anything, less ambitious than my friends. In a way I aimed low. I was perfectly satisfied to write science fiction knowing it would pay very little, that it would be seen by very few people."

In his recent collection *The Bicentennial Man*, he wrote, "My only large interest is in writing. Selling is a minor interest, and what happens after that is of almost no interest." Sitting with him in his library, I quote this to him with some skepticism, but he remains adamant. "I don't care for instance if a book of mine is sold to the movies," he says. "I don't care if a book of mine is advertised or promoted. No, I really don't care. If my publishers for their own reasons are anxious to enlarge my audience I won't stop them. But I'm not sufficiently interested to goad them on to do so. I'm much more interested in writing my next book. As long ago as twenty years my first wife said to me, 'You can make a living if you just type for half a year, and we can have a vacation for the other half,' and I said, 'Sure, but during the vacation, just to give myself something to do, do you mind if I continue typing?' Last year I was in the hospital with my coronary for sixteen days. My wife brought in my manuscript of my autobiography so that I could edit it in pen and ink while I sat there. As soon as I was finished with that they had to discharge me because it was clear that sitting there with the job done was not going to be good for me."

I ask him how it feels to be *prevented* from working. "I suppose partly I feel guilty, because I should be writing. The writing is clicking away in my head and piling up, and unless I get it on paper somehow it's going to create uncomfortable pressure in my skull." Not a very clear explanation, from an expert in the biological sciences; and he seems to realize this. "It's difficult to say; I don't generally analyze how I feel," he apologizes.

He's much more lucid about objective matters. The facts and figures of the future: "My feeling is that the chance of our surviving into the twenty-first century as a working civilization is less than fifty percent but greater than zero. There are several items, each one of which is sufficient to do us in. Number one is the population problem. If we multiply sufficiently, then even if every-thing else goes right we're still going to ruin ourselves. Unfor-tunately it's difficult to make people see this, but I imagine that the time will come very shortly in which a third child will be outlawed, by prohibitive taxation, or forcible sterilization after the second child. Only two things will prevent this: One: If nonviolent means of reducing the birthrate prevail; in other words, if human beings *choose* not to have too many children. Two: If the popu-lation problem overtakes us so that the world is reduced to chaos and anarchy before we can even try drastic measures."

Is he generally pessimistic? "I'm pretty *optimistic* as far as the solving of problems that *don't* primarily involve human beings. For instance I believe it's not going to be very difficult to set up solar power stations in space to supply us with all the energy we need, if we're going to consider it as a technological problem. But if you say, Do you think we will be able to persuade Congress to supply money for it? And, Do you think we will be able to persuade the people of the world to drop their competitiveness and cooperate on a task which is perhaps too great for any one nation? Then you see the problem is perhaps impossible of solution."

I ask what people should do on a grass-roots level. He sighs. "Oh, join organizations. . . . *I* can't participate in a nuts-and-bolts way partly because I don't have the style, the manner of life for it." He looks uneasy and, again, I feel his estrangement, his preference for solitude and retreat. "I tend to send money to lots of people who ask me to send money. I belong to almost any population organization that you can name: Zero Population Growth, the Population Institute, National Organization of Non-Parents, and so on. Also I support women's rights, which I con-sider essential to our survival, because I think the most logical way to reduce the birthrate is to raise the social status of women."

He recites all this quickly and precisely, in sentences that are always grammatical and devoid of the hesitations that you hear in most people's conversation. He must have said it all before, in lectures, in print. It's probably all in one of his 200-odd books.

Before I leave he insists on showing me the 200, each volume neatly numbered and placed in chronological sequence: tangible evidence that you can make a private obsession become a public reality, that you don't need ambition or avarice to achieve success and wealth, so long as you have the willpower to apply your talents unrelentingly enough.

Yet it's not really a matter of willpower. Asimov's daily diary does sound like conscious self-surveillance, monitoring his own performance, and he does seem impelled to work by guilt and a sense of obligation; still it would require willpower for him *not* to work. The work is both his hunger and his feast. He enjoys the occasional diversion—he says he watches TV and his favorite sitcom is "Laverne and Shirley"—but you can tell that ultimately his true delight is retreating to his expensively spartan penthouse workroom, artificially lit at all times, like a basement. There, avoiding interruptions, avoiding self-analysis, he gets on with the job. He doesn't have to tell himself to keep at it, any more than he has to tell himself to keep breathing.

Work first, social obligations second, everything else third. This simple, rigid set of priorities is the "mystery ingredient" in Isaac Asimov's prolific success. For most of us, life is never so simple; our ambitions are mixed, our work lives, love lives, social lives, and fantasy lives compete and conflict, and our priorities fluctuate. Even when we think we know what we really want, we may secretly know that next year we could feel differently. Few can say, *this* is the most important pursuit in my life, and it always will be.

Asimov has apparently been able to say it about his work since he was a teenager. "I started writing in the 1930's when I was eighteen years old. And deep inside me I'm still eighteen and it's still 1938."

This lifelong sense of undeviating purpose and identity has earned him the most honorable kind of success, a measure of his toil, talent, and inspiration. Even more remarkable (for obsessed people are not always happy in their obsessions), his compulsive labors in the ivory tower seem to have brought him contentment.

(New York, June 1978)

BIBLIOGRAPHICAL NOTES

Isaac Asimov's science fiction about robots can be found in *I, Robot* and *The Rest of the Robots* (short-story collections), and *The Caves of Steel* and *The Naked Sun* (novels). There are also some recent short stories that at this time have yet to be gathered in one volume.

His "Nightfall" was voted the best science-fiction story of all time by the Science Fiction Writers of America, and has been anthologized widely.

He is famous for his trilogy of novels, *Foundation*, *Foundation and Empire*, and *Second Foundation*—an epic series that retells the fall of the Roman empire on a galactic scale. Published in book form in the 1950's, it originally appeared as a series of short stories in science-fiction magazines of the 1940's.

Since 1958 Asimov has devoted most of his energy to writing science fact, rather than science fiction. However, his novel *The Gods Themselves* won both a Hugo and a Nebula award in 1972, and his memorable collection of short stories, *The Bicentennial Man* (1976), demonstrates that he has by no means retired from the field.

Thomas M. Disch

New York, city of contrasts! Here I am on Fourteenth Street, walking past The New School Graduate Faculty, a clean modern building. Inside it today there is a fine museum exhibit of surreal landscape photography, but the drapes are permanently drawn across the windows because, out here on the stained sidewalk, just the other side of the plate-glass, it's Filth City, peopled by the usual cast of winos, three-card monte dealers, shopping-bag ladies festooned in rags and mumbling obscenities, addicts nodding out and falling off fire hydrants. Fourteenth Street, clientele from Puerto Rico, merchandise from Taiwan. And *what* merchandise! In stores as garish and impermanent as sideshows at a cheap carnival, here are plastic dinner-plates and vases, plastic toys, plastic flowers and fruit, plastic statues of Jesus, plastic furniture, plastic pants and jackets—all in Day-Glo colors, naturally. And outside the stores are dark dudes in pimp-hats and shades, peddling leather belts, pink and orange wigs, and afro-combs . . . itinerant vendors of kebabs cooked over flaming charcoal in aluminum handcarts . . . crazy old men selling giant balloons . . . hustlers of every description. And further on, through the perpetual fanfare of disco music and car horns, past the *Banco Popular*, is Union Square, under the shadow of the Klein Sign.

9

Klein's, a semirespectable old department store, was driven out of business by the local traders and has lain empty for years, but its falling-apart facade still looms over the square, confirming the bankrupt status of the area. While in the square itself—over here, brother, here, my man, I got 'em, loose joints, angel dust, hash, coke, THC, smack, acid, speed, Valium, ludes, Seconal, Elavil!

Union Square wasn't always like this. Michael Moorcock once told me that it acquired its name by being the last major battlefield of the American Civil War. Foolishly, I believed him. In truth there are ties here with the American labor movement: many trade unions are still headquartered in the old, dignified buildings, outside of which stand old, dignified union men, in defensive lunchhour cliques, glaring at the panhandlers and hustlers toting pint bottles of wine in paper bags and giant twenty-watt ten-band Panasonic stereo portables blaring more disco! disco! disco!

Oddly enough I am looking for an address, here, of a writer who is known in the science-fiction field for his civilized, almost elitist, sensibilities. He has moved into an ex-office building that has been converted from commercial to residential status. Union Square is on the edge of Chelsea, which is supposed to be the new Soho, a zone where, theoretically, artists and writers are moving in and fixing up old buildings until, when renovations are complete, advertising execs and gallery owners will "discover" the area and turn it into a rich, fashionable part of town.

Theoretically, but *not yet*. In the meantime this turn-of-the-century, sixteen-story, ex-office building is one of the brave pioneer outposts. I am admitted by a uniformed guard at the street entrance, and take the elevator to the eleventh floor. Here I emerge into a corridor recently fabricated from unpainted sheets of plasterboard, now defaced with graffiti, but *high-class* graffiti, messages from the socially-enlightened tenants criticizing the owner of the building for his alleged failure to provide services ("Mr. Ellis Sucks!" "Rent Strike Now!") and here, I have reached a steel door provisionally painted in grubby Latex White, the kind of paint that picks up every fingermark and can't be washed easily. There's no bell, so one has to thump the door panels, but this is the place, all right, this is where Thomas M. Disch lives.

Mr. Disch opens the door. He is extremely tall, genial and urbane, very welcoming. He ushers me in, and here, inside, it really *is* civilized. A thick, new carpet and a new couch and drapes and a fine old mahogany rolltop desk—and a view over Union Square, which is so far below that the dope-dealers dwindle to insignificance. It's charming! So is Mr. Disch, hospitably offering a wide variety of edible and drinkable refreshments. Not such an imaginative variety as is available from the natives in the square, but he offers them with considerably more graciousness and finesse.

New York, city of contrasts, also is city of high rents, so that even a relatively well-to-do, quite successful writer nearing forty has to resort to unlikely neighborhoods to beat the accommodation problem. But the point is, Thomas Disch has traveled so widely and is so adept at living almost anywhere, he makes the outside environment seem immaterial. It is Disch's nature to make himself at home by sheer willpower, never ill-at-ease or out-of-place, regardless of circumstances. Perhaps it is his tallness, perhaps it is his implacable control and elegant manners; he always seems to be both part of the environment and at the same time distanced from it, managing it with casual competence.

Similarly, in his writing: he has traveled widely, through almost every genre and technique: poetry, science fiction, nonfiction, movie scripts, mysteries, historical romances. And in each field he has made himself at home, never ill-at-ease or out-of-place, writing with the same implacable control and elegant manners.

Take, for example, his ventures into the science-fiction field. He has logged quite a few years in this literary ghetto. Yet he has always remained a visitor rather than a member, part of the environment and at the same time distanced from it, with his own ironic perspective. This has not always gone down too well with the ghetto-dwellers themselves—the long-term, permanent-resident science-fiction writers and fans. Some of them have been unhappy about an elegant aesthete like Disch "discovering" their neighborhood and using the cheap accommodation for his own questionable ends.

Disch's first novel illustrates the point. Science-fiction readers recognized it immediately as an aliens-invade-the-Earth story, in the tradition of H. G. Wells's *The War of the Worlds* and a thousand others. There was only one snag: in all the other novels of this type, Earth wins and the aliens are vanquished. In Disch's novel (cheerily titled *The Genocides*), Earth loses and the aliens kill everybody. It almost seemed as if Disch were deliberately making fun of the traditional ways in which stories had always been told in the science-fiction field.

Naturally, he sees it differently. "To me, it was always aesthetically unsatisfying to see some giant juggernaut alien force finally take a quiet pratfall at the end of an alien-invasion novel. It seemed to me to be perfectly natural to say, let's be honest, the real interest in this kind of story is to see some devastating cataclysm *wipe mankind out*. There's a grandeur in that idea that all the other people threw away and trivialized. My point was simply to write a book where you don't spoil that beauty and pleasure at the end."

To the science-fiction community, Disch's ideas about "beauty and pleasure" seemed a bit depressing, and they accused him, and have continued to accuse him, of being a pessimistic author. He responds:

"What sort of *criticism* is it to say that a writer is pessimistic? One can name any number of admirable writers who indeed were pessimistic and whose writing one cherishes. It's mindless to offer that as a criticism. Usually all it means is that I am stating a moral position that is uncongenial to the person reading the story. It means that I have a view of existence which raises serious questions that they're not prepared to discuss; such as the fact that man is mortal, or that love dies. I think the very fact that my imagination goes a greater distance than they're prepared to travel suggests that the limited view of life is on their part rather than on mine."

Comments like this lead, in turn, to other criticisms—for instance, that Disch is setting himself up as an intellectual.

"Oh, but I've always taken it for granted that I'm an intellectual," he replies ingenuously. "I don't think of it as being a matter of setting myself up.

"My purpose in writing is never to establish myself as a member of a club. I don't feel hostile to my audience, indeed I'm fond of it, but to write other than what delights *me* would be to condescend to my audience, and I think that would be reprehensible. I think any writer who reins in his muse for the sake of some supposed lack of intelligence or sophistication on the part of his readers is . . . well, that's deplorable behavior."

So Disch has consistently written at a level which pleases himself, and has consistently been misunderstood by science-fiction readers as a result. His novel *334*, a gloomy vision of America in the future, was if anything less well-received by such readers than *The Genocides*, and was condemned as being even more depressing—even nihilistic.

"Well, nihilism is a pejorative that people throw out by way of dismissing an outlook," he replies. "It was one of Agnew's words. Agnew loved it because it means that someone believes in nothing and, of course, we *know* we don't approve of people like *that*. But it also throws up the problem of what do *you* believe in. God? Is he a living god? Have you seen Him? Do you talk to Him? If someone calls me a nihilist I want the transcripts of his conversations with Jesus, till I'm convinced that we're not brothers under the skin."

And about the book *334* itself:

"I think what distressed some people is that it presents a world in which the macroproblems of life, such as death and taxes, are considered to be unsolveable, and the welfare system is *not* seen as some totalitarian monster that must call forth a revolt of the oppressed masses. The radical solution shouldn't be easier to achieve in fiction than in real life. Almost all science fiction presents worlds in which social reform can be accomplished by the hero of the tale in some symbolic act of rebellion, but that's not what the world is like, so there's no reason the future should be like that."

Is this an argument that all fiction should be relentlessly tied to present-day realities?

"I'm not saying that every writer has to be a realist, but in terms of the ethical sensibility brought to bear in a work of imagination, there has to be some complex moral understanding of the world. In the art that I like, I require irony, for instance, or simply some sense that the writer isn't telling egregious lies about the lives we lead."

I reply that it isn't necessarily a bad thing if readers look for some simplification of the eternal problems of real life, or at least a little escape from them now and again.

"People who want that are certainly supplied with it often enough. Of course there's no reason that artistry can't be brought to bear upon such morally simplistic material, but it remains morally simplistic, and to me it will always be a lesser pleasure than the same artistry brought to bear on morally complex material. The escapist reader wants a book that ends with a triumph of the hero and not with an ambiguous accommodation; I suppose I'm inclined to think that you can't have it that way. I don't know people who have moral triumphs in their lives. I just know people who lead, more or less, good lives.

"A literature that doesn't try to mirror these realities of human existence, as honestly and as thoroughly and as passionately as it can, is being smaller than life. Who needs it?"

Tom Disch was born in Iowa in 1940 and grew up in Minnesota, first in Minneapolis-St. Paul ("Always my growing-up image of the big city") and then in a variety of small towns. "I went to a two-room country school for half of fourth grade... finished fourth grade in the next town we moved to in Fairmount, Minnesota, which is in the corn belt...."

At the age of nine he had already started writing: "I filled up nickel tablets with science-fiction plots derived from one of Isaac Asimov's robot mystery stories. If we could find those nickel tablets I'm certain that the resemblance would be astonishing. But I think *my* stories were livelier even then." He laughs happily.

"I remember a moment in tenth grade in high school, talking to my English teacher—I was always the pet of my English teachers and made them my confidantes—and I envisioned two alternatives. One of them would have kept me in the twin cities on the paths of righteousness and duty (I can't remember what that would have been, exactly), the other was to come to New York and be an Artist.

"My first job after high school, after taking some kind of test at the state employment center, was with U. S. Steel as a trainee structural steel draftsman. I stuck it out through that summer till I'd saved enough money to come to New York. Then in New York I got the lowest type of clerical jobs.

"I wanted to get into Cooper Union, to the architectural school. My idea was to be Frank Lloyd Wright. Cooper Union did accept me. Even though the tuition was free, I still had to work as well, and in the end I just collapsed from overwork and possibly from lack of real ambition to be an architect. Architects have to study a lot of dull things for a very long time and I probably wasn't up to it."

Disch returned to college later, but: "The only purpose I had in mind then, for any degree I might have acquired, would have been to become an academic, and I thought it would be better to be a writer, so as soon as I sold my first story I dropped out of college."

Supposedly, a major factor that influences people to read a lot of science fiction, and then write it, is a sense of childhood alienation. I ask Disch if he had that experience. He is skeptical:

"*All* young people are prone to feel alienated, because that's their situation in life. Very often they haven't found a career, don't have a social circle they feel is theirs, and they feel sorry for themselves, accordingly. Certainly it is something real that happens to you, but with luck you work your way out of it and soon your social calendar will be filled and you won't complain about alienation any more. You'll get married. Very few married men with children complain about alienation."

Disch himself seems unusually gregarious, for a writer, and many of his projects have been written in collaboration with various other authors. His first collaborator was John Sladek. "We started writing together in New York in the summer of 1965, just short japes at first, and then two novels. One was a gothic which is best forgotten. The other was *Black Alice*." (A contemporary mystery/suspense novel.)

"My experience of collaborating with other writers is just mutual delight. One person has a good idea and the other says, that's great, and then what-if. . . . It builds. Writing in collaboration with a person whose work you admire—miraculously, sections of the book are done for you, it's like having dreamed that you wrote something, it eliminates all the real work of writing.

"I've planned other collaborations. I've worked with composers on a small musical and an opera, and I just like the process of it. I would like to write for movies. Other writers complain about the horrors of dealing with directors, but if it's a director one admires I would think that it would be exciting, and if it's not a director you admire then you shouldn't be doing it. It would be difficult to share my own most earnest novels; but for comic writing, for instance, I should think it would be so much more exciting to write for *Saturday Night Live* than just to write humorous pieces for magazines, however great your inspiration."

The range of people with whom Disch has worked reflects the range of different forms of writing that he is interested in. "Part of my notion of a proper ambition is that one should excell at a wide range of tasks. I want to write opera libretti; I want to write every kind of novel and story; I've written a lot of poetry and I will continue to do so. I foresee a pattern of alternating between science-fiction novels, and novels of historical or contemporary-realistic character."

I ask if he isn't worried that this will give him too diffuse an image in the minds of publishers, who are generally happier if a writer can be given a single genre label.

"Publishers do feel more comfortable with you if you are, in a sense, at their mercy. They prefer you to be limited as a writer. If you're a science-fiction writer who begins to write a kind of science fiction that isn't to the taste of a publisher whom you've been working with, they will in effect say, stick to what you know best, go back and write the kind of book that has made you successful. If you are a genre writer then genre editors can dictate to you the terms of the genre. In the long term they're asking for the death of the imagination, and a dreary sameness of invention, plots, and characters is the result."

Since Disch has managed to avoid being typecast in this way, I ask him which matters more to him—success and recognition in the science-fiction field, or outside of it.

"I would suppose that *any* science-fiction writer would rather be successful in the big world than in the small world. The rewards are greater. Not simply financially, but the rewards of public acclaim. If the approval of your peers means anything, then the approval of more of your peers must mean more. And not all of the palates that you want to tickle, the critics you hope to please, are within the science-fiction field. In fact the big judgment seat is outside of it."

I ask if Disch's best-known novel, *Camp Concentration*, was an attempt to achieve recognition outside of the science-fiction field.

"*Camp Concentration* was a science-fiction novel, and I think it was probably not strong enough to stand on its own outside the genre. Not as a work of literature. It might have been marketed as a middle-brow suspense novel—some science fiction is smuggled out to the real world in that disguise—but I think the audience outside of science fiction is even more resentful of intellectual showing-off, while within science fiction there's been a kind of tradition of it. Witness something like Bester's *The Demolished Man*, which was in its day proclaimed to be pyrotechnical. Pyrotechnics are part of the science-fiction aesthetic, and that's what *Camp Concentration* was aiming at.

"In America the novel didn't receive very much attention and it became the focus of resentment for some of the fuddy-duddy elements in science fiction to carp about. I never had enough success with the book to make me seem a threat and I'm not much of a self-promoter, so the book just vanished in the way that some books do. And that's not entirely a bad thing. The kind of success that generates a lot of attention can be unsettling to the ego, and the people who have that kind of success are often encouraged to repeat it. It would have been a very bad thing if I had bowed to pressure to write another book like *Camp Concentration*, which was the expectation, to a degree, even in myself. For a while I wanted to write things that were even more full of anguish, and even more serious."

Camp Concentration is, as Disch says, very serious and full of anguish. It is the diary of a character who is locked up and given a drug to heighten his intelligence; an unfortunate side-effect of the drug is that it induces death within a matter of months. The book thus presented a double challenge to Disch: he had to write the diary of a man who knows he is going to die, and he had to write the diary of a man whose intelligence is steadily increasing to superhuman levels. In a way it was a self-indulgence—a conscious piece of self-analysis—in that Disch himself is aware of his intelligence to the extent that it is something of a fetish.

While he was working on *Camp Concentration*, he confided to Michael Moorcock (as Moorcock tells it), "I'm writing a book about what everyone wants the most."

To which Moorcock replied: "Really? Is it about elephants?"

"Elephants? No, it's about becoming more intelligent."

"Oh," said Moorcock. "What I've always wanted most is to be an elephant."

Talking to Tom Disch, I recount this anecdote, if only to check on its accuracy. Disch laughs and comments, "Well, I guess Mike Moorcock and I have both realized our secret dreams."

(New York, April 1979)

BIBLIOGRAPHICAL NOTES

Disch's first novel, *The Genocides*, was published in 1965. It describes the seeding of Earth with vast alien plants which transform the ecology and render civilized existence impossible. Human survivors who attempt to fight back are exterminated as pests. Disch's subsequent novels have depicted equally inhumane environmental and social conditions. *Camp Concentration* appeared in 1968; his next serious science-fiction work was *334* (1972), a complexly linked set of vignettes depicting a near-future New York City in which life is somewhat bleak. Most recently, *On Wings of Song* (1979) is a fantasy which deals seriously with questions of freedom, creativity, and the human spirit.

Disch's output of short stories has been constant and considerable. A good selection is published in *Getting Into Death* (1976) and *The Early Science Fiction Stories of Thomas M. Disch* (1977)

Robert Sheckley

Robert Sheckley reclines amid the disorder of his high-rent Manhattan living room. He's only lived here for a few months. All around him, on the floor and on the new couch which opens out to form a kind of upholstered mattress that you can sprawl across while stoned, there are cassette tapes, magazines, stray items of clothing, cat toys, manuscripts, and books. It's like a rock musician's apartment: an expensive three-level west-village conversion, all white walls and maple floors, housing someone who doesn't take luxury too seriously. "I could move to a tenement in the east village tomorrow and not miss this place at all," he says. And it's obviously true.

Sheckley, at fifty-one, remains an unpretentious bohemian figure, engagingly vague, charmingly unchic. One senses reserves of shrewdness behind his apparent naivety, and maybe even a little ambition behind his antimaterialism; nevertheless he still seems to be wandering haphazardly through life much as his science-fictional heroes stumble around the galaxy, confused, disoriented, and surprised at every turn.

I first met him at a publishing party. It was late and he was quite stoned. We exchanged a few words of mutually inarticulate conversation after which he said, with apparent sincerity, "I feel as if I know you." During the next hour I heard him say exactly the same thing to three other strangers in succession, but I have no doubt he was sincere every time.

Indeed, Robert Sheckley has a habitual, self-conscious air of sincerity, the catch being that he's a relativist whose sincere beliefs are liable to fluctuate from moment to moment. He not only sees the other side of each question, he sees that it's valid and he'll willingly defend it. His ultimate belief seems to be that you shouldn't believe any one thing too singlemindedly; uncertainty is the only thing of which you can be certain.

This shows up in his fiction, which explores a potpourri of philosophical possibilities but suggests at the same time you shouldn't take any of this stuff too seriously. Sheckley the relativist likes to try all manner of beliefs; Sheckley the satirist pokes fun at all of them, and at himself for having been so gullible as to try them in the first place.

His early ambitions were characteristically modest and ambivalent. "I grew up at the time of pulp magazines," he says, "and my fantasy was to become an anonymous pulp writer, one of those guys who turned out cheap detective fiction, *The Black Mask* and all that. I think I was just being self-protective really, because at the same time I was very much into art. I went back and forth between *The Black Mask* and Nietzsche. I had the ideal of being an anonymous craftsman, but that's absurd, because the game is self-aggrandizement."

I ask how he ultimately reconciled this contradiction.

"I'm not sure that I ever did," he says, sounding skeptical of the very idea of resolving any problem permanently. "I guess what I tried to do was reevaluate my idea of what craftsmanship meant. I tried to do it on a higher level."

Craftsmanship on a high level certainly characterized his early output of urbane, witty short stories, many of which appeared in *Galaxy* magazine in the 1950s when it was under the editorship of Horace Gold. "Horace was part of a whole life style for me then," he recalls. "Writing short stories was a part of that style also. You just naturally wrote a story for Horace because you were part of Horace's circle, along with Jerome Bixby, Algis Budrys, Phil Klass (William Tenn), Cyril Kornbluth, Frederik Pohl, Evelyn Smith, Damon Knight, and I'm sure there were a lot more. For some years we had a weekly poker game, almost every Friday night; that was our main social point."

Sheckley's fiction often seemed more sophisticated in its pre-conceptions than that of his contemporaries in the 1950s, and more rooted in real life. I ask if he saw it that way at the time.

"I felt that I wasn't really writing science fiction. I was in some way writing a commentary *on* science fiction, and this sometimes made me feel, a little sadly, that I was not really into it. But I didn't think about this a whole lot. I've never been very much into labeling; I guess it was easier for me to simply write what I wrote and not try to label where I was at.

"I was certainly the resident skeptic. I could and would argue any side of any question. But that was because it was a game of words. I've never, had strong convictions about things because I see how fast they change, and there is something to be said on all sides of any topic."

In due course Horace Gold ceased editing *Galaxy* and to some extent the circle of writers fragmented. Sheckley's output of short stories began to diminish, and in the late 1960s he left the United States and went to live on the island of Ibiza off the coast of Spain. During the next six or seven years he wrote very little and seemed to have retired from the science-fiction field. I ask him what precipitated all of these changes.

"I don't know that one ever thinks these things out. You just sort of feel—oh, the story ideas don't seem magical any more, or they slow down, you don't get them any more in the same way. I was changing, also; I was having marital breakups, they certainly had an enormous effect on me . . . there were a lot of reasons why I finally left the United States, but it didn't feel as if I had any specific reasons at all. I just didn't feel connected with anything here. It felt like there was no reason I should *stay* here.

"What I became a part of, instead, was the expatriate life, and for some years I really felt that those were my people. We were fallout from the hippie generation, slightly longer in the tooth. We were still playing Neil Young records and looking at that big moon up in the sky and trying to love one another still and live a decent clean life off the land." He laughs at his own nostalgia. "Long hair, long skirts, and natural foods. This went on into the early seventies.

"The first thing I wrote at that time was *Options*. It's my mad book. It does not add up at all. It mixes science fiction and surrealist and absurd motifs—to minimum effect!

"Then I got really jammed up. I'd been writing less and less for years, and when I got over to Spain it all stopped. Just about the only stories I was doing were stories which Harry Harrison used to ask me to do.

"Money was always a minor problem. I got in a certain amount of royalty income—not much, because a lot of my books were out of print. But with that, plus a few sales here and there, you could get by. In fact I would have had a really good time, but I was obsessed with my writing problem, so I was not able, except in spells, to lean back and enjoy this very handsome island I was on."

In the end Sheckley left Ibiza and moved to London, England.

"I wasn't unblocked but I worked at it hard and I started getting out some work. And now I'm back in New York and I feel a part of science fiction and I'm happy to be that way. I'm in a better place than I was before. I'm working for *Omni*."

Sheckley accepted the job of fiction editor for *Omni* magazine early in 1980. "I wanted to use some of my skills in a social context. I was getting very sick of being a solitary, isolated writer. I've been doing that for twenty-eight years, from age twenty-two onward. I had had an interest for some while in teaching or something like that. When the *Omni* job came along I had a 100-percent 'yes' response.

"I was very interested to find out what people are writing now. One tends every year to read less and less; it's the encroachment of professionalism, which can have a very bad effect on you. When we started in science fiction we read for pleasure, and then when we started to sell our work we read in order to see what the other boys were up to, and if you ever get confident enough to stop reading what the other boys are up to you find that you don't want to read anything at all except an occasional newspaper or your favorite hobby magazine.

"One thing which I have realized is that it is now harder to write science fiction than it used to be. There's a critique on science fiction by Stanislaw Lem, who raises several good points. One of them is that science fiction has no common, shared background now as it did in the 1930s, 1940s, and even the early 1950s. There were certain background assumptions, then, that you could work with. I think writers started having background trouble once you could no longer put your characters on our solar system's planets. Once you could no longer explore the 'green hell of Venus' something went out, because you had to go out to a new star system altogether, and invent a new planet, and waste a certain amount of head space on what the planet was like, its special characteristics, how you get there, and all that. People hate wasting that much imagination on a short story. When your background takes that much creative energy, and it's that unknown to the reader, another thing that happens is that your foreground suffers from lack of attention. A lot of my early stories were foreground actions with lightly sketched, borrowed backgrounds—future Earths, for instance, that other people had already written about. But things were much simpler then; you could have a future Earth projected simply on the basis of a population increase. These days, setting up a future Earth is a much more major undertaking; you must add in fuel, energy, greenhouse effect, radioactive stuff, all that. Today, I wouldn't even know where to borrow a background from. Whereas I once used other writers' assumptions about things, now everybody rolls his own—usually rather sparsely. And when somebody actually uses all of his brain power and invents a new world, he's in no hurry to let go of it. He's going to write novel after novel exploring the aspects of his thing, and he won't even bother with short stories. And I don't blame him, but for me this does not add up to a good fictional situation. Fiction about *what?* What's science fiction *about*, now?

"A lot of the stories we were doing in the 1950s were *reversals* of standard themes. This doesn't happen now. People are just exploring their own themes, straight. And some of these themes I think are somewhat naive. There's a new sensibility starting to emerge in science fiction now—a much more serious sensibility than we had in the 1950s. People are really *concerned* about things. As an editor, I get a lot of apocalyptic stories; that's very much in people's heads now. Unfortunately, it's only one plot; a lot of writers are doom laden or doom haunted now. But for the purposes of there being a valid fiction, the dance must go on."

Throughout this he seems to be identifying himself with the other writers of the 1950s. And yet I still can't see him fitting in naturally with his more conservative contemporaries from that period. Wasn't he more nonconformist than they were then, and isn't he even more so than they are today?

"Well, I'm certainly not like a lot of people. My life is not the same as a guy, say, who has a house and a family. I could never sustain that sort of role for long; I don't seem to take well to being too settled. But you know these days I don't even know who my 'contemporaries' are. I see people like Norman Spinrad or Tom Disch, so I think of those guys as my contemporaries. But they're all very strange people. I feel quite normal by comparison."

I ask if Sheckley ever had an alternative vocation to writing.

"The only other thing that I did was I was a semiprofessional rhythm guitar player. I played in high school bands, dance bands in the service, and some bands in the San Francisco area when I got out of the service. You see I was in the Korean occupation, in the infantry, stationed on the thirty-eighth parallel. I was a volunteer. I volunteered, to get it over with. I turned eighteen around the end of World War II, and you could join at that time for eighteen months, so I joined. Throughout all the war years I had dreamed I was going to join the army and go over there and shoot enemies. I was quite patriotic."

I ask how this attitude gave way so quickly to the cynicism of his short stories.

"Well, I was wising up fast, of course," he says, deadpan. "No, that was really high school stuff back then; you know, when you're young you try a lot of attitudes on for size. I tried dance bands, dance *class*, patriotism, Nietzsche, I tried to learn Sanskrit, and so forth. I was this shy, nervous, bright kid, spouting adult-sounding theories, but a little socially backward or unsure. Some of it I think was shyness, some of it also was that I never had a great taste for a lot of friendly boozing conversation. It's a little too low-key for me. So, I was a cynic even back in high school, really. I could just about quote the works of Oscar Wilde, and Ambrose Bierce was my man, and H. L. Mencken.

"When I look back at the reasons why I've done anything, it just seems like things left no other choice. It wasn't a question of motivation. Life to me is like falling down stairs; you keep falling through situations; you put out your hand to keep from banging against the wall—and you find you're married; you put up a foot to keep from tripping—and you're unmarried, and you have alimony payments; and the next thing you know you win some sort of prize—but it's all free fall."

I comment that this sounds as if he does not believe in the idea of purposeful thought and action.

"Sanity lies in knowing that *you didn't do it*," he replies. "For example, a lot of the very best artists claim that they are not really responsible for their own work, that they are just plain people who get up there and paint or sing, with someone else directing the operation. You can make a case for art simply happening; there's no 'who' making it do so. Maybe I'm overstating my case here, but if I suddenly get three ideas which cross and synthesize into a story, is that something I've done? To me, it's something that's happened *to* me. I am the recipient of a story I can write, but I haven't planned it."

Surely, however, he accepts the idea of determinism in some areas of life.

"No. I'm a very casual philosophy student, but I've long been struck by David Hume, who came out with the statement 'Sequence does not imply causality.' I think that's sort of where it's at. We infer causal changes which are compounded largely of our fantasies."

I comment that I don't agree with him.

"Well, I don't know whether I agree with myself," he answers. "I'm still exploring this. It's complicated, because you can't say 'There are no motivations' and just sit back on your ass. You have to exercise free will whether there is any or not, really. If for no other reason than for your health's sake."

I realize at this point that our conversation has veered well away from science fiction in general and Robert Sheckley in particular. It has become the kind of slightly serious, slightly flippant conceptual debate that I think Sheckley particularly enjoys.

Trying to get back to my own interest in conducting interviews with writers, I say that the aspect of free will which concerns me here is writers' motivations. I'm curious as to why people do things.

"Yes." He nods, in complete agreement. "But do you think you ever find out?"

(New York, March 1980)

BIBLIOGRAPHICAL NOTES

Robert Sheckley probably remains best known for his short stories. His first collection was *Untouched by Human Hands* (1954), establishing the wry, witty tone and contemporary flavor which was to be developed with increasing sophistication in his subsequent work. This collection includes "Seventh Victim" which was later made into a movie retitled *The Tenth Victim* (1965), describing a comic/horrific future in which death duels have been legalized.

Other well-known Sheckley story collections include *Citizen in Space* (1955), *Pilgrimage to Earth* (1957), *Store of Infinity* (1960), and *Shards of Space* (1962). Most of the stories in these volumes still seem fresh and undated. His novels, such as *The Journey of Joenes* (1962, titled *Journey Beyond Tomorrow* in Britain) and *Mindswap* (1966) are typically episodic, subjecting a naive central character to a series of dire, comic crises with obvious parallels in twentieth-century life.

Sheckley's most recent novel is *Crompton Divided*, (1978), recapitulating some of his earlier themes in significantly more sedate style. His latest short story collection is *The Robot Who Looked Like Me* (1978).

*Photo by
Wide World Photos*

Kurt Vonnegut, Jr.

For more than fifteen years, Kurt Vonnegut was a victim of the genre system of modern publishing. His books were labeled "science fiction" and were distributed as science fiction. Bookshops displayed them only on the science-fiction shelves, where respectable readers seldom ventured. During this period, which must have seemed interminable and horribly unrewarding, Vonnegut's novels (including *Player Piano, The Sirens of Titan,* and *Cat's Cradle*) were known only to the science-fictions fans—and even the reception here was lukewarm, as they suspected him of poking fun at some aspects of their genre (its jargon, in particular).

Then *Slaughterhouse Five* appeared at the end of the 1960s. Suddenly, everyone knew about Kurt Vonnegut. His early work was brought back into print, and it migrated from the science-fiction shelves to the "modern literature" section—where it was discovered by apostles of the counterculture, who adopted Vonnegut as a bashful new folk hero. His work became mandatory reading in college courses coast-to-coast, he went on lecture tours, and he renounced the science-fiction genre which had trapped him in obscurity. *Slaughterhouse Five* was made into a movie, and he received some of the critical appreciation that had been lacking for so long.

Today, the critics are not always so kind to his new work, but Vonnegut no longer needs to worry. Each new book, he says, has an assured sale regardless of how it is reviewed, and the old novels continue to earn royalties. He doesn't have to write short stories for a living any more—in fact he *refuses* to write short stories. He is free to produce perhaps one novel every eighteen months, dividing his time between a residence in Cape Cod and a town-house in Manhattan, which he shares with photographer Jill Kre-mentz.

This is where I went to visit him: a fine, imposing residence in the East 40s, renovated and restored in impeccable taste (cream-and-beige decor, unblemished parquet floors, oriental rugs, mod-ern but unostentatious furniture, just like advertisements in *The New Yorker*). Vonnegut himself looks as if he doesn't quite belong here—he could do with a little renovation and restoration him-self—but that's his public image, of course, the dissipated Einstein look-alike of literature, in garage-sale clothing of middle-aged style and vintage: sleeveless navy-blue sweater, nondescript shape-less grayish-brownish trousers with cuffs, and decaying sneakers.

He makes himself comfortable on a couch in a room upstairs where there is a large TV set, videotape recorder, capacious soft chairs, and many bookshelves. There are no fancy, leather-bound collectors' editions, or antique library ladders, or gilt-framed oil paintings, or other pretentious frills; everything is functional; this is New York City at its most civilized.

A small shaggy dog stretches out beside Vonnegut's knee and becomes comatose. We begin talking. His conversation is spotted with literary references (a kind of erudite name-dropping); he speaks very slowly, with long pauses, smokes a lot, and often scratches his disheveled curly hair. His voice is dry, and so is his humor; at times it is impossible to gauge how serious he is. He says that this is probably the only interview he will give this year. But there have been many interviews in the past—too many, perhaps—and it must be tempting to invent some new answers to the old questions, to make things more interesting, or simply to be playful. I sense a mixture of whimsy, black humor (he laughs loudest when he mentions death), capriciousness, and craziness; but it's all put across in such wonderfully deadpan style, and with such charm, it's impossible to say where sincerity ends and play-fulness begins.

For instance, when I ask him how he feels about science fiction now:

"It's a social milieu. I went to a writers' conference in Pennsylvania years and years ago; they invited me and were glad I came. We got along fine as people, except that I didn't belong to their profession, because I couldn't talk about it. The problem is that I haven't done my homework. I haven't read all the stuff that they have read. I'd hang around the drugstore like anybody else, as a kid, and I was always aware of the science-fiction magazines in the racks, but it never interested me much. You see, one thing that kept me from reading those pulp magazines, was that the *paper* was so unpleasant to touch." He pauses thoughtfully. "It was full of brown specks. Very unappetizing." And he chuckles, as if enjoying the absurdist answer he has just given me.

I ask if he feels that any of his books should have won one of the science-fiction awards that are voted each year. "I thought I should have won several times," he says, sounding considerably more serious, now. "I'm proud of *The Sirens of Titan*, and I thought it should have won that year. It was nominated. But Harlan Ellison said, 'You'll never win, the only way you can win is to have the book serialized in a science-fiction magazine, so forget about it.'" He shrugs.

Does he feel that his lack of acceptance by the science-fiction community had anything to do with the unseriousness in his books, which seemed almost to be satirizing science fiction?

"I can't imagine how you would *satirize* science fiction," he says, in apparent puzzlement. "Unless you were to demonstrate how badly written most of it is." There is a pause, as his mind wanders ahead. "There's a guy named Philip José Farmer—I've never met him but he's a real meat-and-potatoes science-fiction writer, a very nice guy from all reports, and prolific. He asked me again and again, in the mail and through my publisher, if he could please write a 'Kilgore Trout' novel."

(Kilgore Trout is a fictitious character whom Vonnegut has included in several of his books. Trout is a wretched, deteriorated small-town journalist who produces reams of science fiction in his spare time and remains unknown, partly because his work is so atrociously written, and partly because it is distributed only through pornographic bookstores. Farmer wanted to adopt 'Kilgore Trout' as a pseudonym and bring to life one of Trout's imaginary novels.)

"I finally told him to go ahead. There was no royalty agreement or anything. I sort of had the dream of giving a whole lot of people permission to write 'Kilgore Trout' novels, so the bookstores and church sales and everything would just have stacks of these shitty things around." He chuckles. "Anyway, the book came out, sold extremely well, but there was no evidence anywhere that *I* hadn't written this. I got a ferocious review in one science-fiction magazine, as though I had written the goddamned novel, and I got nasty letters saying, You'd do anything for money, you're ripping off your fans this way. Farmer refused to break security and admit he'd written the book; the secrecy was terribly damaging to me."

What about the period when Vonnegut was still relatively unknown outside of the science-fiction field? *Cat's Cradle*, for example, had to wait perhaps ten years to be recognized by the literary establishment.

"Yes, it was never reviewed. There was a newspaper strike on, when it came out . . . but a lot of my books have never been reviewed. A couple of years ago I was at a party for Doris Lessing, and she was talking to me about a book of mine, *Mother Night*, and I happened to tell her it had never been reviewed. So she immediately reviewed it for *The New York Times*, about twelve years after it had first been published."

I remark that he sounds oddly unconcerned about this prolonged lack of recognition for his work. He thinks about this, carefully.

"I figured it probably wasn't much good," he says, with an ironic smile. "I've met so many people I like, who try hard, and really aren't very good. So I'm willing to believe I'm such a person. *Was* willing—I'm less willing now. But I mean, if that were the case, it would just simply be life. I've always been quite grown-up, or tried to be, about underpayments or failures in this business. I've taken it as routine. I got extremely lucky getting in touch with a publisher named Sam Lawrence, who has as a policy putting back into print any author he takes on. He's done this with Richard Brautigan, with J. P. Donleavy. He's connected to Dell books with a handshake; he simply got them to bankroll him. It's a magnificent policy of his to keep all his authors in print. There are damn few authors in this country who are completely in print. If I wanted to get the collected works of Norman Mailer, for example, I'd be shopping all over town for some of the books, and perhaps that's true of Philip Roth, too."

I ask if Vonnegut's body of work is pointing in any particular direction, and if he always has his future output planned.

"I have known people who live that systematically and rationally. Herman Wouk is a friend of mine; he has known since the end of the second World War what books he wanted to write, and in all the books he's written so far there's just one violation of the plan, which is a very brief novel which he was so amused by, he had to do it. But I've just finished a book and I have no idea what I want to do next."

Surely *Slaughterhouse Five* is an exception, then, in that it must have been planned over a period of many years?

"Well, that was a command performance. When I found out that it [the destruction of Dresden] was the largest massacre in human history, I said, my god, I must make some comment on this. It was the first truly beautiful city that I had ever seen. I had no idea that such cities existed. No sooner than I had seen it, it was demolished. The Germans, incidentally, don't give a shit about the destruction of Dresden, or the destruction of anything else. It's a little strange that I should have cared and they don't give a damn. I think they're perfectly willing to rebuild anything." He laughs.

To me, the main message in *Slaughterhouse Five* concerns the futility of human life—a message that I find, more or less moderated, in Vonnegut's other work also. I ask him how he replies when people say that his work is too depressing.

He shakes his head. "But people *don't* say that." He smiles, and I feel my question has not so much been evaded, as stopped in its tracks. I start to protest that I can't be the only person ever to find a spirit of futility in Vonnegut's novels; but he goes off into a digression. "I used to speak a lot for money. I stopped when I had the American equivalent of a command performance before the Queen—to speak in the Library of Congress. I had this innocent country-boy manner there, a speech which had worked pretty well, time and time again. Then about halfway through a guy stood up, he was some recent arrival from a socialist country, Hungary or Bulgaria, I never found out. He said, 'What right do you have, as a leader of American youth, to make the young people in this country so pessimistic?' And I had no answer to this; it was such a startling question, and embarrassing in a way, that my speech ended there. The books are certainly pessimistic . . . but so much of what depresses me is avoidable. Not by strokes of genius, but by ordinary restraint. A lot of the things that are wrong in the world could be put right by restraint. Just the chance of desolating the whole eastern seaboard with this cockamamie way of generating electricity, this crazy way to boil water . . . and the weapons we've built and all that . . . if we just *wouldn't do* a number of things, we'd be much better off."

This leads into my asking about his science background, which is evident in many of his novels and most obvious in *Cat's Cradle*, where one of the main characters is a physicist, apparently drawn from real life.

"Yes, the guy who was Dr. Felix Hoenikker in that book was modeled after Dr. Irving Langmuir, who was one of the few people in private industry who ever won a Nobel Prize. He was a surface chemist; my brother, who is a distinguished scientist, worked with him. But Langmuir was stubbornly absentminded, stubbornly indifferent to worldly matters, and this was a theatrical pose. People don't act that way any more, because it's no longer fashionable. Fashions change in how scientists behave. When I worked for General Electric and reported on the activities of scientists there, it was fashionable for them to be sweetly absent-minded, to have no sense of the consequences of whatever they might turn over to the company in the way of knowledge."

Are there exceptions, whom he admires?

"Well, a scientist I admire a great deal, of the same generation, is Norbert Wiener. At the end of the second World War he wrote a piece for *Atlantic Monthly* which said he wasn't going to tell his government anything any more, because they were liable to do almost anything with whatever levers he gave them. I think that's exactly right, that a scientist should be withholding things from a government all the time."

I ask how he, as a writer, got mixed up with science in the first place.

"My father insisted that I be serious about school, and he had an idea about what serious subjects were. My father and grandfather were architects in Indiana; so I might have been third-generation, that would have been terribly respectable, in an architecture firm in Indianapolis, and I wouldn't have minded that at all. But my father was feeling rather sorry for himself because he hadn't done any architecture for ten years because of the great Depression, so he told me to be a chemist.

"I went to Cornell and planned to be a biochemist. I took these Christ-awful subjects and was at the bottom of my class, always. At the same time they had a daily newspaper at Cornell, and it was easy for me to become a bigshot on that. I wrote columns for it, and fantasies, all sorts of irresponsible writing. Writing was something I could always do better than most of my peers, so, later, when I was working for General Electric and had two kids, and the company wouldn't give me a raise, it seemed to me I could probably make more money as a freelance, and that turned out to be the case. Anyone who could tell a story, in those days, was kind of a fool to have a regular job. The magazines that existed then paid so well."

So for some years he made a living by writing short stories, and took time off to write novels only when he had saved enough from the magazine work. Does he regret having had to do so much money-making writing, to finance his serious fiction?

"It makes me mad that I didn't have more money when I was younger, because I would have had a lot more fun, and so would my kids. There's that sort of regret. If I'd had a rich wife, or something, I would have written more novels; but I don't think I've lost anything, and any time you work in a restricted form you're going to force yourself to be more intelligent than you ordinarily would be. One of the wonderful things about structured poetry is that, in order to make a rhyme work or a meter work, you use this or that wonderful word that you wouldn't use ordinarily, just to bugger the thing to work, and suddenly it's just exquisite. I think to write a conventional short story for a middle-class magazine is an interesting challenge. All the stories had to celebrate the middle classes in some way, otherwise I wouldn't have sold them. But I don't mind celebrating the middle classes that much. I mean, they must rescue the country; no one else is going to do it."

I mention that many writers I've talked to put their faith in science, rather than the middle classes, when it comes to rescuing us from the future. Vonnegut seems to become mildly irritated by this.

"It's just superstitious, to believe that science can save us all. Absurd. It's youthfulness, I think. It's like the science club at high school—they get excited—go out and capture the asteroids—and maybe you can, but these aren't very grown-up people, most of them.

"We're starting to back down on a lot of our technology now. I think the whole country is going to start sorting through our technology to decide what is really good for us and what isn't. That's quite an interesting point to reach."

At the time of this interview, Vonnegut is preparing to go to Washington, D.C. to speak at a rally against nuclear power. I ask about his outlook on politics and economics generally.

"This nonsystem we have here?" He pauses. "Of course, it can't provide nearly enough jobs for people." Another pause. "But we do have these wonderfully motivated maniacs in private enterprise, who will go into, say, the tire business, and do wonderful things with tires, eat and sleep tires. Or TV repair. Or keeping elevators working. This is a very useful sort of nut. Socialism hasn't been able to turn up this sort of person. So I favor a mixed economy where you encourage these nuts to exist and make a few more rubles than their neighbors. They must be paid, although they don't have to be paid as much as they are now—these guys, when they really get going, start working extraordinary extortion schemes and get paid phenomenally for what they do."

The mention of socialism reminds me of an opinion I recently heard from Ben Bova (the science-fiction writer and Executive Editor of *Omni* magazine). I mention Bova, and Vonnegut stops me, trying to place the name. He thinks about it for a long time. After much head-scratching he recalls that it was Bova who took him to an *Omni* lunch just a week ago, no doubt hoping Vonnegut might produce a story for *Omni*. Anyway, trying to get back to the subject, I describe Bova's opinion that socialism is "out of gas," and socialist countries will soon be forced to adopt some form of capitalism, in order to survive economically.

Vonnegut laughs. "That's asinine. It's so silly, no, obviously *we're* collapsing, and there's nobody paying attention at all, nobody has even tried to make a drawing of what the gadget is. I think the socialist countries are quite interesting."

He has continued to speak, on these various topics, in the same offhand, laconic style, ironically disengaged from the matters at hand. It keeps reminding me of the amused fatalism one finds in his writing, perhaps spelled out most clearly in *The Sirens of Titan*, where he depicts humanity as a blind mob pursuing high aspirations—which are in fact arbitrarily manipulated by higher forces, to satisfy trivial whims. To what extent does that book reflect Vonnegut's view of reality?

"Oh, it's just a book, people laugh at parts of it, and it has jokes in it," he says ingenuously—playfully—and yet deadpan. "See, I got curious about—what if there were a God who *really did care*, and had things He *want d done*." For some reason this notion strikes him as wildly funny; he goes into a protracted chuckling fit. "—And how inconvenient that would be. The whole idea of a purposeful God is comical, I think. You know, what on earth could He want, shoving things around all the time, and giving us hints."

Does the book still please him when he looks at it now?

"It's full of typographical errors," he says vaguely. "It began as a cheap paperback, and people have always set type from that original version. I've never changed any of the errors, though it would be the work of an hour to get a clean edition." He ponders for a moment, apparently about errors in other books. "In *Slaughterhouse Five*, I have a person dying of carbon-monoxide poisoning, and I describe the person as blue. In fact the person who dies of carbon-monoxide poisoning is a beautiful golden-rose color." He laughs, at this. "People usually say they've never seen him looking better." At this, he becomes convulsed with giggles.

When the mirth has died down, I try to ask another serious question. Does Vonnegut have a clear idea of his audience? Who, ideally, are his books aimed at?

"A friend of mine, Hans Koenig, a Dutch radical, he's lived here and in London, and he asked me what sort of person I wrote for. It's a person who is more intelligent than his place in society would indicate. Ideally that's the kind of person I would really be proud to have read me."

But was this the audience he was reaching in the late 1960s and early 1970s, when he was a minor hero to the counterculture?

"No, most of those people didn't read. My books and Tolkien's and Heinlein's *Stranger in a Strange Land* were *furniture*, you would come into a person's house and see the books lying around, and immediately know what sort of a person this was. . . ."

Going back to the kind of reader Vonnegut would prefer to reach—does he write novels in the hope of changing that reader's outlook, at all?

"Oh certainly." There follows a very, very long pause. "I would like them to be better sports about disappointment than they are." He says it carefully and decisively. "I think people are bound to be disappointed in this life. I think this is comical, to be the sort of animal that wants this and wants that . . . it's not really the animal's fault, it's the nature of the planet, that most such animals are disappointed. I think this is funny, and something to learn to live with. You don't necessarily die from it." He chuckles. "It's an endearing sort of animal that would want all that. It's sweet."

He seems to be trying to strike a cheerful note. I remark that it still sounds a depressing outlook, to me.

"Well, all right." He seems to decide, wearily, to go through an explanation he has given more often than he would like. He starts counting points off on his fingers. "My mother committed suicide. Three months later, I was sent overseas. Five or six months after my mother's suicide I was a soldier in the Battle of the Bulge, which was the largest single defeat of American arms in history. Three whole divisions with all sorts of supporting crap, all lost. I saw that, and I know what it feels like. There was nothing I could do except endure, and try to integrate this sort of catastrophe into my understanding of life. And I got to Dresden and there's this city without even a cracked windowpane, and it was demolished, I saw the demolition of a major art treasure. And then I watched the Russian army come into Germany, in this irresistible wave. . . . The human spirit must somehow be prepared to survive enormous catastrophes like this, and not hold ourselves responsible for it. What the hell was I going to do in the Battle of the Bulge—climb raging out of my hole blazing from the hip and hurling hand grenades in all directions? This idea that if you're down at the bottom of your society, it's your own damn fault, is intolerable to me . . . broke, sick, or unhappy, very often it isn't your fault." He pauses for a metaphor. "There are sensational weather systems going around the planet, over which you have no control."

(New York, May 1979)

BIBLIOGRAPHICAL NOTES

Vonnegut's first novel, *Player Piano*, was published in 1952. It contains ironic commentary on technology, automation, and American big business. *The Sirens of Titan* (1959) came next, and is the closest thing to conventional science fiction that he has written. *Cat's Cradle* (1963) is notable for its slightly unconventional structure, and its invented religion. Also it is one of the few mad-scientist-menaces-the-world novels in which the scientific disaster is not averted at the eleventh hour; there are catastrophic, irreversible results.

Slaughterhouse Five appeared in 1969, after which Vonnegut announced that he was retiring from writing books. However, he returned with *Breakfast of Champions* (1973) and *Slapstick* (1976), both of which restate his outlook of ironic futility, featuring many characters previously introduced in his earlier work.

Wampeters, Foma, and Granfalloons (1974) is a collection of essays on various topics, including science fiction.

Hank Stine

I am walking down Broadway with Hank Stine, the editor of *Galaxy* magazine. It's nine at night, traffic roars past, lights are bright, the sleazy Manhattan carnival is on the sidewalk stage.

"Let's see," Hank says carefully, "where are we, we seem to be in a busy part of town, there are signs and movie theaters, and it's the midtown area, and there seems to be some sort of major intersection here...."

"You're putting me on," I tell him.

"What? No, I was just wondering...."

"Times Square. This is Times Square."

"Oh really? Well, how about that." He looks around in genuine curiosity. He has never seen it before. He seems spaced out; partly this is because we have just seen *Dawn of the Dead* at a low-class theater where the audience whooped and cheered each episode of looting, cannibalism, and mass-murder. But partly it is because Hank Stine is, literally, spaced out: out of New York, out of touch with the publishing center that most editors and many writers find so unavoidable.

Stine was born in 1945, grew up on the west coast, hung out with science-fiction fans in Los Angeles, and wrote novels and stories there during the late 1960s. In a way he is still a sixties person: he has long hair and a (neatly trimmed) beard, smokes dope, talks idealistically, and likes to experiment with what he calls his "head space." On the other hand, this slim man in a respectable three-piece suit is adept at business and promotion. Through much of the 1970s he worked in advertising as a director of TV commercials in Baton Rouge, Louisiana—which is where he still lives, in retreat from the big city.

In 1978 he heard that the publisher of *Galaxy* was in need of a new editor. Stine got on the phone from Baton Rouge and talked his way into the job. This was the first the science-fiction community had heard of him in five or six years. To many people his name meant nothing, and some resented such an "outsider" taking over a magazine that had been sentimentally revered by many fans for several decades.

Stine's response was to point out that, although he had been on a long vacation, so to speak, he had always cared passionately about science fiction. In fact it is this passion, now, that makes him so angry at current trends. He is certainly the most outspoken and controversial editor we have, and, provided *Galaxy* survives recent financial problems quite outside of Stine's control, he should make a lasting impression—possibly as much of an impact as the British magazine *New Worlds* created fifteen years ago, at the start of the "new wave" in science fiction.

Our interview takes place at my apartment, after three days of local social events in connection with the annual announcement of the Nebula Awards honoring last year's best novel and stories. Stine is dazed by his overdose of late nights, big city, booze, and people. His habitual expression of noncommittal detachment suggests perhaps he won't have much energy or much to say. However, I only need to ask one question, and he launches into an animated, manic monologue, cramming about five thousand words into forty minutes.

For the purposes of this transcript, we'll begin with the background:

"When I was about nine years old I fell in with a couple of friends and we all did what we called movies, which were really story-boards, five or six hundred pages, a picture on each page. We'd show them to each other and say what the story was. All the stories were science fiction.

"By the age of twelve I was like your typical idiot science-fiction fan; I had the typical background—intelligent only-child, moves around a lot, forced into inner resources, develops imagination, discovers science fiction and goes gung-ho. I wrote and submitted my first story at age sixteen, and got my first rejection slip—from *Galaxy*, by the way. By the time I was about nineteen I'd written a first novel, and I tried to sell it to Ace Books, but it was pretty dreadful and the manuscript no longer exists.

"I was a very fast reader as a kid and didn't do much else with my time. Three or four books a day was no problem. So I have a good historical background in the field. By around 1970 I had read eighty percent of all the science fiction ever published in English, period.

"I moved from Sacramento to Los Angeles, hung around, met people, met Norman Spinrad when he was beginning to sell stuff, and met Larry Niven. The first story I sold was a terrible collaboration, with Niven. We submitted it everywhere, to one editor after another. Finally Ted White became editor of *Amazing* and *Fantastic* and he bought it. I was thrilled, and also embarrassed because it wasn't that good a story.

"Around that time Norman [Spinrad] started talking about a new publisher called Essex House. One night he read to me a scene from an Essex House novel, Michael Perkins' *Blue Movie*. It was a satire dealing with the probable sexual head spaces of some famous stars, from Ronald Reagan to John Wayne to Bela Lugosi. It was very funny and grotesque. I thought, well, I could do that.

"Since I was twelve or thirteen I'd had an idea that I'd wanted to write, inspired by a scene out of a Robert Sheckley novel, *Immortality Incorporated*, which was serialized in *Galaxy*. The character's consciousness flashes through the minds of different bodies and he finally ends up in the body of a chick who's about to fuck a guy for the first time, which to a thirteen-year-old reader was highly erotic. I began to have long, strange daydreams about what it would be like to be a chick, you know, which inspired my novel, *Season of the Witch*."

This was Stine's first book. Essex House published it and it had the kind of power and imagery to create a minor cult following. At the time he started writing it, "I had just gotten divorced, I was living by myself, I needed money desperately. I was very excited by the idea of writing the book and I was also terrified. A friend gave me some mescaline, we went out all around town, and ended up seeing a biker movie called *The Savage Seven*— which is actually a fine and sensitive movie in a lot of ways—and at four AM I got back home and couldn't sleep, so I sat down, stranged-out from the drugs, and started typing *Season of the Witch*. I got farther and farther into it, I wrote thirty or forty pages, then I went over to a friend's house and put on earphones and wrote for another four or five hours.

"From 1968 through 1972 I wrote three books under my own name. Then I stopped writing for quite a while. I temporarily burned out as a writer, like a lot of people do, except it doesn't always stop them from going on writing, because they need the money and they have nothing else to fall back on. It's good to be able to do something else for a few years, go into advertising or directing films, and get refreshed, then return to writing science fiction.

"Dean Koontz and Piers Anthony were writers whose work influenced my own decision to stop writing. Their first novels were published about the same time as mine. They were pretty fine first novels. Then their next novels came out and really they weren't as good. And then their third novels came out and they were even a step further downhill. A writer has to make certain choices, especially early-on. You can go right ahead and produce book after book; a lot of the time in science fiction you can sign a multiple-book contract and there's pressure to just keep grinding them out. As a result, people don't take stock and learn. Why do you need to? You're getting $5,000 a book and you're writing four of them, why the hell do you need to learn to write better? But I didn't want to end up writing books that I was progressively less proud of. Piers Anthony, now, is slowly beginning to get his act back together, after a long time writing these semijunk books that weren't nearly as good. Personally I'm glad I just wrote one book that everybody liked a lot, rather than six or seven that left a progressively bad taste in people's mouths. And in the last few years I've finally been able to pull together in my head what I wanted to learn about writing."

We turn now to editing, and what Stine has learned from his first few months of reading submissions to *Galaxy*. He is unhappy with the state of the science-fiction field.

"In the past, in order to write science fiction, you had to care about it enough in order to teach yourself how to write it. That weeded out a few people. The ones who were left had talent, or at least the dedication to stick at it, or were in a few cases, like Lin Carter, so gonzo-crazy that they were going to write it whether they were good or bad.

"Today we have a lot of courses teaching people how to write science fiction, at college. It's codified enough so that if you analyze several science-fiction books, say Pohl and Kornbluth's work or some of Heinlein's early work, you can figure out how to create a future society, extrapolated from ours—you can figure out what pieces to move where.

"One result is that a lot of the new writers are not inventing science-fiction stories any more. They're simply reworking, using the old structure of extrapolation. People learn to write competent stories irrespective of whether they have anything at all to say. I get story after story that is competent, and I've reached the point of writing angry letters saying it is not enough simply to write a competent story that works from beginning to end. Sure, it's *hard*, but it's no longer enough.

"Another thing that bothers me about the field in general is the number of books and stories written around basic ideas that are unworkable. It's unfair to pick on an individual writer, because he may have written better books which I haven't read. But Michael G. Coney's *Friends Come in Boxes* happens to illustrate why I would not read a lot of science fiction for seven years, and why I still will not. That novel suggests that, because of overpopulation, people's brains are cut out from their bodies and put in boxes until there will be enough room. Now the basic idiocy of this is that you can take the most rabid group of people who refuse to stop breeding—rabid Catholics who won't take birth control under any circumstances—and they would *still* rather abandon their faith and submit to birth control than allow their kids' brains to be cut out and put in boxes. Period. Forever, throughout all of history. It's an unchanging variable of human nature. So how can I read a book like that? And yet the book got published, and I see many others in which the authors know what you do in science fiction—how to take a premise and develop it— even though the premise itself is dumb, it's unworkable, nobody's ever going to do it, no human society in history. There are many novels like that, and they get sold, because it's a boom market, and an editor's got a schedule in which there are six books a month, he takes a book because it works basically, except for the premise, and anyway—doesn't everybody have a right to speculate on a different premise? The answer is *no*, not if something is so dumb it's never going to happen in human society.

"There are a lot of people who are very big right now, whom I consider to be very flawed writers. One of them is John Varley.

I haven't read "Persistence of Vision" [the story which won a 1979 Nebula Award] so I'm not going to talk about that and whether he deserved a Nebula; he probably does deserve it. But I will say that I've read several other stories of his, some of which were bought by a previous editor of *Galaxy* when there were some financial problems. I don't know if these problems were what prevented the editor from asking for a rewrite, but I tell you truthfully that I would have had "Retrograde Summer" rewritten, to take just one example, because it's a story in which basically every single thing is extraneous, including the paragraphs to each other. And the climax, or lack of one, renders the whole thing pointless.

"The editor should have helped Varley. But magazine editors seem to just sit on their butts and either buy a story or not buy it. I approve of editors telling writers what they can do to improve their stories. The point of being an editor is not just to be a guy who buys stuff; otherwise, publishers would employ secretaries. An editor should seek out writers who are up-and-coming in the field and work with them. If a writer is getting real close, you don't just take a story and publish it, you should write and tell him what he could do to improve it, and if he agrees with you, fine, and if he doesn't, he can try to sell it some place else. I've read a lot of books which an editor has improved; I know David Hartwell [of Pocket Books] has worked for an entire weekend with Gregory Benford almost line by line, and Benford is a fine, good writer, but he didn't object because an acute editor can see things that can be improved, right down to sentences."

We talk some more, generally, about science fiction, and Stine comes out with an accusation that I cannot recall ever having heard before—that science fiction is basically middle class. It's a convincing argument, as he develops it:

"Somebody once said that most science-fiction writers seem to take Main Street America with them wherever they go. I think that's true. Most of the writers are from the middle class; the few exceptions have brought unusual work and talent into the field. Samuel R. Delany, for instance. Most science fiction to me is far too urbane. They write about all these civilized urbane people, middle-class people in spaceships talking to each other in a civilized way—"

I object, at this point, that many science-fiction writers come from poor backgrounds. Isaac Asimov, for instance. Stine pauses momentarily, then quickly gets rid of my objection:

"The aspirations of a certain kind of poor person are to *become* middle class. I think that was true of Asimov, or of Ben Bova, for example. And some people who are already middle class—Jerry Pournelle, perhaps—have aspirations to become *upper* class, and rich, and of course they become the best apologists for plutocracy, wealth, and conservatism, because that's what they want themselves.

"Science fiction habitually displays a faith in science, or at least some kind of faith in underlying reason, and this again is almost a kind of provincialism. The real truth is that the universe is so much larger than we are, we live in an infinitely small backwater in which, for an insignificant fraction of cosmic time, nothing much really strange from outside has happened. So what the hell do we know about what's going on? What right do we have to take for granted the ongoing process of an existence which is in fact phenomenally insubstantial and fragile? Yet American science-fiction writers, and middle-class Americans generally, are very complacent.

"I think some of it comes out of American textbooks in the 1950s. They suggested that all the problems had been solved, that the racial melting-pot had completely worked, that scientific progress would make everything wonderful, and so on. The textbooks have since then become more balanced, but there's still a lot of that outlook left in America, that this country is something special, it has some kind of historic manifest destiny, and is the perfect experiment. But that isn't really true.

"The entire system is basically running out of almost everything it needs to keep it going. Writers like Bova and Pournelle think that the physical sciences have all the answers; I don't agree. Obviously the physical sciences have created problems. *They* think the physical sciences will go on and solve these problems, and they even go further and admit that perhaps the solutions to those problems will cause further problems which they can then solve, but this is like one of those acrobats who get a bunch of plates spinning on top of poles and then run around from one pole to the next, keeping them all going. Eventually you get tired and the whole thing starts to crash.

"I think the whole problem with science fiction is that we tend to look at things in a very black-and-white way. One set of people assumes that the future is going to work out all right, and the other set says we shouldn't have *any* science or technology, we should go back to a simpler life. The real truth is that most issues in life are infinitely complex and there are no easy black-and-white solutions. Personally I don't think the past was better, I don't think the future will necessarily be better, I don't think the present is bad. I think what is wrong is certain attitudes that writers have and reinforce in their readers—that there are simple solutions, and reason can always solve problems.

"I guess I have a kind of Zen viewpoint which is that you should go very carefully—I guess I'm a Taoist, more or less—we in America think, do,do,do, sort of the Puritan ethic, because there once was a lot to do. But I think people should now examine things more carefully, and shouldn't be fooled into either a romantic or antiromantic viewpoint; they should understand that there's a lot of dichotomy."

I ask how this outlook will be reflected in the policy of Galaxy, under Stine's editorship.

"Well, right now, I have bought four stories that use the subject of feminism. The first is by A. E. van Vogt and will really enrage some people. In a peculiar way it's sort of antagonistic to women's lib. The second is a really heavy recondite women's-lib story, a Planet Stories kind of thing, but with a female central character who is really tough. Then I have a third story by an Iowa housewife who has worked on a farm. Women who are sitting in New York behind desks can see no good reason why being pregnant should interfere in the active pursuit of their jobs; fair enough. But if you're out picking corn in a field, it's different. This story is about an organization that teaches women basic survival skills for work in frontier planets. It's written from the point of view of a woman who understands that there are good reasons why being female should have some bearing on what work you can do under primitive conditions. And then lastly I have a fourth story which is more or less profeminism. So what am I trying to do? People say, Stine, what is your viewpoint? Well the point is to get people thinking about things, seeing that there are different sides, all with some validity."

Through most of this, I have hardly needed to ask questions. I have been barely able to interrupt at all. Hank Stine has wonderful reserves of energy, and he enjoys arguing and thinking and expounding. Editing Galaxy has been a frustrating experience thus far, because six months have passed and not one of his issues has yet been published (there have been delays while the magazine was refinanced). But his enthusiasm is just as strong and his ambitions are just as grand as when I talked to him when he first started the job, in 1978.

We wind up the interview, not because everything has been said (at least another hour could have been taped) but because there isn't space for a transcript of anything more. It's hard to pick a quote that summarizes who Hank Stine is and what he's doing, but this, at least, expresses his feeling for science fiction:

"There are two kinds of people that read science fiction. There are people who read it occasionally, out of curiosity. Then there are people who are hip to some kind of weird dream, a spiritual resonance, some kind of thing that lights in their souls, and they become crazy about it. I'm in that group. I've spent most of my life involved with science fiction. I've been lucky to escape occasionally, because the centrifugal force of love always keeps dragging us back to our loved object."

(New York, April 1979)

BIBLIOGRAPHICAL NOTES

Hank Stine's *Season of the Witch* was published in 1968; it describes the transformation of a man into a woman as punishment for acts of rape and murder. His other science-fiction novel is *Thrill City* (1969). In addition Stine has written some non-science-fiction suspense novels.

His editorship of Galaxy magazine was announced in 1978, and the first issue under his control was published in 1979. The magazine has since been sold to Galileo Magazine, and Stine has gone on to become the editor of Starblaze Books.

Photo by
Paul Turner and
Dorothy Simon

Norman Spinrad

"Whenever he comes up here he looks as if he wants to bite someone." That's how an editor I know described a typical visit from Norman Spinrad.

Certainly Spinrad has built a reputation as being a "difficult" author. His best-known novel, *Bug Jack Barron*, was abrasively radical, challenging the science-fiction establishment at a time when the so-called "new wave" had already antagonized the more traditionally-minded people working in the field. Editor Donald Wollheim (who subsequently founded DAW Books in New York) called the novel "depraved, cynical, utterly repulsive, and thoroughly degenerate." Published in the USA by Avon Books, it was despised by hard-core science-fiction fans who saw it as an attack on the values of their literature—as, in a sense, it was.

Spinrad went further with "Fiawol," a notorious magazine article which (as he now describes it) "Defined science-fiction fandom as a warped subculture that was fucking up the publishing of science fiction." This diatribe offended amateurs and professionals alike, to the extent that one magazine editor spent an entire editorial attacking Spinrad and condemning him, as an influence, as a writer, and as a person.

Other miscellaneous incidents followed (such as Spinrad's telling science-fiction fan Bruce Peltz that he was a "fat fascist prick" at the Los Angeles science-fiction convention that Peltz had helped to organize). To many people Spinrad seemed contemptuous of the science-fiction world, at the same time that he was earning his living through its readership. Certainly his was a radical stance, coinciding with the antiestablishment mood of the late 1960s generally.

Most radicals of that decade have long since sold out or subsided. Norman Spinrad himself did go through a period of reduced visibility; he published no science fiction in the seven years after his *The Iron Dream* in 1972. But when his new novel, *A World Between*, finally appeared in 1979, it turned out to be at least as controversial as *Bug Jack Barron*. Spinrad's vacation from the field is over, and there is every indication that he is just as ready to bite someone now as he ever was.

The obvious question is, why? Does he relish conflict for its own sake? Or does he harbor sincere dissatisfactions with the status quo? Either way, is he, like the heroes of his novels, really a no-bullshit, macho wheeler-dealer, scheming to manipulate his world?

Certainly he lives more modestly than his fictional characters. His Manhattan apartment is a "railroad flat," a string of four tiny interconnecting rooms on the fourth floor of an old walk-up building in the West Village. It is the kind of 1880s apartment house that was once full of poor immigrant families, before the Village became fashionable.

Spinrad's apartment has been partially renovated by some previous tenant (a shower installed, a loft-bed built). He took it over three years ago; there are few signs of his having made it his own since then. The furniture is simple and basic: yellow plastic chairs in the kitchen, a rather grubby pillow-couch in the living room; discount-store bookshelves. I have the impression that he lives there as he would live in a hotel room, and as we begin to talk it becomes clear that, indeed, he has always tended not to commit himself inextricably to any one place—or any one field.

"I'm from New York City originally. I grew up part of the time in the real hard-core Bronx, and part of the time in a backwoods section of the Bronx, a countrified part. I lived other places as well, I don't want to have to go down the whole long list."

His curriculum at City College was just as varied—or indecisive. "I took courses in short-story writing, constitutional law,

Japanese civilization, oriental art. I got out with a pre-law major by lumping everything together and getting accepted by some law schools, though I never went to any of them. I went straight into writing short stories, which I started selling after about a year. In the meantime I worked in a sandal shop, a carpentry shop, and at the Scott Meredith Literary Agency."

A colleague at the agency sold Spinrad's portion-and-outline of his first novel, *The Solarians*. "I was collecting unemployment insurance, writing the novel under contract and being paid under the table, so I saved enough to travel. I'd always wanted to see California so I loaded all my shit into my car and drove out there. I found myself an apartment in Culver City, a pismire-dull place. Lived there for half a year, then San Francisco, then back in L.A. because I liked it better."

He wrote pieces of film criticism. He wrote *The Men in the Jungle* and *Agent of Chaos*. He was offered a lucrative script-writing assignment on *Star Trek*. And he wrote *Bug Jack Barron*, which drew on the interest he had already developed in the movie/TV scene. However, "The visual stuff I'm interested in is secondary to novels, and always has been. You go too crazy chasing after screenplay deals. It drives you nuts."

Still based in Los Angeles, Spinrad wrote numerous articles on contemporary social and political themes for *Knight* men's magazine; he contributed regularly to the *Los Angeles Free Press*; and he followed *Bug Jack Barron* with *The Children of Hamlin*, a novel that was serialized in the *Free Press* but has never been published anywhere else. "It's all about the East Village and drug dealing, and a literary agency that operated in a certain manner," he says. The Scott Meredith agency? "I refuse to answer that question on grounds that it might tend to incarcerate me." The novel has been rejected by all the major New York publishers; it was bought by MacDonald, in Britain, but they subsequently decided not to print it, even though they had paid Spinrad for it. "I don't know why it never made it into print as a book anywhere, though I have a lot of paranoid theories. Maybe there are political reasons, or people afraid of being sued by the literary agency, I don't know. I've thought of self-publishing it, which I might end up doing. The theme of the book is the correspondence between dope-dealing, gurus, cults, and the way that the business world operates. It's set in 1965, so there's stuff about the birth of the counterculture, as well. In the end the hero throws it all up and goes to work for a porno publisher in California."

His next novel was *The Iron Dream* (heroic fantasy written as if by Adolf Hitler; recently reissued by Jove). And then came the ill-fated *Passing Through the Flame*, a Hollywood novel that reaped poor reviews and was the cause of a violent dispute with Putnam/Berkley who, Spinrad felt, almost went out of their way not to sell the book. The dispute was so acrimonious that Spinrad is sure he'll never again be published by Berkley, whether he wants to be or not.

A World Between, which signals Spinrad's return to science fiction, is set on an alien world which has been colonized by Earth people and made into a Californian-style, media-conscious utopia. There is an idealized Jeffersonian democracy, and almost total equality of the sexes. This idyllic status quo is threatened, however, first by a deputation of "transcendental scientists" and then by a faction of "femocrats." Both are extremist organizations attempting to plant the seeds of their ideologies on all colonized worlds of the galaxy. The scientists appeal to what Spinrad sees as male traits: abstract dreams of power, ambition, discovery, and destiny. The movement is autocratic, ruthless, and subtly male-supremacist. The femocrats, conversely, are ultra-radical feminists whose secret aim is to foment revolution, institute a matriarchy, and use men for breeding purposes only.

A three-way battle ensues between male-supremacists, ultra-feminists, and the moderate utopian government, whose democratic ideals compel it to allow full freedoms of speech to the extremists. The resultant battle of ideologies is fought mainly via political TV commercials.

A World Between would offend a Gloria Steinem more than an Archie Bunker. Spinrad's femocrats exemplify the most extreme male fears of feminism. They are lesbians, they are unattractive, they spout dogma, and when their leader spends some time alone with an arrogant male cop, the sight of his "piercer" (the book uses an odd amalgam of science-fictional sex terms and 1950s euphemisms) rouses a deep-seated heterosexual urge in her, making her want to . . . suck it.

By contrast, the male-dominated transcendental scientists in Spinrad's novel are portrayed as relatively sympathetic characters—a trifle unscrupulous in their pursuit of idealistic goals, but beset by occasional twinges of doubt, and no more oppressive to women than, say, a modern American corporation.

I ask Spinrad if he would agree to being biased against feminism. "Only to the extent that feminism becomes an 'ism'. I distrust all ideology, any 'ism'. When any movement becomes an ideological mind-set it becomes just another form of fascism. Any philosophy which becomes a prescription for the way the world should be . . . that's a fascist trip and I don't like any of them, including feminism.

"Men and women both have their techniques for getting their own way. Where I particularly object to feminists is their attempt to get rid of this dialectic. There *are* psychological differences between men and women; trying to create a unisex 'personhood' will not work, for psychological reasons if not for physical or biochemical reasons. We're different—and that's not bad.

"We're in a period where all the old values aren't valid any more, and nothing that really works has coalesced to replace them. That's part of the thing with feminism now: they're trying to find something that works, but actually it doesn't seem to work for them very well. I think most women who are really into it are not all that happy."

And is there an overall message of the book?

"Part of what it's about is the paradox that faces all democratic systems when confronted by totalitarian systems trying to subvert them: how do you preserve your liberties while fending off a system that isn't playing by your rules? How do you destroy the enemies of democracy without losing what it is you're fighting for?"

I point out that the book shares interests and themes with other novels that Spinrad has written. There seems to be a recurring obsession with power-games, cults, scheming, ambition, fascism.

"Well, I believe there are only four things, basically, that you can write about," he replies. "Sex, love, power, and money. To that you can add transcendence—higher consciousness, psychology. That's all there is."

Certainly his male characters seem to be motivated only by this assortment of basic qualities. Their dreams are bold; their style is macho. And yet they all have another level, too—an almost self-conscious, apologetic gentleness, as if Spinrad, though attracted by the *idea* of ruthless men of power seducing the inevitable glamorous women, isn't happy to present the type in its purest form.

Is this a reflection of his own personality? Are his heros modeled on himself in any way? "Only insofar as I identify with *all* my characters, because I write from various viewpoints. I don't think any of my characters are me, but on the other hand nothing in any of them comes from anywhere else. The major characters are never based on people I know. They're theoretical. Yes, I have been obsessed with powerful and charismatic figures, and how love and sex fits in with this. But only because, as I say, I don't see much else to write about, outside of the sex-love-power-money-transcendence framework."

I feel he isn't happy with my question, in that it demands self-analysis of a kind that he is reluctant to indulge in—in an interview, anyway. I ask instead about his love-hate relationship with science-fiction fandom. This question puts him immediately back on easy territory; he launches into what is obviously a familiar polemic. "I think fans are okay in their place, which is to be fans—go to conventions, read the stuff, and produce amateur publications. I don't like it when it goes beyond this—when science-fiction fans influence professional publishing. So many of the editors and writers started as fans and still think of themselves secretly as fans. Writers who *didn't* start as fans have discovered fandom and gotten sucked into that pocket universe and had their subsequent work judged by fannish standards. Fans think of science fiction as their own genre, and it isn't, it's a field of literature. I don't think science-fiction fans as a group are competent to control the evolution of a field of literature. That's a ridiculous notion. It's as if all the rock groupies got together to decide the future of rock music."

This attitude was relevant in Spinrad's running for office in the Science Fiction Writers of America (he was vice-president for two years). "The organization was really fucked up—it was being run in an amateur fashion and there was excessive fannish influence. It was a question of either resigning, like other people who were resigning, or trying to do something about it. Actually I think despite its shit-headedness, despite squabbling about membership requirements and Nebulas, it's done an awful lot. The SFWA got a quarter-million dollars out of Ace Books, it got Tolkien the money he was entitled to . . . when it has functioned as a quasi-union it's worked well, and when it has functioned like an amateur jack-off society it's worked . . . like an amateur jack-off society."

Spinrad is now, once again, involved with the SFWA, this time as its East Coast Publicity Director. But his main preoccupation these days is his work. He has started on another science fiction novel, for Pocket Books. "It's called *Songs from the Stars,* and it's a post-catastrophe novel of a kind, postulating a world in which science is divided into black and white sciences, and there are remnants of the O'Neill space people . . . instead of the usual sword-and-sorcery set-up of science-versus-magic, here, because the world has been destroyed by the evils of certain kinds of sciences, those are the sciences, especially physics, atomic physics in particular—the people who practice those sciences are regarded as sorcerers. It's taboo to make artificial molecules; to use power other than natural power derived from sun, wind, water, and human muscle; and so on."

Beyond this novel, he has ideas for other books, including: "A book about Cortez's conquest of Mexico, written from a modern sensibility, and not entirely realistic. Something on the order of *Gravity's Rainbow* in a funny kind of way. And another vague plan that I have is to do a kind of Arabian Nights novel."

Behind this work, I sense a renewed ambition. Certainly Norman Spinrad is producing more fiction now than during the middle years of the 1970s, selling it for much larger advances, and *planning* his writing career. He maintains a close concern with the publishing process: the sales of his work, the reviews it receives, the impact he is making, and, yes, the size of his name on the covers. *A World Between* seems to have been written with talk-show appearances in mind (he agrees he'd enjoy debating someone like Joanna Russ), and he tries to ferret out the hard figures involved in book promotion and publicity—an area that many authors feel they have neither the stomach nor the time to investigate.

To this extent, perhaps, it is fair to portray Norman Spinrad as a would-be media-manipulator. Certainly he is at his meanest and angriest when he feels the media have manipulated *him*, as in the alleged Putnam/Berkley mishandling of *Passing Through the Flame*. It comes down to a question of who is going to push whom around. If Spinrad suspects he may be the one who gets pushed, whether by a careless art director, an unenlightened editor, or a convention organizer who wakes him unnecessarily early in the morning—the notorious ire and abuse are at once drawn forth.

The power fantasies of his novels do not translate accurately into his own life. I ask about his private ambitions; he says, "I have a dream about making movies over which I have complete creative control, as both producer and director, or writer and director—you have to occupy at least two of the major positions to have any assurance that things are going to be done your way."

To me, this sounds more like a fantasy about freedom from interference—freedom from getting screwed—than a fantasy about power.

And: "I also have a fantasy lifestyle of being able to hold onto a house in L.A. and my apartment here and bouncing back and forth in airplanes as much as possible. I like fluidity. I like mobility. One main reason for being a writer is not having to be in any particular place when someone tells you to." Again: freedom from interference.

Does he see himself ultimately settling? Does he feel the instinct to retreat (possibly with some future wife) and hole up, like primitive man in his cave?

"Not a cave," he says. "Maybe a castle."

(New York City, November 1978)

BIBLIOGRAPHICAL NOTES

Of Norman Spinrad's novels, *Agent of Chaos* is notable for having influenced young American radical-anarchists in the 1970s, and *Bug Jack Barron* is notable for its pyrotechnic style and development of a science-fictional idea (cryogenic storage of those who contract currently incurable diseases) in a realistic, media-conscious context. The frank sexual language of this novel offended some science-fiction readers in 1969, but is unlikely to bother present-day readers of contemporary fiction. *The Iron Dream* was published in 1972, and is Spinrad's idea of how Adolf Hitler might have written a fantasy novel; Hilter's style is authentically bad. Spinrad published no further science-fiction novels until 1979, when *A World Between* appeared. *The Mind Game*, a novel about cults, appeared also in 1979.

His short stories are collected in *The Last Hurrah of the Golden Horde* (1970), *No Direction Home* (1975) and *The Star-Spangled Future* (1979).

*Photo by
Brian M. Fraser*

Frederik Pohl

In *New Maps of Hell*, a notorious, eccentric study of science fiction published at the beginning of the 1960s, British novelist Kingsley Amis singled out Frederik Pohl as the best American science-fiction writer.

This choice surprised a few people—not because Pohl had a mediocre reputation (quite the contrary) but because he was not so noticeable as writers such as Asimov, Bradbury, Clarke, Heinlein, or even Bester. Pohl did not have such a distinctive voice; indeed most of his well-known novels of the 1950s were duets performed with C. M. Kornbluth. His prose was always efficient, but unmemorable. The subject matter he chose, and the worldliness he applied to it—that was what mattered.

Together, Pohl and Kornbluth pioneered and excelled in a completely new kind of science fiction. They invented and played with "Sociological SF"—alternate futures here on Earth, exaggerating and satirizing real-life social forces and trends that most other science-fiction writers seemed too removed from contemporary reality to understand or perceive clearly. This sophisticated material was a powerful but difficult form to write. Few people handle it with finesse even today, and Hollywood has never begun to master its subtleties (movies like *Soylent Green* and *THX 1138* are hopelessly inadequate, simplistic attempts).

The problem is that good sociological SF requires such broad-ranging insights—into everything from politics to organized crime, economics to advertising, mass-media to big-business. These are the forces that have molded twentieth-century life, and they are likely to endure, stemming from such bedrock motivations as greed, ambition, power, and fear. Pohl and Kornbluth understood it all, better than anyone else around, and so their future scenarios remain the best of their kind, unfailingly plausible and unsettling.

Kornbluth died tragically young, in 1958, but Pohl has continued to work vigorously as a writer, as an editor, and as an activist who has gone out and tried to apply some of his socio-political perceptions in the real world. He has written a nonfiction guide to politics, has run for political office himself, has addressed business groups, and has even worked for the State Department, lecturing throughout Eastern Europe. In the science-fiction world he has edited various magazines, including *Galaxy* and *If*. As an editor at Bantam Books he published controversial books such as Delany's *Dhalgren* and Russ's *The Female Man*. Most recently he has written new, memorable novels (*Gateway*, *Jem*) which are winning at least as much praise as the work which first attracted Kingsley Amis's attention twenty years ago. Born in 1919, a published writer by 1937, magazine editor by 1939, Pohl has ended up not necessarily the "best" but undoubtedly the most realistic, multifaceted, and enterprising writer of his generation.

His home is in Red Bank, New Jersey, which is one of a series of smallest towns along the East Coast about forty miles below Manhattan. There is a center of old buildings around the railroad track; further out, there is the inevitable sprawl of gas stations and shopping plazas and drive-ins and modern factories that have grown up as the population has grown. Once, Red Bank might have been an idyllic retreat; now, it is enmeshed in a long wide, suburban strip.

Pohl's residence is a charming, old three-story wooden-sided house, set back a little from a two-lane highway, and overlooking the Navesink River. Traffic moves slowly along the highway and over the bridge that spans the river. Small boats pass by, and occasionally you hear a train on the railroad just across the water. These noises filter into the comfortable old building, as if one is on an island surrounded by methodical, unseen movements of trade and commerce.

Various family members occupy the lower two floors, and Pohl has the whole of the top story to himself. There are four rooms, and the decor is, shall we say, casual: painted floorboards, faded cream-color walls, dusty carpets here and there. At some point in the past, well-constructed and well-finished bookshelves were installed in each room, but it's been a while since then and things have become less well-organized. Not all the books are on the shelves; in fact they are stacked anywhere they can be stacked, and the place looks like a middle-aged bachelor pad. Odd items of clothing, old envelopes, boxes, empty coffee cups, tape cassettes, mementos, ashtrays, and so on, are scattered across floors, chairs, and tables. The roof has leaked over some of Pohl's collection of magazines which he once edited. His shelf of Hugo, Nebula, and other awards is covered in dust. But it doesn't matter; he's seldom here any more—he travels a lot.

Personally I find the place immediately comfortable, a relaxed, lived-in, worked-in space without pretensions. It is a world unto itself (most of the drapes are closed across the windows), obviously the retreat of a man whose imagination is more vivid to him than, say, the scenic view outside across the river.

In the sort-of living room where we will sit and talk I find a pile of glossy color prints on the edge of a cluttered tabletop. They are photographs of Jupiter and Jupiter's moons—a NASA press release. Pohl himself was down at Cape Canaveral when the data transmissions were coming in from the Voyager probe that took these pictures. He and other science-fiction writers had to wait forty-five years to see pictures like these; through all that time, they only had their private faith in an unrealistic dream to sustain them, in the face of apathy or ridicule from a general public that didn't even believe in space travel until the 1960s.

Looking at these close-ups of the face of Jupiter, a truly alien world of infinite mystery, I feel a twinge of the old so-called sense of wonder that made me start reading science fiction in the first place. And I feel frustrated at the impossibility of ever going out there in person and seeing it with my own eyes. Pohl says he feels the same way, "but I've just about reconciled myself to it." To judge from his tone of voice, he isn't reconciled at all. He is, I think, an uncompromising man.

He offers me instant coffee made with hot water straight from the faucet ("An awful habit for which I must apologize"), we clear some papers off a once-fancy, now-dusty fifties-style couch upholstered in gold fabric, and make ourselves comfortable. He talks very quietly, chain-smoking, and almost seems shy, which is surprising in view of the time he spends giving lectures and interviews. Indeed, he says he likes the sound of his own voice, and (unlike many writers) is quite happy to promote his work. "Last fall I did a two-month tour for *The Way The Future Was* [his autobiography] and covered sixteen or eighteen cities. I enjoy doing that, in moderation."

More often, his public appearances have been in some consultancy role. "I've been involved in a great number of symposia and panels and management consultancies in the past. My impression is that the corporations and management groups that employed me wanted me to shake them up a little bit and perhaps give them some new perspectives, but they were not inclined to heed what I said very seriously. I remember talking to a group in Chicago once and saying that the primary requisite for achieving a viable relationship between our society and the planet's ecology was individual self-control. They stood up and cheered me. Then the next speaker said exactly the opposite and they stood up and cheered him too.

"As a writer, I don't consciously try to spread a message most of the time, but sometimes in the process of writing a story it becomes clear to me that there is something I want people to feel. I *am* a sort of a preacher. I like to talk to people and get them to change their views when I think their views are wrong. One way of doing this is to write; also, I have actually preached. I've taken the pulpit at the local Unitarian church eight or ten times, and probably twice that number of times at other churches. I was a trustee of the local church for a while. I think if I were not a writer, I would have had to be a preacher."

His most recent sermon in print prior to this interview was a conservationist message in the form of an article for *Omni* magazine, defining growth limits that are imposed by heat that is generated in civilized life on Earth. Beyond a certain point, the heat will produce climatic changes, melting the ice caps and inundating coastal areas. Of all the limits to technological growth, this is the most immediate and unavoidable.

However, "An article like the one in *Omni* won't reach very many people who are not already of the same opinion as I am. Many people will say that I'm just telling them more gloom and doom and they don't want to hear it, because surely someone will think of something and there'll be a way around it. People who think like this are wrong, but I don't know how to get through to them.

"Generally, the human race avoids doing *anything* radical until forced into it. Having done it, I think people find they are better off. They don't go exploring until they're forced to, by famine, discomfort, or some sort of political or social force, but then once they get to the new place they kind of like it. This has been true in my own personal life. Most of the changes I have resisted most violently have turned out for the better. . . . So I don't think that any real change in our global lifestyle is going to happen until things get pretty rough, and that part is *not* going to be a lot of fun. But after that, in the next stage, I have a lot of hopes."

Pohl believes that it may be more effective to preach indirectly, and science fiction can be a tool for accomplishing this. "In science fiction one can say a great many things that are unpalatable and that people prefer normally not to think about; because it's expressed as fiction you can slip it through their defenses. Science fiction can provide all sorts of insights, into technology, natural resources, the grandeur of being out there in space, and they're all valuable. But that's not all that science fiction is good for. It is the only kind of writing that allows you to look at the world we live in and change one piece at a time. What I mean is the process of taking the world apart, taking some elements and throwing them away, replacing them with others and seeing how the thing works after that. I think that that is very valuable."

Certainly this technique, in its purest form, recurs in almost everything Pohl has written. I ask if there are particular themes or obsessions that recur, also.

"There are some doctrines or dogma, I suppose. One is that most of the problems of the human race are human inventions. We don't have severe natural enemies any more—wolves don't come through the streets of London carrying off babies. What endangers people in London or any large city are taxicabs, muggers, and so on. Therefore I think that the solutions to most human ills must be social solutions. I'm not as convinced as I once was that political solutions are possible, but some sort of social solutions are necessary, and that shows in most of what I write.

"Politically I was a Marxist as a teenager and a Democrat for about twenty years. I was a member of the Democratic party and a committee man here; I ran for office once or twice and helped to elect other people. For the last ten years or so I've been an agnostic politically. I just don't know."

With all his other activities, I ask how he manages to fit writing in.

"I write while I'm traveling. Four pages a day, wherever I am.

About two years ago I reinvented the lost art of handwriting; I was getting in trouble with stewardesses, using my typewriter on planes. Since then I've been quite free.

"When I first began writing I taught myself to do first drafts only. The trouble with that was that although I got some of it published, it just wasn't any good. Because I have no willpower, and can't trust myself to continue to do anything for very long simply because I know that it's right, I had to *trick* myself into revising, by writing first drafts on the back of correspondence, envelopes, circulars, any typeable surface that I couldn't possibly submit as a manuscript. So I *had* to rewrite them at least once. Now, I do at least one complete rough draft, and one complete retyping, and I often rewrite sections, some of them over and over again, and then when it's finished I edit it carefully. I spend more time revising than I do writing; I'm not sure why.

"I feel very badly if I don't write. I think I write unless I feel so depressed and miserable that I can't get out of bed, which doesn't happen often. I like to write; it's partly an escape and partly therapy. It's a good way to release tensions and sublimate aggression and dispel hostilities."

I am curious as to whether these purely internal needs were what motivated Pohl to start writing originally, and what ambitions were involved.

"Like most immature and incompetent writers, the principal thing that I wanted was to see a story that I had written in print, because of the vanity and the romantic notion of being a writer. I suffered from that for a long time, but something happens after you've done it for a while, and you begin to feel other desires and other ambitions. I'm not sure that I can articulate them, but they involve saying something that hasn't been said before. I don't know how often I succeed, but I sure as hell try. I've often failed: I have cabinets full of stories and books that are failures and are not ever going to be published." He gestures to a pair of black four-drawer file cabinets. "Seven or eight times," he goes on, "I have been under contract to write a book, and have received an advance, and have later returned it because the book didn't work out."

I ask what his ambitions are now. Does he, in fact, have any left?

"It's true, I have very few unfulfilled ambitions. I'd love to be president of the United States but that's not really an ambition, that's only wise counsel to the voters, which they are not prepared to accept. I don't really have urgent ambitions, except to do specific things, like write specific books, and if I live long enough I'll do them. There's nothing that seems to be out of reach, there's nothing that requires the grace of God. It's just a matter of completing projects, rather than trying to attain something that I can't find the handle for."

Through all of this, we have discussed Pohl's personal decisions and preferences. In reality, though, an individual writer has limited free will, if he is writing for money. To what extent has Pohl's work been influenced by commercial factors?

"I think most of the books that I published up until five years ago certainly would have been rewritten a little more if I hadn't needed to deliver them to get paid. I don't know if they would have been different books. On the occasions when I have tried to do something because I thought there was a lot of money in it, it has usually bombed disastrously. The stuff that I wrote for love has worked out much better. All of the science-fiction novels I wrote, alone or in collaboration, are still in print somewhere and are still producing income. The buck-hustles are dead; none of them ever amounted to very much.

"Science-fiction writers as a class, I think, respond poorly to money. If they have too much of it they either become impossible to live with or they stop writing. When I left *Galaxy* it was my own firm intention to spend a lot of time writing, in the spring of 1969. Unfortunately Ballantine Books reissued eighteen of my books and paid me for all of them, so I had no incentive to write, and I didn't, for a year or two. And I didn't feel good about it. I felt unemployed, not doing anything and not wanted for anything. But if I'd had to finish a book in order to pay the mortgage or feed the kids, I would have done it.

"I think during the forties and fifties, in particular, the pressure of getting work written to sell to a magazine for the only check you ever expected to see produced some really good work. The best work of people like William Tenn and Damon Knight, Robert Sheckley and twenty or thirty others, came around that time for that reason. Cyril [Kornbluth] too—he was writing against the mortgage payments all that time, under pressure, and doing some great stuff.

"Today, for some writers, that pressure is not so intense. Science-fiction writers are better-paid than they used to be. I understand the floor [minimum acceptable bid from a publisher] on Heinlein's new novel is $500,000. Incredible. Half a million would have paid every science-fiction writer alive for everything they wrote for ten years, in the thirties. In fact there would probably have been a couple of hundred thousand left over."

Can people be taught to write, in college courses?

"I have mostly negative feelings about such courses. They emphasize the wrong things about writing: how to spell and punctuate, use alliteration, how to take apart a published story. They do not emphasize what seems to me to make one story better than another, which is the personal viewpoint of the person writing it—his own perception of the world. You really can't teach that. People either have something to say or they do not. There are many people who want desperately to be writers and have no talent; there seems to be no way to graft it into them, and they're the ones who show up for writing courses."

Pohl is more positive about the role of an editor in influencing the development of a writer. Like many science-fiction authors, he admires the late John W. Campbell, Jr., who edited *Astounding Science Fiction* magazine (later retitled *Analog*) and strongly imposed his ideas on the writers who sold stories to the magazine. However, times have changed:

"There could not be a John W. Campbell today. He would find some new writer, as he did with Heinlein or van Vogt or L. Sprague de Camp. He would hang on to him for two stories, and then Bantam Books or Pocket Books would be bidding for that author's novel and he'd be gone, which would be very satisfactory for him, but would make it impossible for someone like John to change the whole field around as he did. In fact it would make it impossible for him to help writers learn their craft.

"There is no editor in the science-fiction field now who has any real control over what happens. Not even David Hartwell at Pocket Books, in spite of the fact that he can spend six-figure advances. There just is not a place or publisher who defines the field or even defines his part in it. It has become big business, where books are merchandised and promoted and distributed and placed on sale like slabs of bacon or cans of soup.

"One of the reasons I left Bantam [where he had been their science-fiction editor] was that the joys of editing, for me, involve finding something that no one else has seen the wisdom of publishing, and making it go. That is not the skill that's in great demand in major paperback publishing houses. They don't forbid it—I had complete freedom at Bantam and they encouraged me to do what I wanted to do. But I was playing the wrong game for their field.

"What I really like is editing a science-fiction magazine. The big advantage of a magazine is that it should reflect the insanity of one individual, so it has a personality. I would have liked to take over at *Analong* [following the departure of Ben Bova, who inherited the job after John W. Campbell's death]. But I think probably they were reluctant to see any changes in the magazine, and I would surely have changed it."

I remark that in the time Pohl worked for Bantam Books, he bought some remarkably experimental and innovative material, which seems surprising in that during the late 1960s some "new wave" science-fiction people had condemned him for being a conservative.

"But back then I was editing for *Galaxy* magazine, and I *published* the majority of 'new-wave' writers," he points out. "Aldiss, Ballard, Ellison . . . it wasn't the stories I objected to, it was the snottiness of the proponents. I don't think the 'new wave' has actually died; it still survives in everything that is being written today, just as James Joyce survives. The thing that the 'new wave' did that I treasure was to shake up old dinosaurs, like Isaac [Asimov], and for that matter me, and Bob Heinlein, and show them that you do not really have to construct a story according to the 1930s pulp or Hollywood standards. This is a valuable thing to learn. I don't think I could ever have written *Gateway* if the 'new wave' hadn't happened. And I'm more pleased with that than any other book I've ever written."

I inquire what other influences have affected his work, and what his reading habits are.

"I read most of the science journals and magazines. I average about a book a day, and from time to time I realize there's a big hole in my education that I need to fill. Lately I've been reading nineteenth and early twentieth century writers; and Shaw plays, most of which I had read before when I was a teenager. I found myself with a copy of one in my hand and enjoyed reading the passage from it, so over the last couple of months I've read almost all of them over again. Then from time to time I go back and reread science fiction that I love. Edgar Rice Burroughs, and E. E. Smith. Of the newer writers, I'm impressed by John Varley and George Martin. I think they're very promising."

It all sounds very busy—even the reading seems more like a

workload than a recreation. I can't help wondering if he allows himself, or needs, any real leisure. The question causes a temporary halt in the conversation. "Well, I was wholly addicted to watching Kojak, as long as it was on television," he says. "I guess I loaf around a lot, too—my writing time is largely spent sitting at the typewriter mulling over the story and the world. I spend anywhere up to eight hours sitting at the typewriter without hitting one key, before I can find my way out of an impasse."

To me, it all sounds as if work is recreation and recreation is work, and Pohl is equally active in each. He is currently making some attempts to find a retreat.

"I'm shopping around for a new place to live. I'm not really living here," he gestures at the room, in its casual disorder. "I'm only here when I'm not traveling. I haven't yet found the perfect place, but I can describe it. It needs to be warm in the winter and not to have hurricanes or revolutions or civil disobedience or too much street crime, and it should be within reasonable distance of a major airport in case I want to go somewhere else. I've been looking in the Caribbean lately . . . a couple of months ago I tracked down an island called Grand Cayman, but that didn't work out. . . . I like being isolated. I think I'm overexposed to people because of doing so much lecturing and conventioning, and have become a lot less gregarious. A little isolation knits up my soul."

And I have no doubt that he will find it, and satisfy this need as he has satisfied his others. Frederik Pohl seems a slightly shy man, more self-analytical than other writers of his generation, carefully modest, and extremely complex. But he has a clear, quiet, deliberate determination; despite his low-key presence and his lack of a flamboyant identity he has asserted his will on the world as much as, or more than, any other science-fiction writer.

(New York, May 1979)

BIBLIOGRAPHICAL NOTES

The Space Merchants (1953) was Frederik Pohl's first collaborative novel with C. M. Kornbluth, and is still the title most often associated with his name. The novel cynically but accurately visualizes space travel as a commercially exploitable enterprise; it remains a classic. Pohl's other collaborations with Kornbluth include *Gladiator-at-Law* (1955) and *Search the Sky* (1954); in the latter, there is considerable comic relief, in addition to social awareness and invention.

Pohl's solo work includes classic stories such as "The Midas Plague" (1954), a satire on consumerism; his early work is represented in *The Best of Frederik Pohl* (1975). His earlier solo novels, *Slave Ship* (1957), *Drunkard's Walk* (1960), and *A Plague of Pythons* (1965), made a less enduring impact, but in 1977 he won a Nebula award for his novel *Man Plus*, dealing realistically with the biological adaptation of human beings for life on Mars, and the strength of his recent work continues through *Gateway* (1977), which won both the Nebula and Hugo awards in 1978, and *Jem* (1979).

Samuel R. Delany

Mystery novels are not usually written in stream-of-consciousness form. Likewise, westerns do not normally include sections of concrete poetry, and historical romances don't employ techniques of the avant-garde.

Science fiction, however, is different. Alone among the popular genres, it dares to experiment. Alfred Bester introduced unconventional prose and typography in his work of the 1950s; since then, Aldiss, Ballard, Moorcock, Ellison, Sladek, Disch, Farmer, and even a technologically oriented writer such as Joe Haldeman, have written stories and novels in ways that go outside of plain-and-simple storytelling.

Samuel R. Delany has gone furthest; his novel *Dhalgren* contains more than 300,000 words of difficult, esoteric, avant-garde writing, including some passages in double-column format (like a split-screen movie), streams of surreal, impressionistic prose, and strange syntax. This book alone confirmed Delany as the most prominent innovator in American science fiction, one with high literary aspirations. His critical essays, dissecting the work of his contemporaries in relentless detail, have also demonstrated how serious he is about things like style, semantics, and literary standards.

He is not an easy person to interview. His academic habits of analyzing prose and speech make him self-conscious about the act of communication, so that, as he talks, he runs a commentary on himself, and adds digressions and asides, and tentative propositions that are subsequently amended, and footnotes and parenthetic remarks. . . . The skein of words grows longer, and the stream of abstract thought becomes hard to follow, and it is difficult to disentangle the real essence of what is being said; and if you *do* grasp it, the subject itself often turns out to be a question of semantics—as if, to Delany, the message is the medium.

The only way I can convey, fully, the problems involved in listening to Samuel R. Delany is by quoting a portion of the interview in raw, unedited form. Here, he responds to a skeptical question about the importance of college literature courses specializing in science fiction:

"For instance, there are lots of sentences that can appear either in mundane fiction or science fiction, and one uses the term *mundane fiction* both with a sense of irony and also (the word simply means, *mundis*: world, that fiction which takes place in the world), by extension: the here-and-now, or in some historical real world. And any other connotations, well, it's just a matter of turnabout-is-fair-play. There are all sorts of sentences where the actual words could appear in both kinds of texts, for instance, 'Her world exploded': if this sentence appears in mundane fiction it is probably going to be a more-or-less muzzy emotional metaphor, referring to some internal state, whereas in a science-fiction text it reserves the margin to mean that a planet belonging to some woman blew up. Or, 'He turned on his left side,' in a text of mundane fiction probably refers to an insomniac; in science fiction it could mean that someone reached down and flipped a switch. So there's a little margin to the language in science fiction that mundane fiction frequently doesn't have. Also we store the information differently, reading a science-fiction story, to make it make sense. In the first couple of pages of *The Space Merchants* there's a sentence, 'He rubbed depilatory soap on his face and rinsed it away with a trickle from the fresh-water tap.' The depilatory soap marks it as science fiction because, you know, you don't use depilatory soap—but it does exist in the world—but it's telling you something about the world, it's telling you something about the world of the *story*; the fresh-water tap is a way of implying that in this particular world there are fresh-water taps and salt-water taps in every house, and the trickle is telling you that the fresh water is—is—you know, *low*. Whereas if this sentence—at least, the second half of it—appeared in a mundane fiction story, it would be, well, you know—and the point is when you start storing the information differently, then you are reading science fiction. No matter what the actual words may say. I think this kind of—the way you organize the information from the text, the way you read some of the sentences more literally, and of course science-fiction writers make use of this, but this is what essentially establishes the genre—which is what happens with any other genre.

"One of the things, when teaching science fiction, I've noted: you do have—in any situation with science fiction there are—two populations; there are those people who *won't* read science fiction, and there are also people who really *can't* read it, and are to be distinguished from people who just *won't* read it. I know I've come across more and more people who've actually tried to read science fiction and can't make it make sense. When I actually worked with some people who expressed their goodwill, claiming very seriously they had tried this, that, the other science-fiction novel, and it just didn't make sense—when we began to read the thing sentence by sentence, and you worked over it with them the way you would work with a child just learning to read, I began to discover that what they couldn't do is put the *world* together. They couldn't take the little hints, the little flashes, the little throwaways that any science-fiction writer uses, to make the world coherent, and make a world out of it. They were actually having difficulty, unless there was a page of exposition. All those little hints and what-have-you which are the essence of a science-fiction story—by which the author makes the whole thing vivid and makes the whole thing glitter—they literally didn't know how these were supposed to be read. And you'd also discover that by working with them through a science-fiction story literally phrase by phrase—you know, what does, and what does 'what does this mean about the world' mean about the story—you discovered they got better and better at it and eventually they learned it. But it is a language; in that sense science fiction really *is* a language; because, again, mundane fiction...you read it against a given world, or a view of the world that is a...you know, you don't have to construct the world for every single story, you just have to—the story's telling you which part of the world to pay attention to. But you're not, you know, always being given things that tell you that the world operates in an entirely different way from the way it does. And this makes one of the, you know, one of the problems with teaching science fiction, for those people who have not been reading it for years and years and years, anyway, and haven't learned the language simply by osmosis."

And so listening to Delany can be every bit as demanding—and prolonged!—as reading Delany.

In person he is open and affable, with a sincere manner and a good-naturedness which allows him to be unfailingly polite, even when replying to hostile critics or belligerent readers who complain that they weren't able to understand *Dhalgren*. Like Disch, Bryant, or Spinrad, Delany is one of the science-fiction writers who became notable in the 1960s, and brought more intellect, more analysis to bear on the genre than had been usual in the past. At the same time, Delany seems in love with the jargon, the hardware, and the spirit of old-fashioned space-adventure fiction, or "space opera." Surely (I suggest to him), this is a contradiction in terms: adventure fiction is most effectively written in simple, terse sentences, rather than in the heavily-styled or avant-garde prose he prefers.

"Obviously I don't see it as a contradiction in terms," he replies, "or I wouldn't be able to do it. I do like the basic 'space-opera' construct, the basic field in which it takes place—a field which has many worlds and exists as a set of relative centers. There is a kind of linear, gravitic thinking that organizes so much of our thinking; I do think just that basic image of several worlds relating to one another undercuts this up-down, higher-lower metaphorical thing, so that, somehow, there is good in the space-opera construct *per se*. I like the freedom that it gives."

I decide to be persistent. Isn't it an affectation, to overlay a popular art form with artistic pretentions?

"The question is, is it simply an overlay, or does it get down to something deeper? I don't think of it as adding a level, I think of it as exploring the entire construct in ways that it hasn't been explored before. I don't see it as a layer on top; I see it as going down into the whole thing and breaking it open."

To this I reply (focusing on what I see as the core of the matter): Is it better for a book to be finely written, or for it to be a bit clumsy, but full of primitive vitality?

"Primitive vitality is usually a kind of illusion. If you have a gut response to a story, you are not responding to something new; you can bet your bottom dollar that what you are really responding to is a story you were told when you were six or seven, which has been so overlaid, you don't recognize what it really is. But your subconscious recognizes it. If you're going to work with those old things, I think you do better to work with them with a sense of irony, to know that you're telling the old story and indeed keep your tongue somewhat in your cheek as you tell it. You also have to know what those old stories are and what they mean in order to actually say something new, because, if you don't, what you will do is end up saying the old things without knowing it. In that sense I think that a lot of the people who respond to the 'primitive vigor and vitality' of writing are fooling themselves."

Delany's mixing of forms—applying a kind of civilized sensibility to the writing of adventure fiction—has a parallel in his upbringing, which allowed him to experience an unusual mix of cultures. As a black youth, he grew up in Harlem; but, "I spent my days downtown at a white upper-class school at Park Avenue and 89th Street. Either my father or one of his employees would drive me down there. My parents felt there was a better education to be had.

"In Harlem we had a fairly nice private house—one block north of the most crowded tenement block in New York City, by the 1951 census. It gave me perhaps a misplaced sense of superiority that I had two worlds to play in whereas most of the people I knew had only one. I had a chance to compare different cultures in a way that still influences what I do and what I write. In one sense I've always been writing about people making trips through that kind of barrier—although not necessarily a racial barrier."

At the time of our interview, Delany is living on the top floor of a Manhattan walk-up tenement on the Upper West Side. The apartment's many rooms are sparsely, ascetically furnished. There are a lot of simple bookshelves of unpainted wood. Outside the living-room window, traffic roars up Amsterdam Avenue.

"I've always lived in more rundown parts of town," he says. "I always think that when society is beginning to fall apart, you can get a better view of how it operates, when everything is not absolutely squeaky-clean, because so much of that surface is there to mask the way things actually run."

Scenes of decay are indeed the most obviously recurring theme in Delany's work. Another theme which he returns to, especially in recent years, is feminism. I ask why he seems to have a special commitment to this cause.

"When I was nineteen, Marilyn [Marilyn Hacker, the poet whom Delany married in 1961] had just gotten a job at Ace Books editing manuscripts, and one of the things she came home constantly complaining of was the fact that the women characters were all either bitches or quivering simps. I just wanted to write a book with at least one feminine character who was slightly different. That was *The Jewels of Aptor*, where my one female character comes on for one chapter at the end," he laughs self-deprecatingly, "and looks different."

I feel Delany hasn't really responded to the sense of my question, so I go further and mention Norman Spinrad's outlook, which is to distrust any social movement that becomes an "ism."

"I think that's a kind of dishonest naiveté," Delany replies. "If Norman is saying that the reductionist version of any view of the world is not terribly interesting, sure; but the point is there are going to be people who do not see the world the way you see it; I mean, when I say that I think feminism is a very serious thing, I think the situation of fifty-three percent of the population—their rights and struggles—is a very serious matter. I don't see how anyone can fault that."

I mention that my only objection is to fiction which takes up the feminist cause (or any cause) to the point where it becomes not so much fiction as propaganda.

"I think the Marxist critic Lukacs said, back around 1916, the novel is the only art form in which the artist's ethical position *is* the aesthetic problem," he replies. "I think one realizes this when any kind of narrative begins to move toward some kind of maturity or some kind of sophistication."

I press him to restate this perhaps a little more simply. He willingly obliges:

"All fiction is propaganda, and the fiction we like is the propaganda we believe in, and the fiction we don't like is the propaganda we don't believe in."

Which fiction does Delany like? Which authors is he enthusiastic about?

"Disch. Russ." He pauses. There is a long silence. "Among the younger writers I like John Varley, M. John Harrison, very much. I still go back to some of our old war horses, Bester, and Sturgeon, who, at their best, were establishing the genre."

I ask what his future ambitions are.

"To keep doing science-fiction novels, but also to broaden what *is* science fiction. I do have all sorts of grandiose ambitions, to make the world a better place, and all those kinds of things. Not so much to influence people's thinking, but to influence their ways of reading. I want to write texts that *are* worthwhile reading, with a sense of imagination and with a sense of play, but a play of a much more complex kind than frequently is supplied through most science-fiction texts."

And regarding innovation:

"The choice is between saying what you do want to say, and saying what has been said many, many times before. Unfortunately, too many of the, quote, *experimental* writers, unquote, are—" He gropes unsuccessfully for a word. "You have to dispossess yourself of the illusion of meaningfulness," he says, more decisively. "If you start writing 'meaningful writing,' but you're not exactly sure *what* it means, chances are, it's carbonated crap."

(New York, March 1979)

BIBLIOGRAPHICAL NOTES

Samuel R. Delany's novel *Babel-17* (1966) is probably the best known of his earlier work. It tackles questions of semantics, given that our perception of reality is molded by the language which we think in. *The Einstein Intersection* is also a significant early novel, in which aliens attempt to interpret symbols of popular culture remaining on Earth after the disappearance of humanity.

Dhalgren (1975) is a novel-within-a-novel, chronicling in impressionistic style an odyssey of a youth through surreal, ruined, urban landscapes. It was commercially successful though controversial because of its length, style, and (according to some readers) its obscurity.

Delany's essays in literary criticism are collected in *The Jewel-Hinged Jaw* (1977).

Barry N. Malzberg

I have always been drawn to that land of domestic fantasy, American suburbia, where nothing is real. Cruise down Main Street, see the plaster facades molded to look like solid brick, plastic fashioned to resemble wrought iron, plywood treated to look like oak, Formica patterned to look like plywood. Mary Hartman land, where the International House of Pancakes is a bizarre architectural mutation, part Swiss chalet, part prefabricated Transylvanian castle, and the Household Finance Corporation is headquartered in a miniaturized mansion, a kiddieland version of a New England town hall, complete with cute little white columns at the entrance.

Once I dreamed of marrying and moving out of Manhattan and buying a house in the suburbs, where I would be comfortably wealthy and own a large car and become enduringly, dedicatedly depressed. I saw it as entering a kind of simplified stasis, a barbiturate nirvana. For me, it never happened; but for others, blessed with more ambition and initiative, it has all come true. For Barry Malzberg, in particular.

He lives in Teaneck, New Jersey. If you drive out of Manhattan across the George Washington Bridge, proceed for five miles along a drab divided highway, and make a sharp left, you find

Teaneck. Streets of well-spaced, solidly built houses, surrounded by trees and overlooking well-sprinkled lawns...housewives driving home from the supermarket with bags of groceries beside them on the front seat...mailboxes, utility poles, kids' bicycles lying in the driveways...serene, stable, and in a way dignified: no ostentatious wealth here, just a sense that people have done well enough to afford a comfortable family life away from the dirt and noise—and traumatic reality—of Manhattan.

The house of Barry Malzberg and his family fits right in: a middle-aged two-story building of some integrity, on a quiet block, a Cadillac in the garage, all very middle-American and conventional. Malzberg himself blends less easily with the suburban landscape. "I'm not very happy here," he says, "but I would be even more unhappy in New York." As for the local people, they make him feel alienated. They learn he's a writer and they say, "Oh really? Have you ever sold anything?" He tells them he has published more than thirty novels, and they say, "Oh really? What name do you write under?"

But alienation is nothing new; Malzberg says he has always felt alienated ("It seems to be the common denominator not only of science-fiction writers but of all fiction writers"), and depression, likewise, is another fact of life.

If this sounds too flippant, it is because in the face of too much pain one can only try to make gloomy little jokes. Certainly this is what Barry Malzberg manages to do himself, having experienced an extraordinary career marred by what must have been truly a crushing sequence of disappointment, frustration, and bitterness.

Prior to my visit, Barry N. Malzberg had always refused to give an interview to anyone. Still I found him approachable, and his answers quickly built together into a speech as succinct and cohesive as the rap of an experienced talk-show guest. The transcript speaks so eloquently I present it with a minimum of interjection or explanation:

"I wanted to win the Nobel Prize and be celebrated as the greatest living American writer. And I still do." (He laughs, self-deprecatingly.) "I had large ambitions, very large, from the beginning. I mapped out a course for myself, a large, ambitious career as an American novelist. My first model was Mailer, and a little bit later Philip Roth, whom I don't think is a first-rate writer, but had the kind of career that I would like to have had.

Brilliant short stories in the right places, National Book Award at the age of twenty-six, major critical recognition well before his thirtieth birthday. That was the career that I mapped out for myself. I failed, utterly.

"I realize, I do judge myself rather harshly. I operated from what F. Scott Fitzgerald called the authority of failure, very early in life, since I was maybe eighteen or nineteen. I never felt I was as good as I needed to be, ever to fulfill my ambitions.

"I had always known that I was going to be a writer. I've known it since I acquired the tools of literacy, at age seven. I didn't want to write for the money; I wanted to write because it was the only way I could deal with, control, and shape my experience. I wrote my first short story in second grade; I went to Syracuse University from fall of 1956 until 1960, spent six months in the army, two-and-a-half years in the New York City Department of Welfare. . . . I won a Schubert Foundation playwriting fellowship, 1964–1965. Once I was in the academic environment, writing, I achieved recognition very easily at that level. I was simply faster and better than anyone else around. But I felt a self-contempt, because it wasn't hard to be better than anyone around, and the work wasn't selling anyway. I wrote seven one-act plays, and one full-length play, none of which have ever been produced. I wrote some poetry, some of which was good, none of it ever published. I submitted some to the little magazines, unenthusiastically; it didn't seem to me, even at that nascent state, that I wanted to be in little magazines. Nobody read them and they didn't pay, so why bother.

"I became a science-fiction writer because I failed in my attempts to succeed in the literary world. I quit the largest writing fellowship in the country—the Cornelia Award Creative Writing Fellowship—in 1965, because I was being rejected. I was writing literary short stories and drowning in rejections and I just did not want to go any further.

"In October or November of that year I read in *Galaxy* magazine Norman Kagan's story *Laugh Along with Franz*. It was a brilliant, savage piece of science fiction, except it wasn't science fiction at all, it was a serious, savage work of American fiction by a young American fiction writer. I shook my head as I read it and I cynically said to myself, if this son of a bitch can get away with this kind of stuff in the commercial science-fiction genre then I've got a future, because I can do this just as well myself right now, and I can do it a little better in a couple of years, given a little training. If he can get away with this, I can too. And it was at that moment that I knew, viscerally, that I could sell science fiction.

"By sheer chance I had become a ninety-dollar-a-week employee of the Scott Meredith Literary Agency. I became familiar with the commercial markets, studied the science-fiction markets for about a year, and then started to write for them, with a mixture of literary ambition and cold commercial focus, and I was quite successful. I had a terrific run. Between 1968 and 1975 I had, in quantity, an unduplicable career. There have been writers who wrote more, and writers who wrote better, but nobody ever did as much work of *ambition* in science fiction within such a short period of time. I wrote twenty-five novels and 200 short stories within those seven years.

"Philip Dick with his forty or fifty novels and his 100 short stories is ahead of me. Silverberg is ahead of me. But I don't think that either of those boys squeezed it into seven years. Actually Silverberg and I had very parallel careers; it's close. As for Phil, I admire him more than I admire myself; to be able to do work of that intention and ambition and sustain it from 1954 to 1975 is stunning. He carried it on for two decades.

"In April 1976 I renounced my association with the science-fiction field. Since then I have written a body of work outside of science fiction which by any standards other than those I set myself would probably be sufficient. I have written three commercial suspense novels in collaboration with Bill Pronzini. I've written a pseudonymous novel, *Lady of a Thousand Sorrows* by Lee W. Mason, a roman-a-clef in the first person by a character who was consciously modeled on Jacqueline Kennedy. It was a story that had obsessed me for years. I wrote it at a very high level of ambition, it was published as a Playboy Press paperback original, and they literally threw it in the sewer, thank you very much, Playboy Press. And lastly I novelized my novelette *Chorale*, for Doubleday, who published it to stunning indifference. And then of course I have continued writing short stories: fifteen for Hitchcock's magazine, three for *Ellery Queen*, and about twelve science-fiction stories. By the standards I set myself—for instance in 1973 I wrote sixteen novels, thirty short stories, and a poem— my current output is minuscule.

"I found writing therapeutic when I was young. Until perhaps my thirty-first birthday, it was serving short-term purgative needs. It was cathartic, it was controlled, it was expressive. Relatively late in life, around my thirty-fifth birthday, it occurred to me that writing was actually dealing with the most neurotic, deteriorative, defensive aspects of my personality, and at that point I became very unhappy.

"People tend to want to become writers to compensate. We know this. Most people who want to write fiction want to do so to compensate for real or perceived flaws or inadequacies in their real lives. That's okay except that I began to feel somewhere in mid-life that perhaps compensating as a way of life was kind of a sad thing for an adult.

"Now, writing never makes me happy. Of course many writers say this, and then add, however, that *having written* is ecstacy. I myself would have said that, as recently as five years ago. But I can't even say that any more.

"I get nothing out of seeing my books in print. Absolutely nothing. I stack them up on the shelves; I collect them. I'm an obsessive collector of my own work; it's all I have, these fragments I shore against my ruins. I want my own work, and I want it displayed, and that's probably symbolic of the fact that I am still *connected* to being a writer, but it's virtually the last thing. That and the money. I get no satisfaction out of having my work in print."

We pause at this point. I find it hard to grope for another question to ask; anything I say seems to lead back to this steady litany of grief. I am sitting beside Malzberg on a couch in his comfortable, lived-in living room. He has been talking in a low-pitched voice, shy and self-conscious but determined to spell everything out in full, metaphorically hammering the nails into his own literary coffin, with grim satisfaction. He has only paused to refill his glass with ice and vodka occasionally.

His wife, Joyce, has been sitting quietly in a chair opposite us, listening. Now he turns to her: "How'm I doing, Joyce? Too self-expository?"

She smiles. "A laugh here and there wouldn't hurt."

"Perhaps we reach the funny bits later," I suggest.

"Oh, no," says Barry, firmly. "No, what I've been saying, *that's* the *good* news."

Joyce turns to me. "If you didn't feel miserable when you came in, just wait till it's time to leave."

I get the impression that the Malzberg condition of despair has become an accepted fact of life here, like air pollution or rising real-estate taxes. You can't do anything about it, so you might as well learn to live with it.

I try a different approach. I ask him which, out of all his stories and novels, he is most pleased with.

"The best short story that I ever wrote in my life—which nobody has ever noticed—is 'Uncoupling,' which appears in Roger Elwood's *Dystopian Visions* anthology and in my *The Best of Malzberg*. It has been read by about four people, I guess. I wrote it on January 14, 1973, a Saturday night, between 8:15 and 8:50, while Joyce was getting dressed to go to a party. Four thousand two hundred words in thirty-five minutes, and that's as close to joy in writing as I've come since I was fourteen. I never even read it—I never read a lot of my short stories. I addressed an envelope, we walked an extra block so I could mail it, and then we went to the party. It wasn't till the story got into print two-and-a-half years later that I read it, and then I said, boy, this is sensational!

"Of my novels, *Underlay* is my favorite. Avon Books bought it; they couldn't publish it as science fiction, because it wasn't science fiction; but literary novels by science-fiction authors go nowhere either, so they didn't know what to do. They settled for printing 15,000 copies, and before the rights to the book reverted back to me my royalty statements indicated it had sold 3,500. *Underlay*, which I thought was the best novel I ever wrote or was capable of writing, received one review, in a fiction roundup in the *Hudson Review* in the summer of 1975, covering forty or fifty titles. They thought that it showed 'remarkable energy and talent' for a paperback original, and showed how pervasive had become the tools of the literary novel. Malzberg, an ordinary paperback hack, showed a surprising command of bravura technique. That was the only review I received. The book has reverted to me; I cannot now resell it; it looks like a flaccid, detumescent penis oozing brown semen—is that all right, can that be transcribed? I'm noted for my imagery, yes."

Underlay was a novel of charm and gentle comedy, but many of Malzberg's other books have been criticized as being grim and depressing (the same sort of complaint that has been leveled against Thomas M. Disch's work). How does Malzberg respond to accusations of being a gloomy writer?

"First I was delighted to be noticed. Then the disappointment, then the rage, the contempt. They don't understand my work. They don't understand what I was trying to do. I don't think I'm a particularly gloomy writer. I find far more gloom in Poul Anderson or Christopher Anvil. First of all I had a comic vision; I truly did. And secondly, nobody can write with this precision and passion, about anything, without being life-confirming. I believe that profoundly. That's why I think J. G. Ballard's *Crash* and *The Atrocity Exhibition*—this is not death, this is life. To be able to write in such a poised and beautiful fashion and control it so well is affirmation, is optimistic. I'm not as good as Ballard; I wish to hell I were. But I know exactly what that man was trying to do, and that's what I was trying to do."

I ask if he ever imagined an alternative career, other than writing.

"I'd like to be the first violinist in a symphony orchestra. I wish I could play the violin at all well. If I could, I would then be like any one of a number of musicians who are infinitely better than I am and can't get a job. But being a violinist strikes me as being infinitely more satisfying than being a writer. It pleases my soul."

What about being an editor? Briefly, Malzberg took over editorship of *Amazing* and *Fantastic* science-fiction magazines, in the 1960s.

"I never thought of myself as a very strong or memorable editor. I had an ability which I thought was the minimum requirement of an editor, which was simply that I could tell good from bad. That doesn't seem like much, does it? But almost no contemporary editor seems to have it.

"If I were a manifestly unqualified person with cachet of one sort or another, then I'm sure I could find an editing job. But I'm a moderately qualified person with no cachet.

"I think the level of editing and publishing, now, is as debased and corrupt as I've ever known it to be. The field's in a bad way, now. But that's always been my perception of the field. Even when I was twelve years old I knew that most science fiction was bad. Dreadfully written, dreadfully imagined, clumsily handled at every level."

I remark that he says this with something close to satisfaction, as if he's pleased, in some strange way, when life fulfills his worst expectations.

"There's an American expression: shit-kicking. That's when you get an Academy Award and you say, 'Oh, man, me get an award for acting? I can't even enunciate an English word! If it weren't for my mother and my director and my scriptwriters, I'd be lucky to work in a diner slinging hash!' That's shit-kicking, okay? It's shit-kicking maybe when I say, 'My work doesn't matter to me at all; now, tell me, *tell* me it doesn't matter.'

"But I honestly believe that. It's not a pose. I don't think it matters at all and I think my career in science fiction to have been a mistake at best, a tragedy most likely. But if I had to do it all over again I would do it exactly this way. I had to run the course, I had to find out. I'd do it all over again, to the same conclusion. In a way it's satisfying because there's no sense of loss, I will never have to lie awake at night thinking, *what might have been if*—Or, *could I have been a writer*. I have become the best version of what I could have been"

After the interview, the Malzbergs invite me to stay for a meal of Kentucky Fried Chicken (so this is what one eats in suburbia!) and then Barry suggests I play their piano while he accompanies me on violin. His taste is classical, whereas my ability is limited to blues and rock; his violin pursues the chord progression (more or less) about two bars behind. It's quite painful.

But his appetite for excitement is as fresh as ever; he insists on a game of chess. It turns out that we both play with the same foolhardy aggression, flawed strategy, and crass blunders. I win only by luck and his errors. He immediately insists on a rematch; and this second game is played in grim, tense silence, punctuated only by sudden cries of excitement or despair. Finally I pretend to make a mistake, sacrificing a piece; Malzberg seizes on it in mad triumph; and then discovers—too late!—he will be checkmated on my next move.

"Tricked!" he shouts, leaping to his feet. "You set me up! And I fell for it! I fell for it like a babe in arms!" He snatches his fallen king from the board and throws it across the room, then strides from the dining area to the living room and back again, hurling more chess pieces in various directions. He's very tall, with amazingly long arms and legs; I have to back away from the flailing limbs and flying chessmen.

I apologize for having won in an underhanded fashion. "No! No! It was a coup! You deserved to win! I was a fool!" And he groans and subsides into his chair by the fireplace.

Later, just before I leave, he shows me his workroom. It is a little annex off the living room, without even a proper desk. His typewriter is a Smith-Corona portable electric—one of those cheap machines painted in bright colors, for students and part-time home-workers. "I like it because you can pound it hard," he says. "When the carriage bangs back, the whole thing jumps, you have to hit it back into position." He glowers at the typewriter, and his gesticulations make him look as if he's shadow-boxing with it.

A couple of weeks later, I encounter Mr. and Mrs. Malzberg at a Manhattan party. We leave the place together, and walk out to the street. Malzberg gets out his car keys, and unlocks the door of a new, pale-blue, totally anonymous, middle-class, Chevrolet Impala.

"My god, what happened to your Cadillac Coup-de-Ville?" I exclaim.

"I had to sell it. It was falling apart."

"This actually has more passenger space inside than the Cadillac," his wife points out hopefully.

"It's a horrible car." Malzberg eyes it malevolently. "Horrible. It makes a noise as if there's a *grasshopper* in the engine."

"But I was going to mention, in my profile of you, your Cadillac in the garage," I protest. "It was part of your image."

"Good! Fine! So now you can add a postscript, about how I had to sell it and buy *this!*" and he glowers at the Chevrolet with the same manic fascination he showed toward his typewriter. Maybe it's my imagination, but I see him, facing his car, sizing up yet another adversary—and savoring its inexorable victory over him, and his glorious defeat.

(Teaneck/New York, May 1979)
•

BIBLIOGRAPHICAL NOTES

Barry Malzberg's earliest work was written under the pseudonym K. M. O'Donnell; short stories from this period are collected in *Final War and Other Fantasies* (1969) and *In the Pocket and Other Science Fiction Stories* (1971). As O'Donnell he wrote *Gather in the Hall of the Planets*, an accurately-observed comedy whose scenario is a science-fiction convention of writers and fans.

Writing under his own name, in the 1970s, Malzberg achieved recognition with *Beyond Apollo* (1972), an innovative and ironic commentary on the U.S. space program. It won the John W. Campbell Memorial Award. Of Malzbug's substantial output of science fiction, *Overlay* (1972) is notable for its absurdist interplay between aliens and a race-track bettor;

the book is related to *Underlay*, a charming comedy, without science-fiction content, in Damon Runyon tradition. In *Herovit's World* (1973) Malzberg dramatizes the antipathy and alienation he feels, confronted with commercial publishing, in his role as a science-fiction author.

*Photo by
Arlene Solomon*

Edward Bryant

Edward Bryant has come from his home in Denver to New York City, for the Nebula Awards ceremony. What is a Nebula? It is a block of lucite with a spiral of silvery dust suspended inside it. Who awards this prize? The Science Fiction Writers of America, a professional guild, which casts an annual ballot to pick the best science fiction, in various categories.

And this time it has been Bryant's turn to win, for "Stone," judged the best short story of the year.

He's happy to be a winner—of course!—and yet . . .

What about the eleven long years in which he has been writing stories, never enough stories, and no novels at all, except for one failure that he didn't even submit anywhere? What about the next few years, and the stories that he should be working on (but isn't), and the whole problem of *producing*? He consoles himself by remarking that many writers do their best work around the age of fifty, so Bryant, aged thirty-four has some time left. But it seems hollow consolation. He knows what he ought to be doing, yet he hasn't been doing it. He's acknowledged as a very talented newer-generation writer who produces fine work, but it's not enough. Cynical as he may pretend to be, and laid-back as he may seem to be, he cares, and worries, and is his own enemy. He is of a post-Freudian generation whose self-analysis is honest, clever, but unhelpful in alleviating the problem which it has identified. Even worse, in a way, analysis itself is part of the problem: you can end up analyzing yourself so thoroughly that there's no time for actually getting anything done. And this problem, too, can be analyzed.

Meanwhile, some of the stories that Edward Bryant *has* managed to produce are published, interconnected, in his book *Cinnabar*, and others are in a large new collection. In a year or three he may be making a bigger impact on science fiction's mass audience; right now, he is only well-known within the science-fiction field itself, and among its more completist readers.

His situation, his outlook, and his talent are important, as counterpoint to the successes and methods of older writers who never had the double-edged weapon of analytical introspection.

Bryant has a moustache, is slim, and wears his hair long, straight down to his shoulders. In the 1960s his appearance would have been seen as a radical political statement; these days it somehow looks anonymous and even respectable (the long hair and moustache are neatly trimmed). He is not an expressive person; his face seldom shows much, and he has a slightly studious air. To some extent this is a misleading image.

The interview takes place at my apartment in New York, and we start at the beginning:

"My father had a romantic idea about our family being cattle ranchers. So we went to southern Wyoming when I was six months old and did it without benefit of electricity or other civilized amenities; it was very much an Abraham Lincoln cliché. I walked half a mile to a one-room school, for the first three-and-a-half grades.

"I was an emotionally stunted case. I spent a lot of time reading. When I was about eight I was in the bunkhouse on my parents' ranch, and I found two paperbacks: *Mandingo*, and *Donovan's Brain* by Kurt Siodmak. The latter was the one I chose to read, and I think my writing was predicated on that choice. Had I read *Mandingo* instead I would probably be very prosperous by now, because I would be writing whip-and-chain slavery-oppression novels; *but*, I read the science-fiction novel."

His first sale was to *Again, Dangerous Visions*, the anthology of new fiction edited by Harlan Ellison. Ellison "discovered" Bryant at one of the Clarion science-fiction writing workshops, from which have emerged several new authors over the last ten or so years. Bryant comments, wearily:

"Yes, I'm a Clarionoid. Eleven short years, from Clarion to a Nebula. Another overnight success. Oh, Christ.

"I was pretty prolific from 1968 through to the middle 1970s. Then for three or four years I averaged only three short stories a year. But I have somehow kept away from getting a full-time job outside of writing; there's something symbolic about just packing it in and becoming a counterman at Burger Chef. So I scrounge jobs; I've worked a lot in the last few years in Writers in the Schools programs for various arts councils, going around to places like Austin, Nevada, population 400, staying anything from one day to two weeks and handling classes, telling people they should never become writers because it will do them no good at all, and discouraging them in any way I can.

"I get the teaching jobs basically through word-of-mouth. It started when someone at a science-fiction convention, who taught English at a junior college, said, 'How would you like to come to speak to my class, I'll give you $50 and a meal.' That sounded good to me. It still sounds good to me. So I did it, and somehow it led to that person talking to someone else. . . .

"Every state technically has an arts council, and you can just write to them and ask for application forms. It doesn't take very much of a credential to qualify, and generally you're paid anywhere from fifty to one hundred dollars a day, and expenses. Of course these things tend to be very spotty and there's a lot of time involved traveling back and forth, and you don't make much money when all's said and done. But it assures me that in a given month I'll have $400 or $500 to pay some rent and minimum charges on Visa and Master Charge.

"I've lived for months at a time on food purchased with Master Charge from a Denver grocery. You can't charge indefinitely, of course, and I was reaching the end of the lines of credit; but my Master Charge and Visa were each issued from a different bank, and each bank suddenly sent me a letter saying, would I be interested in obtaining the opposite card. So now I've started a second Master Charge account. This has potential for an enormous financial disaster. I think I'd better see about getting another Social Security Card . . . and a fake passport. . . ."

I ask what led to this dire state of affairs.

"*Not writing*, that's what led to it!

"After selling my first story, for $150 in 1968, which was

pretty impressive to me, there was the promise of fame and further riches. I thought, if I write only one short story a week, I've got it made, I don't even have to write novels. At that time I was finishing my Masters degree in English, which was futile. I spent most of the next year writing short stories and working part-time at my uncle's stirrup-buckle factory in Wyoming. Most of the stories were science fiction and fantasy, and nobody wanted any of them; I sold one story, and that was a collaboration. But there's a syndrome that other writers have told me about, which worked the same for me: once I started selling stories regularly in 1969, those old practice efforts, usually without any rewriting, sold too. I went out to California, and there I started selling to *Knight* and *Adam*, these sleazy men's magazines, for $200 a shot, which is twice what I would have made from the science-fiction markets. That supported me for another year—a kind of subsidy to young writers.

"In Clarion we had been urged to write novels, because short stories were a financial cul-de-sac. Finally in 1972 I did a 'college novel.' If it's really done well this is the kind of novel in which a usually-young writer talks about what he or she has learned, the epiphanies of learning the truth about real life and growing up, usually centered around college experience. I determined to do 3,000 words a day until it was done. No matter what, I wrote 3,000 words a day. It took me three weeks and it's the one piece of writing that I've never sent even once to an editor. It's horrible. Four people have read it, ranging in reaction from loathing it to merely despising it. But I should be able to cannibalize perhaps half of it and incorporate it into a rather different framework. It's the one true novel that I've done.

"Three or four years ago, I did get a contract with a publisher to write three novels. At the time it seemed a great idea, but as soon as I signed the contract I felt the glacier closing in around me, I felt the weight of three books dragging me down. I became literarily impotent; I have continued to write short stories, but very slowly.

"I feel very angry with myself. I put myself through all sorts of neurotic hell. I count up the years that I haven't written books. I think about the books that haven't been written and probably never will be written. Some of them might have been decent books, at least transition books. And of course that's one of the ways I avoid writing—by going through all the mental games, emotional games about it."

He states all of this seriously, yet with ironic humor, as if he is amused by his own hopeless traits, at the same time that he despairs of them. I ask if he knows a way of avoiding the excesses of self-analysis which seem a barrier to getting on with the job and getting something done.

"When someone is getting something done, they minimize the self-analysis," he says, with irony, turning it around. "But I don't think it ever goes away. Unless through enormous amounts of drugs, or some other artificial means."

Does he have a notion of the kind of writer he would like to be?

"If there were to be a role-model it would be John Fowles. Part of his being a good writer is that he tends not to repeat his own successes. He is relatively adventurous. It is not lost on me that when Fowles does a new work of fiction he is both lionized by the critics and enormously successful in commercial terms as well.

"My fantasy is that I go into a very small-town public library, and find my books on the shelves, with each call-slip showing an incredible number of rubber-stamped entries. Because I've certainly walked into small-town libraries and notice *Cinnabar* on the shelf and then found that the slip informs me the book was checked out once in 1977 and twice when it first came out in 1976, and that's it."

Fantasies aside—does he have ambitions for specific achievements?

"I don't have great plans for literary achievement. The Nebula—in some ways I was delighted to get the Nebula; I had a terrific time on Saturday night after I got it, it was very enjoyable, but it was also anticlimactic. It's a beautiful hunk of lucite crystal, but it doesn't mean anything ultimately, because what's important to me are the stories that are going to come.

"I brought with me to New York the beginnings of three stories, all of which will be finished. That multiple-book contract will be renegotiated so that my first obligation will be to do a major short-story collection—as opposed to a minor short-story collection or just an ordinary short-story collection? I suppose it means 100,000 words instead of 60,000. And then I'll follow that with a novel of my choice.

"Sometimes when I remember it took me only twenty-one days to write that terrible first novel, it seems, well, if I allow a week between novels to recover, I could do twelve novels a year. Then sanity grabs hold, and I know exactly what those novels would turn out to be. And then I slide back to a different level and say, yes, but, if I did those twelve terrible first-draft novels, I could afford, then, to let them lie fallow and then come back and rework each one and turn it into some splendid work of fiction. And then again I say, no, no way, it's crazy. Ultimately I suppose it's all a delaying tactic—to delay opening the typewriter and putting in the paper and typing the first word.

"There's a wonderful couplet: 'When I've died I hope it may be said/My sins were scarlet but my books were read.' That's a great one to use at writers' workshops. It amuses the crowd, it's a wonderful ice-breaker. And then," he says with a deadpan weariness, "you can get on to talking about narrative hooks."

(New York, April 1979)

BIBLIOGRAPHICAL NOTES

Edward Bryant's best earlier stories were collected in *Among the Dead* (1973). His book *Cinnabar* (1976) gathers together interconnected stories, all on the same theme. Thus far, his only other published work in book form is *Phoenix Without Ashes* (1975), the novelization of an original script by Harlan Ellison for the U.S. television series, "The Starlost."

A new collection of stories, *Particle Theory*, is scheduled to be published late in 1980.

Alfred Bester

New York, summer 1970: I was sitting in my horrible five-feet-by-ten-feet thirty-dollar-a-month room, on my thrift-shop chair, at a table I had dragged in from the street. Trucks on the avenue were roaring past, belching diesel fumes. Puerto Rican kids were on the roof of my building, pounding their conga drums. Next door a radio was blaring WABC bubblegum music. But I was blissfully unaware of these low-rent surroundings; unaware, even, of the ninety-degree heat. I was fully absorbed in reading, for the eighth or ninth time, *The Stars My Destination* by Alfred Bester.

When I had finished the book and returned to reality, I wished, as always, that Bester had written more. Only two novels, and a dozen or so short stories, in the 1950s—a handful of work which had been so unusual and so excellent, it had made him one of the enduringly important names in science fiction. Few of his contemporaries had ever matched his vitality, and no others—none at all—had matched his innovation, sophistication, and satirical wit. Bester alone experimented freely with typography (in both his novels, and short stories such as "The Pi Man"), and even combined first, second, and third-person voices in a multiple-viewpoint narrative ("Fondly Fahrenheit"). And he alone, among science-fiction writers of his generation, seemed truly keyed into

93

modern media and the arts, urban style and fashion. One sensed that he must have contacts on Madison Avenue; that he would be a connoisseur of wine, and he'd dress rakishly.

It struck me as odd that this science-fiction innovator and influence had never received much critical attention. Where Heinlein or Bradbury had been checklisted, indexed, surveyed, and critiqued to the point of total boredom, I had never seen an appreciation of Bester's work, or any explanation for why he had stopped writing science fiction.

I felt an impulse to satisfy my curiosity. I didn't know where he lived, but I had a hunch that it must be New York City. I picked up the Manhattan phone book. Sure enough, his name was listed. I hesitated, and then I dialed the number.

He answered right away, brightly: "Hi, this is Alfie Bester."

It was an odd moment. A disembodied author-figure had suddenly become real; I might just as well have gotten through to Santa Claus.

I told him who I was, and, to provide an excuse for the phone call, I mentioned I would like to interview him some time for *New Worlds* magazine.

"Why certainly, when do you want to do it? How about now?" It was a playful challenge, very New York-style, as if saying— you mean it? You seriously want to do it? Then why procrastinate? What's stopping you?

So I went over and met him. It turned out he not only had Madison Avenue contacts, he *lived* on Madison Avenue. He got me drunk, delivered a virtuoso renaissance-man monologue strewn with first names of the famous (from "Sir Larry" Olivier on down), told me a simple formula which I should use in writing my article, and sent me home. I have been using that formula ever since to write most of my nonfiction work, including the profiles in this book.

Nine years have passed. Alfie (as I now know him) has grown even more opinionated, slightly more eccentric, and no less challenging. In fact, his strength of character and identity would be unbearable, were it not buffered with such friendly, gentle charm. We should remember that this man was not only science fiction's first stylistic innovator, but that he did it entirely *alone* in the 1950s. He had no movement, coterie, or clique around him to tell him that he was right and his techniques were valid. He was a solitary radical, whose classic novel *The Demolished Man* was at first turned down by "every publisher in New York" because it was so different from anything that had been done before. It takes a lot of willpower to pursue that kind of career. (When I asked him in 1970 how to cope psychologically with having one's work rejected by editors, his advice was "Drink more!")

And now, at the beginning of the 1980s, he still seems determined to continue being an innovator and polemicist. While others of his generation have either retired or slowed down, Bester has returned to science fiction, aiming high, refusing to repeat himself, and experimenting with unorthodox methods which he freely admits are a gamble. His most recent work is a truly visual novel, incorporating collages and some artwork that he drew himself; as for his next novel, he says (name-dropping incorrigibly, as always): "It's based on the old philosophical concept of *anima mundi*—the soul of the world. In the book, everything is alive. The furniture, the pictures, the people, the chairs you sit on. It's going to be pretty wild. I was talking to Steve King about it [author of *The Shining* and other best-sellers] and I threw it on him, I said, Steve, the philosophic concept says that flowers talk to us, furniture, everything has this world soul, and the only reason we don't hear them is because either they talk too slow or too fast, which I buy, that's fine, that's wonderful, but Christ, typographically how am I going to do it? I still haven't decided."

He talks energetically, jovially, often using early-1960s hip slang, like a New York sophisticate of that era who refuses to grow old. His return to science fiction in 1974 came after years of working on *Holiday* magazine: "I had my ten years with *Holiday*, and that was enough. Curtis Magazines fell apart completely—*The Saturday Evening Post* went out of business, and *Holiday* was bought by some cockamamie manufacturer from Indianapolis who had made a fortune manufacturing housemaid plastic aprons. They asked me to go out to Indianapolis, and I went and took one look and said, Forget it, I'm quitting. I can't work with second-rate people, I really can't. And these people were *fifth*-rate.

"I went back to science fiction to try a few experiments and stuff like that, and my first experiment was a disaster, as you know. That confounded book *The Computer Connection* [titled *Extro* in Britain]. There is something vitally wrong with that book, and I knew it when I finished it, and I couldn't patch it then, and to this day I think about it, because there's no point in making a mistake unless you understand the mistake so that you don't make it again. I don't understand it, so I can't profit by it. It's infuriating. Of course my redheaded old lady, and a few other people, say 'No, no, it's much better than you think,' and I say, thanks a lot, but—I think of it as Beethoven's Fourth Symphony. It comes between the Third and the Fifth. I hope."

Having written for many other genres and almost every branch of the media, Bester still retains a fundamental loyalty for science fiction: "It's the one literary medium left in which we have a free hand. We can do any damn thing we please. And we know we have a creative reading public who will go along with us. You're not, shall I say, stunning them with the unexpected. They may disagree with your unexpected, but they're not stunned by it, whereas the constant reader of, let's say, women's magazines and women's fiction, if she or he tries to read science fiction, will be absolutely bewildered, flabbergasted, won't know what to make of it."

For many years, Bester has relied on other fields, such as TV scriptwriting, as his primary source of income. Science fiction he writes for fun, rather than profit:

"I feel very sorry for so many first-rate, splendid writers who earn their livings solely through science fiction and as a result have to turn out an awful lot of junk, because the rates have been very low in the past. Fortunately I have not been forced to do that."

Rates of payment in science fiction are much higher now; does he approve of this?

"Yes, that's splendid."

But surely, the commercialization of science fiction, with larger sums being offered by publishers, tempts an author even more to write for the money and produce whatever seems appropriate to the market.

"Of course they will," he says, cheerfully. He refuses to be baited by my line of questioning, and goes on into an ingenuous laissez-faire philosophy: "Sometimes, I imagine, an author will be writing exactly what he or she thinks the market wants, and without their knowledge they're turning out a masterpiece. As for second-rate, commercial writing—ass-licking writing, as it were—what's the harm in that? Good god, people who read books in subways don't want to be startled too much, they like nice convenient stories, and these *are* convenient stories. Good for them, good for all of them, that's great."

I remark that this sounds a very optimistic outlook.

"I'm afraid I'm an unregenerate optimist. What can I do? You know, it's so easy to be sour and to beef about things—stuff like that—well, I think that's just a sign of frustration, that's all, and since I don't happen to be a particularly frustrated guy, I'm very happy to let anybody else do anything they damn well please. Fine, great, have a good time."

I ask who the writers are whom he particularly admires.

"Harlan Ellison is just the greatest. Even when Harlan goofs, I just love everything he does, because, by god, he goes for hell and high water, to do something different, startle you. It's like Heinlein, once I said, come on, how do you write, kid? And Robert said, I'll tell you what I do. He said, it's like a man in the street is passing by; I reach out, I grab him by the lapels, and I pull him into a doorway, and shake him until his teeth rattle. And that's what Harlan does, and I admire him tremendously.

"There's a marvelous writer named Ballard—what is it, A. G., E. G. Ballard? Jesus Christ, that son of a bitch could write. Christ, he's written some stories I wish I had written. There's one called "The Voices of Time"; whew! What a piece of work. It makes no sense to me at all, but I am absolutely enchanted by it, it's great. And of course *The Crystal World* is a hell of a novel.

"Brian Aldiss—brilliant—*too* brilliant. I've had this argument with Brian for ages. I say, look, Brian, if I can't understand you half the time—and I can't—how the hell do you expect your readers to understand you? But Brian's off on this brilliance kick, I don't know why. I think his greatest novel was *Hothouse* [also titled *The Long Afternoon of Earth*]. You know, Bob Mills, when he was editing *Fantasy and Science Fiction* magazine, received the manuscript and was terribly worried, and sent it up to me and said, Alfie, should I print it or not? I read it and said, If you don't print it you're a damn fool, it's one of the greatest things that's ever been done. He said, But, it's so different. I said, That's exactly *why*. Some of my contemporaries who started with me, I think—I don't want to mention any names—have either been repeating themselves over and over again, which I think is criminal, or else have lost their energy, lost their drive. And some of them fortunately have quit writing altogether. And I'm sorry about that." He looks embarrassed at where his conversation has taken him. "Crikey, I don't know what to say."

I suggest that he seems to be setting himself just a little apart from the rest of science fiction, as if it is a world he doesn't really fit into easily.

"It's true, I don't. In Brighton [at the World Science Fiction

Convention in 1979] I felt terribly out of place and rather embarrassed by it. This is a tough one, because I'll be accused of snobbism; but the truth of the matter is that my background is the entertainment business—studios, the theater, publishing offices, *Holiday* magazine, where I was senior editor. As a result, the science-fiction colleagues of mine—I mention no names—seem rather sophomoric to me, and their jokes [at the convention] were rather like fraternity jokes from my freshman year, and the fans of course with their dressing-up and costumes seemed just like overgrown kids, so of course I felt out of place. One might say, Oh, Alfie, come on, don't be a snob. But the truth is that all that's way behind me, and I can't get into the swing of it with any ease." He pauses, almost shyly. "So, I drink too much." And he laughs.

"The few times I spoke to the kids [at the convention] I just leveled with them. I talked plain, ordinary, realistic shop to them, as I would—for example, Peter Benchley came in with a piece that he had written down in DC on sharks, and nobody in the *Holiday* office wanted it, and I was new in the office, and I loved it. I had a violent battle with the art director and my editor-in-chief, I fought for it, so they took it. Then Peter came in, and I leveled with him, I said now, Peter, this is a hell of a piece, but this is the first chapter of a novel. Now, are you going to put your back into it, and do the goddamn novel, or are you going to let it go at this, and go on being a drifter, writing odd pieces for *Holiday?* This is the same way I talked to the kids at the convention. Well, Peter took my advice and put his back into it, and turned out, of course, as you know, *Jaws.* For which I take no credit at all; I just use him as an example of the way I talk to all my colleagues on a professional level, and the way I talked to the kids at Brighton. I don't know whether the kids at Brighton understood. But you've got to do your best."

And he does always seem to be trying to do his best; trying to top himself, in his fiction, to the point where it sometimes seems a self-conscious duty for him to be dazzling and memorable. The result could be embarrassingly pretentious, were it not always coupled with such charm and such severe self-criticism.

"I am my own worst editor," he says. "I'm my worst critic, I'm a son of a bitch when it comes to me. My father, who was born and raised in Chicago, never really learned to speak Eastern English, he spoke Chicago English, he always pronounced my name 'Alford', and when he was very angry with me he would say [Bester goes into a deep, solemn voice] 'Alfoord, what have you done now?'—that sort of thing. Well I now use that for myself, when I've let myself down. I look at myself and say, 'Alfoord, you have to do better next time, Alfoord.'"

There's a pause at this point, as I try to decide which line of questions I want to pursue next. Bester seizes on this pause as a sign of lethargy on my part. "What, have I run you out of gas?" he exclaims happily. "Come on!" I think he likes the idea of being twice my age (he was born in 1913) but still as quick-witted, or more so.

I ask what his ambitions were, when he started out as a writer. Did he ever imagine he might end up well-known? Did he aim for that?

"I was an apprentice trying to learn my craft, that's all. I broke into writing for pulp magazines—detective magazines, science fiction, too, adventure—I used to write for a magazine called *South Sea Stories*. Oh boy, my south sea stories were really something! And then from there, a couple of my editors got brought over to that brand-new thing called comic books, where there was a desperate need for writers. It was a new medium, a new challenge. From there I went on to ghosting *Mandrake the Magician* and *The Shadow* for Lee Falk for a couple of years, and from there I went on to radio. By that time I had been trained in compression, and writing to the point. Of course I'm obsessed with simplicity and compression, which is one of my big hangups."

I remark that a danger of it is that it can oversimplify fiction—especially characters and their motivations.

"Yes, sometimes. Sometimes I condense too much, and oversimplify too much. But you know, I write in two, three, four, five, or six drafts. I go back and I look it over and I say, A little too fast, baby; now, take it easy."

How would he ideally like his readers to respond to his fiction?

"All I want to do is entertain them, so that when they're finished, they say, Jesus Christ, wow, hey, crazy! And then go about their business doing what they always do."

And yet Bester's work sometimes seems to have a message in it. For example, I point out, the idealistic ending to *The Stars My Destination*.

"That's one of the big headaches. I remember I discussed it with Paddy Chayevsky once, after he had finished *The Tenth Man*, which went kind of philosophic at the ending. I said to him, Paddy, I know why you did it, you build to a certain climax, and there's no way to go to finish it off, except mystic. Is there any other way, Paddy? I haven't been able to find it. And he said, Me neither, you gotta go mystic, it's all you can do. And he's right, you know."

This facile and irreverant explanation doesn't convince me, because I sense Bester is rewriting history, refusing to take his old work as seriously as he used to. I point out that when I talked to him in 1970 about the climax of *The Stars My Destination*, and its message, he told me then that he believed in that message quite sincerely.

He looks slightly chagrined. "Well, I forget the message. What the hell was it?"

I remind him that at the climax, his hero distributes a super-weapon among the common people, telling them that they can transcend themselves.

"Oh, well, I may have believed it then. Now, I don't know. I have great faith in people on the one hand, but on the other hand I think there are an awful lot of idiots running around. I think maybe today what I'm looking for is a new educational system that'll grow people up a little more, I don't know. At least, the American people. I can't speak for the Continent, or England; they may be a hell of a lot more adult than we are in the States, where three-quarters of us are children, children with delusions."

At this point he seizes the microphone that rests on the table between us, and turns it around. "Now, let me interview you." He's playfully aggressive, and it reminds me of when he once told me that he tends to resort to "attack-escape": escaping from a problem by attacking it.

I protest I haven't yet finished interviewing him. He brushes my objections aside. He spent most of his ten years on *Holiday* magazine conducting interviews, mainly with celebrities. He's a lot more experienced at this than I am. I'm in the position of a filmmaker trying to photograph Orson Welles.

Bester starts quizzing me about the various people I have interviewed so far, and my interview techniques: "How do you cope with people who only say 'yep' and 'nope' to questions?" (I tell him that I don't have this problem, because most writers are extremely articulate and voluble, just like him.) "Now, the toughest thing when you interview people who've really been interviewed a lot, I find that they have canned replies for everything, and I need at least two interviews to break past that and get down to basics. How about you?" (I say that most of the people I've talked to haven't been interviewed that much, with the exception of Kurt Vonnegut, whose replies I still haven't entirely figured out.) .

Throughout this, I keep turning the microphone toward Bester, and he keeps turning it toward me. It's ludicrous. Finally I turn it halfway back to him, and he accepts that as a compromise. He continues:

"I find it best to establish some sort of bridge of common interest, with the interviewee, no matter what it is." This sounds as if he is about to tell me his formula for interviews, just as he once told me his formula for writing nonfiction. "The funniest bridge that was ever established with me was when I was interviewing Kim Novak," he goes on. "Somebody had loaned her an apartment in New York on the East Side, and I would go over there, two or three times, and it was always very guarded and careful; she was on her best behavior. The third time I went over there, at three or four in the afternoon, she put some records on. She said, Do you want to dance. Come on. So we danced for fifteen or twenty minutes. And after that everything was *fine*. I was very curious; I went back to the *Holiday* office and told them about this, and I said, *Why,* for god's sake? They said, That was the only way she could test you, to see if you were a right guy, with a little physical contact. You know she was a simple kid, like a high-school sophomore from Chicago. But as a result of my going back to the office and telling them about the incident, of course, they were convinced—wrongly!—that I had had an affair with Kim Novak. I said, Oh, come on, fellas, it's so *unprofessional*, I could never do that."

These days, Bester's interviewing work is taking him away from show business, into the sciences. *Omni* magazine has given him a list of Nobel Prize winners whom they want him to talk to. He says it's a lot harder to set up a meeting with an eminent scientist than it is with a personality who wants the publicity; but he's pursuing it.

I remark that he never seems to run out of new projects, and new things to try, in general. He agrees: "I'm always looking for new adventures. For example, we went to the Royal Albert Hall, I'd *never* been there to a concert before; it was marvelous. Or I remember in Paris last year, we were walking where they were jackhammering, digging up the cobblestones, so I said, in my broken French, that I would like to try it. So the guy handed the thing to me, and I dug up a street in Paris. You know, you try anything, there's always a new adventure to have, you just have to be willing to take a chance on making a damn fool of yourself, which I *am* willing to do, all the time."

Does he ever plan to retire?

"Retire? Yeah, I want to die with my head in the typewriter. That's my idea of retirement. Arthur Clarke told me that he's retiring, and he's going to do nothing but underwater photography. I said, Oh, Arthur, really, you and your deep-sea photography! Preposterous! Go write another book.

"But he wouldn't listen."

(London, September 1979)

BIBLIOGRAPHICAL NOTES

Alfred Bester's two science-fiction novels written in the 1950s are *The Demolished Man* (1953) and *The Stars My Destination* (1956, also titled *Tiger, Tiger*). The former is a murder-mystery set in a future society whose telepathic police should make crime impossible; most of the drama involves the desperate and ingenious attempts of the antihero to evade detection. The second novel is an odyssey of revenge, loosely based on the plot of *The Count of Monte Cristo*; the hero, a common man turned criminal, transcends himself and becomes the savior of humanity. Both books use vividly decadent scenarios, are packed with high drama and wild innovation, and feature characters who are memorable, if melodramatic.

Bester's short stories are collected in *Starlight* (1977), which also includes a short essay about his love affair with science fiction.

The Computer Connection (1975, also titled *Extro*) was his first science-fiction novel in twenty years; though structurally erratic, it shows undiminished vitality and wit. At the time of this writing, his fourth science-fiction novel, GOLEM100, is due to be published in a few months.

He has written one non-science-fiction novel, *The Rat Race* (1955), whose plot deals with writing for the media and for the advertising world, but shows some similarities to *The Demolished Man*.

My own 1970 interview and critique appeared in *New Worlds Quarterly*, number 5 (U.K. edition), containing material about Bester quite different from that used in the profile here.

C. M. Kornbluth

When I was planning this book, one of the more tasteless suggestions was that we should set up an Ouija board to interview the late Edgar Rice Burroughs.

Science fiction is a relatively young branch of literature, so most of its practitioners are still alive. But a few have died, and died young. Some of us respond to death by mourning, others by making flippant jokes in poor taste, others by feeling helpless anger and frustration. Personally I tend toward all three of these responses, but especially the last, since I seem incapable of coping rationally with the outrageous injustice of a great talent dying at an early age. Of course, it does no good to be angry at fate; yet I *am* angry, and I get even more irate when the memory of a dead writer fades in people's minds.

C. M. Kornbluth died in 1958, when he was only thirty-five years old. He was undoubtedly one of the finest writers in the science-fiction field; he worked at a time when fine prose was rare indeed. In collaboration with Frederik Pohl he produced classic, enduring novels; since then it has become fashionable for some people—such as Lester del Rey—to suggest that Kornbluth played some kind of lesser role in the collaborations, though there is no evidence for this whatsoever. Kornbluth's solo work, especially his short stories, showed great inventiveness, meticulous writing, and outstanding maturity. He is given less credit now than is due.

Like Pohl, Kornbluth had a sophisticated awareness of the dark undercurrents in life and society—the elements of greed, crime, power, and fear which mold much of twentieth-century America, whether one likes it or not. In almost all of Kornbluth's stories these forces shape future societies with dramatic, often unpleasant, realism. The grimness of these visions may be one reason for their not being more popular, now, among readers who may prefer more optimistic material.

One of Kornbluth's earliest stories was "The Rocket of 1955," published in 1941, when he was still a teenager. While other writers were reveling romantically in the glory of man's forthcoming adventures to the stars, Kornbluth cynically visualized the space program (fifteen years before any such program existed) as a great opportunity for con men. The story is a confessional; its narrator describes how he used blackmail to enforce the assistance of "that old, bushy-haired Viennese, worshiped incontinently by the mob" (an irreverant reference to Einstein?), and how he bought radio time to publicize his patriotic plan to "plant the red-white-and-blue banner in the soil of Mars!". As a result of this media-hype, legitimized by the name of an eminent scientist, contributions flood in. A fake rocket is built, as cheaply as possible, from tinplate. As soon as it takes off, it blows up. Newsmen exclaim over this "tragedy" while our narrator counts his millions of dollars of pure profit . . . until "Einstein" confesses the part he played in the sordid affair, and our narrator is cornered by a lynch-mob carrying a rope.

The story's cynicism, its elitist contempt for the gullible masses, its grasp of the power of the media, and its concise, terse narration—all are remarkable, and are qualities that recur in later, well-known stories such as "The Marching Morons" (1951). In this blatantly elitist doom-warning, the large families of the proletariat have outbred the birth-controlled intelligentsia, with disastrous results. It takes the abhorrent tactics of a corrupt real-estate salesman (conveniently resurrected from the past) to implement a Hitlerian final solution. Kornbluth, a Jewish intellectual, deliberately scrambles our sensibilities by depicting genocide as a practical solution to an intolerable social problem. Yet he is not so much demonstrating how one evil can be cured with another, as he is showing evil begetting evil, and the consequences, tomorrow, of being socially stupid today.

Weaknesses in human nature are a recurring theme in his work. "The Little Black Bag" (1950) is probably his most famous story;

in it, a disbarred MD turned wino bum finds a doctor's bag that has traveled backward through time from a technologically-advanced future world. Aided by the instruments in the bag, and by the shrewd business sense of a sharp little ghetto girl, "Doc" becomes the only quack in town whose cures really work. Ultimately he decides he must donate this wonderful discovery to science; but Kornbluth, never willing to allow an unrealistic or sentimental happy ending, arranges for the greed-crazed young woman to kill the well-intentioned old man before his altruism can be put into effect. Good does not triumph over evil. . . .

. . . But at the same time, usually, in Kornbluth's work, evil defeats itself. "The Mindworm" (1950) is the fable of a modern vampire who feeds not on blood but on mental anguish. He is the incarnation of evil. His gratuitous acts of mental sadism against innocent people (to invoke the tortured emotions which he savors telepathically) are horrifyingly vivid. His feeding, however, kills his victims; and after one death too many, a crowd of old peasant folk corners the Mindworm and dispatches him according to ancient tradition.

Kornbluth's preoccupation with evil is not so much a morbid obsession as a genuine concern for ethics. Sometimes this is expressed in his work a little clumsily. In "The Goodly Creatures" (1952) an advertising man is forced to face his own shoddy retreat from idealistic literary values when he hires a young copywriter whose ambition is to be a "space poet.". In "With These Hands" (1951) Europe has been atom-bombed, "culture" is therefore dead, and the last artist has been put out of work by computerized sculpting technology; he makes a suicidal pilgrimage into the radioactive wastelands, to catch one last glimpse of a true art treasure. Such messages are a trifle heavy-handed, but there can be no doubting the sincerity of these fables—and no denying their eloquence and power.

Kornbluth's social awareness is an extension of this concern for ethics. He dwells on exploitation, corruption, and unprincipled greed as if he is too tormented by these flaws in society to write about anything else. "The Altar at Midnight" (1952) depicts a young astronaut whose space-work as a company employee is disfiguring him and ruining his health. It turns out that his barroom buddy, an alcoholic who narrates this tale with flippant irony, is the inventor of the space-drive which has made interplanetary travel possible. Thus the astronaut is victim of the narrator's scientific genius, the work of genius has been expropriated to unscrupulous ends, and both men have been exploited by powers which they are unable to fight. Of course, in reality, the space program hasn't turned out exactly like that. But anyone who is familiar with the psychological crises of astronauts who found themselves no longer of much use to NASA, and anyone who reads about (for example) the life expectancy of workers in mining industries, will see how grimly accurate Kornbluth was in his general picture of forces of twentieth-century capitalism impinging upon the individual.

At the same time, in other stories and especially his novel *Not This August* (British title: *Christmas Eve*) he showed strong patriotism and total commitment to the ideals of the Free World. In 1973 I was able to talk with his widow, Mary, who now lives in a retreat in the Adirondacks, in upstate New York. One of the first questions I asked her was about the apparent contradiction in Cyril Kornbluth's work, between his love for his country, and his angry disgust at the crimes of capitalism.

"I think that Cyril, in discussing this with me, once pointed out that criticism and patriotism are necessarily part of the same thing," she replied. "Cyril and I spent a lot of time in the 1930s, when we were both teenagers, hoping for this brave new world, so to speak, that was supposed to come up out of the Depression, which was a very creative time in America—despite all the disasters there was also a lot of creativity. Cyril and his writing began to evolve during that period. Subsequently, we were both somewhat disillusioned. For instance, we were both intensely pro-union, and it's very disillusioning to see what happened to the unions. They were supposed to make life better for the common man, but they became quite corrupt."

What were Kornbluth's politics? In today's terms, could he be called a liberal or a conservative?

"The thing he discussed most often was Jeffersonian democracy. Cyril was not a liberal, because of his intense interest in semantics. It's impossible to be a liberal and a semanticist. On the other hand, 'conservative' is too simple a label. He examined each issue separately, critically.

"His general feeling about capitalism was that it may not be the most ideal system imaginable, but it was the best game going. But he was extremely ethical and high-principled, and he not only believed in his principles but acted on them, so, naturally, he felt that capitalism could be improved."

Was he optimistic about the future?

"He definitely didn't feel that a past with bad teeth, slavery, child labor, and all the rest of it, was good. But he did not feel we were headed toward anything better. I remember, for instance, the day they admitted building obsolescence into cars. Cyril walked into the kitchen where I was diapering one baby or another and said, 'Will you look at this?' Out of the whole paper he'd picked out a little one-inch paragraph, and at the time I didn't pay too much attention, but in a few minutes I got involved because he had a facility for getting you involved . . . the point is that our junkyards, our international oil purchases, our shipments of ore from Africa, along with the destruction taking place in our woodlands, are all aspects of what he foresaw and described at that time. He saw it all, as soon as they announced obsolescence in American society. He said, 'Americans don't like to keep things,' and I remember feeling somewhat insulted at the time, myself. But he saw it all, horribly accurately."

What was his home background?

"His father was a second-generation Jew, and ran a small tailor shop. He seems to have been an authoritarian man. Cyril always believed that father knew best. He (Cyril) had a very precocious childhood, learned to read when he was about three, graduated from high school when he was thirteen, won a scholarship to City College when he was fourteen, and got thrown out for leading a student strike. He started to write when he was about seven. He was writing whole issues of magazines by the time he was sixteen."

I mention that I understand he went back to college twice.

"That's right. Both times, he dropped out. He couldn't see the point to it. I was thoroughly disillusioned with education myself, and so was he. Platitudes bored him inexpressibly and he heard a lot of them at college. He was a semanticist in an age when no one else had heard of it. He understood language as no one else I've ever known understood it. His earliest training was as a poet, I mean when he was seven, eight, nine, in junior high school. We used to write poems to each other, and I would look for the most difficult form I could find, and finally I would get it into shape with great labor, much burning of midnight oil, and give it to him, and then of course he would cap it with something even more complicated."

As a writer, did he ever complain of editorial interference?

"I don't know whether you're aware of how much editorial interference he had. Science fiction wasn't exactly the most rewarding field to work in, in editorial terms. They generally wanted a certain type of ending. Cyril did his best work when he could devise the whole thing himself, and was not subject to any editorial restraints. That's why the short stories, I think, are better; not because the novels couldn't have been better but because there were things about them that had been influenced by other people. I don't want to draw any personalities into this . . . but if he'd been left to himself he might have devised other endings. He didn't believe in happy endings, you know."

Regarding his story "The Mindworm":

"When he wrote that story he was attending the University of Chicago. There was a housing shortage and we were both stuck back at the stockyards in a fantastic old neighborhood. There were ancient Polish people there, whom he described in "The Mindworm." When the story was written I believe it was written pretty accurately about what would have happened, and what a real, modern vampire would be like. At that time I was a little more innocent than I am now, and I pointed out to him that life doesn't have to be like that. But his point was that it *is* like that. Now that I've been involved with a couple of conservation battles [Mrs. Kornbluth has opposed the construction of an interstate highway through unspoiled land] all I can say is that I have to agree, now, he was right. He said that the people who do the destroying are like that [like the Mindworm] and now that I've seen some of them and talked to them myself, I have to say that they really do enjoy destroying, and the more beautiful a thing is, the greater their enjoyment is."

So he did not in any sense contrive that story? He was writing from the heart?

"Yes, he was."

> (Dialogue excerpted from a taped telephone conversation, New York—Northville, summer 1973.)

BIBLIOGRAPHICAL NOTES

Kornbluth, like many short-story writers, had difficulty in producing a well-integrated, evenly-paced novel. Of the three he wrote in the science-fiction genre, *Takeoff* (1952) suffers from hasty writing, *The Syndic* (1953) has an amusing premise (the Mafia have completely taken over America and turned it into a utopia) which is never developed fully, and *Not This August* (1955, titled *Christmas Eve* in Britain), after a chilling opening, degenerates into an episodic quest. This last novel is probably the most memorable, however, being an extremely perceptive vision of how the U.S.S.R. might have invaded America in the late 1950s.

Almost all of Kornbluth's short stories written in the 1950s have been collected in book form, and do not seem at all dated, despite the twenty-five or thirty years that have elapsed since their original publication. *A Mile Beyond the Moon* (1958) is an excellent selection of stories; many of them were re-collected in *The Best of C. M. Kornbluth*, edited by Frederik Pohl, published in paperback in 1976. Pohl's introduction describes his association with Kornbluth, but is frustratingly vague and superficial.

*Photo by
Anthony Rogers*

Algis Budrys

I'm a foreigner here; the most ordinary routines are strange. Here, Chicago, is a world away from New York, which is a world away from my small-town British origins; it is a culture of conveniences, so everything is easy, but still strange.

Close by the airport I collect my rented car from a fenced compound. Then out along a concrete highway, in humid heat, following route directions typed meticulously by Algis Budrys (who is a meticulous man and, like myself only more so, a foreigner here). I traverse run-down Chicago suburbs, toward Evanston, just on the edge of the metropolitan sprawl. Totally mundane but alien scenery drifts past the windshield: Photomat, Wendy's Hamburgers, the White Hen Pantry, Mira-Kleen cleaners, a towel factory, Futuristic Fashions. The bumper sticker on the red Chevrolet ahead of me asks, Have You Hugged Your Kid Today?

As a foreigner, one has no skepticism. One believes anything. Change is an assumption of life. One expects to be surprised. At the same time this breeds a suspicion that nothing is as it seems, nothing is permanent, nothing is, ultimately, real. This is a recurring theme in Budrys's writing.

Past a decayed shopping center, and across many railroad

tracks, here is Evanston, population 79,300. It looks greener, less industrial than its neighboring urban subcenters. I see tennis courts and baseball diamonds; and on Budrys's block there are ample trees, and grass beside the sidewalks. His front lawn is a cheerfully undisciplined carpet of bright yellow dandelions.

He is in his basement, amid a jungle of bicycles and power tools, camshafts and dismantled washing machines, stacks of books, garden implements, coiled rope, and old overcoats. It's like a giant thrift shop run by an auto mechanic. He works in one section, divided from the rest by bare brick walls. There are stacks of papers on shelves and on the floor. He sits on an office chair, applying an X-acto knife to a cardboard mask which he is making for a large black-and-white photograph. It's part of a promotional campaign for a Chicago jewelry designer. Budrys, like the thoughtful, gentle men in his novels, has many areas of special knowledge. He applies them, methodically. His role today is Free-lance Media Consultant; down here in the dusty, cluttered, but cool and quiet basement he has been creating a whole advertising campaign—writing the copy, choosing the markets, supervising the photography, and handling little details like the photographic mask he is now finishing under the fluorescent light of his desk lamp. It's a long way from science fiction; but Budrys actually spends very little of his time writing science fiction, for reasons he explains to me later.

Before he leaves the basement he notices that one of the arms of his spectacles is loose. He opens a drawer and takes out a box of jeweller's screwdrivers. He selects the correct size of blade, and carefully tightens the tiny screw in the hinge of his glasses. For a moment I see him as Martino, the prosthetic hero of his novel *Who?*, lecturing on the proper use and maintenance of machines. A gentle touch, and the right tool for the job; every item meticulously maintained.

He is a shy man, who falls back on a kind of uneasy protocol when dealing with strangers; but, as he later tells me, he recognizes a kind of science-fiction brotherhood. So I, a stranger, am welcomed into his home and meet his wife and two of his tanned, blond sons, and a large black cat which has no name, but does have a license—the Budrys family, concerned with local politics, believes there should be a local ordinance making cat licenses mandatory; they are working to this end. Evidently, they are an active part of their community. And yet, as I say, Algis Budrys labels himself a foreigner. He has no passport. He is a citizen of

Lithuania. His identity is as complex as Martino's—or those of his other protagonists, searching for the final bedrock truth in worlds where they suspect nothing is, ultimately, real.

The ground-floor rooms are shadowy and hot, strewn with books. It is a large, comfortable house. After dinner we talk out on the front porch. He speaks very slowly, with constant attention to the function of each word and the precise meaning of each sentence. He talks as if the parts of speech are like mechanical components, which must be selected and assembled carefully, in an exact sequence, in order to function efficiently and elegantly. Later, when I transcribe the interview tape, I find it almost impossible to trim away any surplus wordage; Budrys only repeats himself when he feels phrasing was not quite accurate the first time.

I often feel an author's origins are not very pertinent to his work. In many profiles in this book, I have summarized the person's background as briefly as possible. But Budrys's conversation leads inexorably to his background, because his background not only explains who he is, it explains what he writes and how he sees the world. In his words:

"I'm basically a Lithuanian peasant, and there are centuries of acculturation behind me. I sit here passing for a middle-class American, but I'm not. I was raised by parents who had to endure a hell of a lot and had built in all kinds of cultural safeguards. I think the most noticeable ones were that you should toil incessantly, that you should let no opportunities pass to do something solid, and that there's something essentially rascally, insincere, and impermanent about someone who rises too high. The thing to do is not to rise, but to broaden out and let down more roots. I can laugh at all that stuff, but that does not change what happens inside my head.

"When my mother was eighteen or nineteen she already had an extremely responsible position in Lithuanian military intelligence. She came from a house with a tin roof that belonged to her father, the village tailor and sexton of the local Roman Catholic church. I don't believe there was any inside plumbing; the source of water was a well outside; all the vegetables, and most other food, they raised themselves. The purpose of her going to the big city and getting a government job was to send money home and keep the land going.

"My father came from essentially the same kind of family, except that his father had already achieved a certain amount of status in the imperial Russian civil service, Lithuania then being a province of the Russian Empire. Dad followed him into it and had all kinds of adventures. When the Russian revolution broke out he was stationed in Vladivostok as a member of the imperial Russian military intelligence; he had to get home to Lithuania somehow, and it took him three years to do it, and he did it by way of China. When he died and I took a look at his insurance papers, it turned out there was a long list of significant scars including bullet wounds and saber cuts that he had picked up along the way, and I know he came extremely close to dying of typhus. His entire motivation was to get back to Lithuania, and do his duty. In fact he's the model for Colonel Azarin in *Who?*; put a little bit more of a smile on Azarin's face, and add the fact that somewhere there was a wife and a child of whom he was fond, though he wouldn't have much time for him—and Azarin is my father.

"My father was transferred into the Lithuanian diplomatic corps after about 1927, and he and my mother were stationed in East Prussia. We always lived in a hostile environment. The only two people that I could talk to intensely day after day were my mother and father; everyone else around me was a German. They were nice, pleasant people, very neighborly, and very loving toward this very Aryan kid. I had ash-blond hair—not merely blond, it was white—and I had these enormous blue eyes and these wonderful clean-cut features. That was before I got to weighing 250 pounds. I spoke German with such an impeccable East Prussian accent, and carried myself like a little soldier, they doted on me. And then they did something that completely changed my life.

"Adolf Hitler drove by our house a couple of times, and they went insane. Hordes of German housewives and househusbands, people that I knew, who were all living in the same apartment complex together, were tearing themselves psychically to pieces all over the sidewalk, just watching the man go by. They weren't simply shouting or clapping their hands or going 'hooray,' they were going through an animal frenzy to the point where some of them were having what I guess were epileptic seizures. Others were defecating in our bushes, couldn't control their bowels. I was four years old. I remember a guy hopping across our lawn with his pants around his knees, tugging desperately at his underpants, trying to get to a bush; and men and women rolling on the ground, writhing, clutching at each other. A hell of a thing to see; I'm four years old and I suddenly realize that I know absolutely nothing about the world except that it is populated entirely by monsters—werewolves. Naturally, I cling even tighter to my parents. But my mother has the duties that are attendant on her position, and my father is in a hostile country, doing everything he can to keep the Nazi revolution from spilling over into Lithuania. He has a very hard row to hoe, extremely conscious of the fact that with the first bad breeze that blows, Lithuania's going to be reoccupied by the Soviet Union.

"He indoctrinated me with self-discipline and patriotism. I used to hear very long, fervent speeches when I was five or six years old, and the last line was always, '*I* liberated Klaipeda [a seaport he attached to independent Lithuania], *you* will liberate Vilno.' It was going to be my duty in life to restore it to Lithuania, when I grew old enough. [It had been annexed by Poland.]

"A lot of my life when I was a small child was spent in cars, on trains, talking to strangers, speaking a variety of languages, never settling down anywhere, and feeling a great deal of hostility because German governesses hate the kids that they raise, and because I could look out the front window at night and see the Germans out there throwing bricks with swastikas chalked in them. Sitting in the dark on my mother's lap with no lights on in the apartment at all, except for the little green pilot light on the radiogramophone, and my father with a pistol in his lap just waiting for the Brownshirts to break in.

"And then, we moved to New York City, and there was a whole new set of things to learn. My father was consul general of Lithuania in the United States between 1936 and 1964. It was at his knee that I learned what's important about being a P. R. man. He eventually died at his desk, at the age of about seventy-five, having lived a life full of sixteen-hour days. He was on his eighth heart attack when it happened. Each time they released him from hospital, he went right back to sixteen-hour days.

"So, I came over to this country when I was six. I very quickly acquired the accent and mannerisms of a born American. I'm almost totally American-educated. I'm married to this nice American lady and I have these fine strong sons all born in this country and they don't speak a word of Lithuanian. But I do not come from the same place that most people in this country come from.

"I've always had the consciousness that there were larger destinies to be worked out, responsibilities extending beyond one's personal family; you spent your life in the service of an ideal, and toiled for it. I think this accounts for a lot of my naiveté when I was in my early twenties; and it explains to some extent what it was about science fiction that really got to me, that made it a very special thing. It offered me the thought that although life contained some very wild changes, it was possible to live with change.

"My way of looking at science fiction is all wrapped up in a series of quasi-mystical ideas that I gained as a kid, having to do with the nature and the worthiness of science fiction. I'm now forty-eight years old, and I think I read my first science-fiction story when I was eight. The books that I had read before then that I can recall were aviation books and the complete, as-written-by-Defoe, *Robinson Crusoe*—not a child's version. My sister started reading it to me, and I grew impatient with the process and learned to read so I could finish the book.

"Around the age of ten or eleven I decided that it would be a rare and wonderful thing to be able to produce science fiction; this was the very best thing there was to be. I developed the delusion that science-fiction writers were not only a breed apart, but extremely high-cut, and if you were the kind of person who was capable of having his name published in *Planet Stories* or *Thrilling Wonder Stories*, the world would yield up Rolls Royces and homes in California. I assumed that people had cars and homes and girlfriends like that because they were *worthy* of them, not because they had done something that was then paid for, and they converted the money into acquisitions. I'm alarmingly stupid in many ways and still to this day I'm equipped with any number of pieces of hard-won practical knowledge which I don't really believe in, because they are not in accord with the instinctive notions I developed as a kid. I'm a romantic. I think worthiness is the key concept behind it all. One of the questions I consider when a story occurs to me is: This story might be all right for somebody else to write, but is it worthy of me?

"When I came to Manhattan from Long Island, as a fellow who had sold a couple of stories, I had absolutely no compunctions about turning to people who were practically strangers, and saying, Do you mind if I move in with you for a while? Because we were all members of the great science-fiction brotherhood. It was as if there was this big house populated entirely by science-fiction people and by right I had a place in that house somewhere, as we all did. It's amazing how tolerant the world can be. My first story had sold to Campbell; I had made it, essentially, first-crack. Somewhere in my mind I equated that with reaching a permanent niche.

"In the 1960s, it was a persistent rumor that I had at that point quit science fiction in disgust. When *Rogue Moon* did not get the Hugo award [as best novel] . . . the award went instead to *A Canticle for Leibowitz*, which in that year appeared as a reprint, which I do not believe was eligible. I was extremely angry, because *Rogue Moon* represented a maximum effort and I frankly think it is a better book than *A Canticle for Leibowitz*—as a novel. The original short story, fine; the novel I don't think is that good. I was angry, and in some circles very vocal about my anger. That apparently led people to think that I had renounced science fiction in disgust. Actually I knew my fourth child was going to be born in January 1962, and it was just too much for a freelance to carry; I had to get a salaried job.

"When I get a job, I tend to bury myself in it. From then until essentially January 1974, I was almost always doing something other than science fiction, very intensely.

"When it was my responsibility, for instance, to put out the introductory news-release package for a new truck, I had to work as hard as I think anyone would work in order to completely plot out a novel. A new model of truck can make or break a multibillion-dollar enterprise; it's not like manufacturing family cars at all. If you turn out a product in the truck business that can be proven to be not as good as somebody else's, you are in serious trouble. You may be unable to recover your position, over a period of years. So I researched the news-release package more heavily than I have ever researched a novel. It was intellection and sweat, and some moments in my life that I'm extremely proud of, because by God I worked for them. Whereas in a science-fiction novel, I may put in an enormous amount of labor, but I never regard it as intellection or work. On *Rogue Moon* I would drive myself to a point of fatigue such that I was suffering from auditory hallucinations; but what I was doing was shaping something, I was having some kind of psychic experience. It took me until I was in my forties before I realized: these damn things are not stories, they're utterances. Some of the time a story comes out without my supervision at all. I just sit at the typewriter and watch my fingers move. A great many times I surprise the hell out of myself with some feature the book will develop.

"I think I have written every science-fiction story that I ever felt was worth writing, at the time that I felt was the right time to write it. I've got to do something with the rest of the time. It's no longer necessary for me to be on any kind of salary or retainer, thank God, simply because so much time has passed and there are so many properties [books and stories] around that keep getting reprinted. Generally speaking we need less money than most people do, because we set our standard of living at the poverty level, and have been very happy with it ever since! I love doing the public-relations work and advertising copywriting and the other things I do, because I think I'm pretty damn skillful at it. I do it very quickly, glibly, and it comes out better than average because I'm a better observer and reporter than the average person who's working in advertising or P. R. and I've had a lot of training in finding the exact word and the right sentence.

"The only thing that happens is that some science fiction doesn't get finished quite as *soon* as it might, though it gets started when it's ready to get started. *Michaelmas*, for instance: the first sixty pages of a 240-page manuscript were written over a period of about forty-eight hours in January 1965, and if I had stuck with it at anything like that pace, obviously I would have finished it in 1965. It would not have been a substantially different book. As it happens, there was a ten-year hiatus in there, when I was doing something else. But there was no other book clamoring to be born.

"It's a simple test: if a science-fiction idea doesn't make it, doesn't get written, it wasn't good enough. There are no other science-fiction books that I want to write at the moment, although I have the idea that I may in fact write a sequel to *Michaelmas*—which shakes me, because I told a lot of people I never would. But it occurred to me that it would be very interesting to continue the chronology from the viewpoint of one of the minor characters, a very interesting chap who's in there and hardly speaks. Michaelmas is going to die some day, and Domino is going to be looking for his successor.

"I think that all forms of fiction and art are actually survival mechanisms. Far from being frills and decorations on the face of some kind of practical world, they are just about the most practical thing there is. They consist of a series of affirmations or denials of conventional reality, and of tests of various facets of reality. Science fiction has unique capabilities in that respect. I can talk seriously in science fiction about otherwise-unattainable aspects of very important situations. When I wrote *Rogue Moon* I was able to talk about love versus death in a way that conventional fiction cannot handle; the whole thing is fueled by a situation in which a man can deal death repeatedly, experience death repeatedly, and can talk about the essential nature of the immortality that love confers, which is that immortality rests in the memory of the beloved. The beloved remembers with love, and confers immortality, without respect to the fact that the object of her love is not in fact the same man that he was yesterday. It is possible to discuss the illusion of reality as an artifact of memory, by having a character in the story who remembers being the same man, but is not in fact the same man. I think that what science fiction is—and this is my definition of it—is drama that has been made more relevant than ordinary drama, by social extrapolation. By which I mean, conditional reality."

His monologue didn't come out exactly like that, all in one piece, of course; but it had a coherency that made it seem to fit together best without any interruptions.

After leaving the Budrys family, I have some thoughts on what he said. His sense of duty, of course, manifests itself through the main characters of almost every novel and story he has written; and it is obvious, too, in his writing style. Just as his heroes proceed quietly and with dedication, motivated by an almost abstract sense of moral obligation, so Budrys's writing is quiet, careful, and executed with his strange sense of dedication to science fiction as a world apart, a field of worthiness, a brotherhood which claims one's fundamental patriotism.

Paradoxically, the intensity of Budrys's loyalty toward the genre probably accounts for his having written so little science fiction, and so much commercial journalism and advertising copy instead. Despite his very rational arguments (for example, his claim that if a story doesn't get written, it wasn't good enough), I almost feel he avoids writing science fiction much of the time, not because it is too demanding, but perhaps because it is such a special area to him, the work would somehow become devalued if it ever became part of a frequent routine. It's as if he only allows himself the pleasure of science-fiction writing on birthdays and national holidays; the rest of the year, he has to get his hands dirty and apply himself to the mundane jobs—"doing something solid," as he puts it, "and not rising too high." Indeed, he has broadened out and let down more roots—in just about every commercial writing field. This is frustrating for those of us who admire his science fiction for its unusual depth, humanity, and political sophistication. One hopes that, when he starts his next novel, he doesn't do what he did with *Michaelmas*, and put the half-finished manuscript aside for ten years, before coming back and finishing it.

(Evanston, May 1979)

BIBLIOGRAPHICAL NOTES

The two novels for which Algis Budrys is probably best remembered are *Who?* (1958) and *Rogue Moon* (1960). Both deal with crises of identity, and with technology as a factor affecting human psychology. In *Who?* a prosthetically rebuilt physicist must attempt to prove that he is not a Russian spy; his sensitively described emotional difficulties are juxtaposed with accurately visualized political game-theory. In *Rogue Moon*, a tense psychological study written as a kind of cinematic, obsessive melodrama, a scientist agonizes over the ethical implications of his matter-transmission machine, which in effect kills and resurrects the death-obsessed test-pilot who uses it to travel across space and investigate an enigmatic alien construct on the moon.

Budrys returned to science fiction with *Michaelmas* in 1977; it is his most impressively integrated vision of interplay between man and machine in the near future, and shows a uniquely thorough and sophisticated grasp of the workings of electronics and communications in the modern world.

Budrys's most recent collection of short stories is *Blood and Burning* (1978).

Philip José Farmer

Traffic is at a standstill all around us. Above the murmuring of car engines, I hear Scottish bagpipes. The music's getting louder. The bagpipes are playing "When the Saints Go Marching In." I look at Philip José Farmer, sitting beside me. "What the hell is going on?"

"Must be the Shriners," he answers.

I get out and climb onto the roof of the car. The traffic has been held up by police at an intersection, a little way ahead of us. Crossing the intersection is a procession which boggles the mind.

First the bagpipers, in full Scottish regalia, including bearskins. Then a phalanx of middle-aged men wearing pastel-tinted, pink-and-orange turbans with MOHAMMED written across them. Then an all-male brass band, followed by a squadron of men wearing business suits and rainbow-striped "beanies" (skullcaps with propellers on top). Then a formation of men in sports jackets riding mopeds, circling one another in an intricate ballet pattern. Then comes a parade of identical dark-blue Volkswagens—at least a dozen of them. Why Volkswagens? Why blue? And why, next, are there clowns riding bicycles, towing painted wooden dachshunds, whose legs move realistically? Why Middle-Eastern warriors in garish gold and crimson robes, brandishing silver-painted wooden swords? Why a school bus full of men leaning out of the windows chanting and waving paper flags?

"Where are they all going?" I ask.

"Oh, the Mohammedan Temple," Farmer tells me, as if this should have been obvious.

"But—why?"

"Well, I don't exactly know," he replies, as if he had never really stopped and wondered about it.

It's fair to say that there is a strong element of bizarre fantasy alive here in this amazingly conventional town of Peoria, Illinois. Maybe the conventionality drives them to it. Either way, that Farmer should live here is appropriate. He is both conventional and bizarre himself.

A very quiet man, he is always respectably dressed, proper, polite, hard-working, conscientious, embodying every Horatio Alger virtue. He is also the man who shocked science-fiction editors in the 1950s by writing stories full of sex. He was the first to give aliens a love life, and have them share it vividly with human beings, in his classic story "The Lovers"; and he wrote *Flesh*, an uninhibited fantasy of lust; and *A Feast Unknown*, in which his two childhood heroes, Tarzan and Doc Savage, were endowed with superhuman sex-drives, described in pungent, pornographic detail.

This brings another scene to mind:

When I first met Farmer, ten years ago, I was in America for the first time, shell-shocked and shy. There were other people in the room, who all knew each other, and were talking. Farmer and I sat in silence to one side, like a pair of wallflowers at the prom. Finally I made the most obvious conversational gambit and asked: "What are you working on now?"

He paused, as if wondering whether to take me into his confidence. "Well, you see, Charles," he began carefully, "I really believe that Tarzan existed."

Huh? Oh, really, Phil?

"You see, I think he was related, distantly, to Jack the Ripper."

And so on. Farmer, like Peoria, has a rich fantasy life. Most of it goes back to the myths of his childhood, which are as alive for him now as they were then. During my visit to Peoria he refers constantly to the landscape around his new house, on the edge of woodland where he used to play as a kid. We walk along a railroad track that has fallen into disrepair, and he talks of a swamp somewhere near here, of which he has special memories—in fact he starts checking each lowland to see if it is the right one. His school friends called him "Tarzan" when he was young; he climbed trees and literally swung from branch to branch. He recalls playing at Indians, too; and building a raft of logs; and being Robinson Crusoe. Even now, in his sixties, he seems very young, and still has an athletic physique; he's a tall, strong, handsome figure. He gives me an inventory of wildlife that once lived in the woodlands: wolves, cougars, bears, bobcats, and even, he claims, parakeets. And he says there used to be an Indian tribe which had unique customs—including sexual cross-dressing.

I have to look twice to see whether he is putting me on. He seems not to be. I suppose it makes sense: in a region where local businessmen now dress up in turbans, robes, and kilts, why shouldn't bygone Indian braves have dressed up as women?

The woodlands have largely been built over—with houses such as the one in which Farmer lives himself, with his wife Bette. It's single-story, very modern, with new furniture and wall-to-wall carpets throughout, and in the basement there is a bar with an imitation marble top, and wood paneling and a touch of imitation wrought-iron here and there. The radio in the living room is tuned to a sweet-music station, setting a mellow suburban mood in the house, complementing the furnishings; and there's an air-freshener in every room, complementing the music.

Farmer seems only peripherally aware of these things, which are no doubt orchestrated more by his wife. His working space is down and around a corner in the basement, through a long passageway, to a cool, windowless den at the end. The wood paneling extends here, too, but there are rather different pictures hung on it—erotic art, for instance, drawn to illustrate his early work. And shelves—endless shelves—of reference books, reflecting his fascination with language, myth, and legend; plus a row of copies of his own books, five or six feet long.

In Freudian terms (which Farmer's fiction has often used) this hideaway of his, where he works, is buried like a subconscious underneath the conventional American home.

Farmer's motives and sources of creativity, as a writer, are equally well-buried, and hard to learn about. Even after talking to him through a two-day stay at his house, I still don't know to what extent he works consciously, as opposed to naively, or by pure instinct. When I ask him about these things I get very matter-of-fact answers, in terms that are so general, they almost become platitudes. For instance: "You have to keep the reader interested in the story, and even though there's a serious theme you still have to keep it moving. You have to make your characters as real as possible....I never sit down thinking I've got to entertain people, I just write the story the way I want to." And so on.

Partly, I think, it's true: he just does what he does, without analyzing the operation. At the same time, he doesn't talk about himself easily, especially when a tape recorder is running. Before we begin our interview he pours himself some Glenfiddich whiskey and sits down, rather stiffly, saying "I warn you, I tend to get self-conscious in front of these things," as he looks warily at the microphone. And as soon as he starts answering my questions, his voice doubles in volume, as if he were addressing an audience, and he chooses his words as if suspecting they may later be used in evidence against him.

What emerges, in the end, is simply a story of a lot of very hard work, in the face of repeated disappointments; a dedication to acquiring knowledge, as an end in itself; and an idealism so pure, it verges on innocence.

"I was born in January 1918," Farmer begins, formally. "That's the year von Richthoven was shot down," he adds, with a shy chuckle, mentioning another of his favorite legendary figures.

"I was going to be a newspaper reporter, which, as I look back on it, seems pretty ridiculous. Because I don't have the aggressive personality you need for it. In 1936, to put me through college, my father started an extra business on the side, and then went bankrupt. I had to drop out of college to help repay the debts, because, even though he went bankrupt, he insisted on repaying the money he had borrowed. I worked for Illinois Power and Light, repairing electrical lines, fixing high-tension wires in the country sometimes.

"When the war came along I was going to be drafted so I joined the Army Air Corps, as an aviation cadet. But after four and a half months I washed out because of inconsistent flying. So I went to work for Keystone Steel and Wire Company, and waited for the draft. But they never took me. So I was there [in the steel mill] for eleven years, doing some of the hottest, hardest work you can imagine. I could have gone around and looked for another job, but what could I do? I didn't have any real training."

He says it matter-of-factly, in his slow, deep voice. Really he is describing an early adulthood of frustrated aspirations and sacrifices. But he would never make it sound that way. I can't imagine him ever complaining about his lot in life.

"During those eleven years, I wrote about ten stories, but only sold one, and only two of them were science fiction. See, I had no desire to be a science-fiction writer. I wanted to be a mainstream writer. I sent stories to *The Saturday Evening Post* and *Redbook*. Even there, I wasn't very aggressive. If I got two rejections on a story, I didn't send it anywhere any more.

"In 1949 Bette and I went back to college. I was still working a forty-eight-hour week, doing nights down at Keystone, and also carrying seventeen semester hours of school, which meant that I would work six nights a week, go home, eat breakfast, go to school till about one or two in the afternoon, then I'd come home and sleep, and then I'd study and then I'd go back to work. This went on for a year and a half.

"I was a voracious reader. I even managed to read at work. When I was a billet inspector. Twenty-foot-long rods were sent down a trough; I was supposed to look at the ends of them to see if they had any impurities. There was a little gap in between the time one batch quit coming and the next came, so I'd run into the little hut I had there and read maybe half a page, and then run back and do my work, and then run in and read some more. And when I was working the shears, there was a little gap there, too. It was awfully hot and heavy work, but still I managed out of eight hours to maybe get thirty minutes' reading. That's how I studied, too. At the end of a year and a half, I came down with what they call a case of nervous exhaustion. So I rested two weeks and then I went out and got a job." He laughs.

"In 1952 I sent in 'The Lovers.' It was bounced by John W. Campbell, as being 'nauseating.' H. L. Gold [of *Galaxy* magazine] had somewhat the same reaction. Then I sent it to Sam Mines, who was editing *Startling* and *Thrilling Wonder Stories*. *Startling* published it.

"I decided I would go into full-time writing. Shasta Publications, a little publishing firm in Chicago, had made a proposal to Pocket Books, to arrange an international fantasy-novel award. The prize would be $4,000, which in 1952 was a lot of money. I sat down and typed anywhere from twelve to sixteen hours a day. Then I'd go over it and correct it, and Bette would type part of it, and a neighbor next door would type part of it, and I got it in just under the wire, and it won."

However, this was just the beginning of a new series of disappointments. Shasta Publications was involved in fraud, which ultimately robbed Farmer of his prize money, and the rights to his novel (for many years), and temporarily forced him to abandon the idea of being a freelance writer:

"The publisher of Shasta had kept the money which Pocket Books gave him, and secretly put it into another project, which failed. He not only kept the money, but told Pocket Books nothing about it, so they never got my manuscript, and I couldn't understand why. In the meantime, he kept telling me that Pocket Books wasn't satisfied with my novel, and wanted a complete rewrite—which I did. But of course during this time I wasn't making any money from my writing.

"He not only screwed me, but John Campbell, and Murray Leinster, and Raymond Jones. He went bankrupt, so there wasn't any use in suing him. We lost our house—had to sell it and buy a smaller one. And then I went back to work, for a local dairy. Meantime, I was doing a little writing on the side. But not much. It had really shattered me."

Farmer then moved through a variety of jobs. He was a technical writer for General Electric, for a couple of years. Then he moved to Arizona, where he worked for Motorola, for about seven years. Finally to Los Angeles, where he worked as a technical writer for McDonnell-Douglas. But:

"They had a big cutback of space funds and I was laid off along with thousands of others, in 1969, a month before the first moon landing. I'd been helping to put that ship up on the moon, and then they laid me off. Things were really bad. There were engineers with Ph.D. degrees, pumping gas. Some engineers committed suicide. I looked around, couldn't find a job. I decided, well, I'd been writing on the side, on evenings and weekends. I'd try it full-time again. Maybe I'd do better this time. Well, there were some grim periods, and after we moved back to Peoria there were six months when the publishers weren't putting out the money they owed me. But I just persisted, and kept at it. Now in the last five years, things have been steadily improving. And now they're getting pretty good."

Farmer's early novel, which won the fantasy contest, was the first of his "Riverworld" series. "Actually that publisher did me a favor, because there wasn't any market for a 150,000-word novel in those days, in science fiction. So I put it in a trunk. Many years later I took it out and sent it to Ballantine; Betty Ballantine returned it with the comment that it seemed to her just an adventure novel. So I sent it to Fred Pohl, who at this time was editing *Galaxy*. He said it was a great idea, in fact it was too big to put into one novel. Why didn't I write a series of novelettes for the magazines, and later put them together if I wanted to. And that's what happened. There's very little of the original novel, aside from the basic concept, in the new Riverworld books I've done."

The books have been Farmer's most popular so far. *To Your Scattered Bodies Go* collected a Hugo award in 1972. Twenty years after being cheated out of his prize money, he was finally reaching the audience he deserved; and they were showing their appreciation of his work.

"My development in almost anything has always been a lot slower than most people. I don't put it down to a low intelligence. Just the fact that that's my temperament. When I went to high school I never dated. I was just too shy. I never had a drink of liquor till I was nineteen. I was very naive. I was a bookworm. At the same time, of course, I was an athlete. I was a track man. I ran the 440 and the 220, and did the broad jump. But what can you learn from knowing a bunch of jocks?

"I have the feeling that, even though I'm sixty-one now, I'm not the least bit fossilized and I'm still developing. And ten years from now, if I'm still alive, I'll be a much better writer than I am now. At present I'm not satisfied by any means, because I haven't really done what I set out to do. I set out to be a mainstream writer, and would like to go back to that, maybe part-time. I want to satisfy myself that I can do it. I think if *Fire and the Night* had got the distribution and the recognition it deserved, when I first wrote it, I might have turned to mainstream then." (The book is an intense story of an interracial love-affair against the background of a steel mill, with symbolic overtones. It is eloquently written. Its theme was controversial, for the time of its original publication.)

I ask Farmer if he is pleased with the work he has done.

"Every time I reread some of my stuff—which I don't do very often, because it pains me too much—I can see where I could have done a lot better. I can see innumerable cases. But it's no good to go back and rewrite them, because if you did you'd lose a certain primitive vigor that they have. The thing to do is to go on and write new stuff.

"There have been cases where I have been just too rushed, not only in the prose but in the structure and characterization, and so forth. I've been too busy making a living writing science fiction, and getting too many contracts, one after the other. But I took my time on some things. 'Riders of the Purple Wage,' for instance.

[A long experimental story published in the *Dangerous Visions* collection edited by Harlan Ellison.] But of course that was a lot of fun, it wasn't labor. Then when I wrote *Venus on the Half Shell* [under the name Kilgore Trout, who is a fictional character invented by Kurt Vonnegut], I wrote it very fast, but I'm well satisfied with it."

Farmer has more to add about the genesis of this book:

"Vonnegut may pretend to have trouble, these days, remembering my name. But I'm sure he remembers me quite well. We've talked over the phone a number of times. He's spoken about me in at least one lecture I know of. We've exchanged letters. And he's suffered a lot of unnecessary and masochistic anguish over *Venus on the Half Shell*.

"I wrote it (with great enthusiasm and glee) because I thought people would flip their minds if they saw a book by Trout, a supposedly fictional character, on the stands. Also, I did it as a tribute, the highest, to an author whom I loved and admired at that time. And I identify with Trout.

"Vonnegut says that it was his intention to have many people write Trout books. In another publication he said that he'd thought about writing a Trout novel himself. In all the talks and letters between us, he never mentioned these ideas. I firmly believe that they are after-the-event thoughts. Vonnegut is as confused about time as Billy Pilgrim.

"I understand that in his interview for this book of profiles, Vonnegut's main concern was that I refused to divulge that I was the author of *Venus*. But Vonnegut knows better. When he suggested that I make people aware of who the real author was, I did my damnedest to comply. If he was so anxious about it, why did he turn down my offer to put on the dedication page of *Venus* that Vonnegut was *not* the author?

"Any speculations about Vonnegut's strong tendency to reconstruct the past would be out of place here."

Farmer is now known as a playful writer who has borrowed all kinds of names from history and from famous fiction, and used them as pseudonyms, or told fantasies from their viewpoints. He explains that he got into this when he had a writer's block; he found he could only write fiction if he did it pretending to be a different person. The block soon disappeared, but by this time he was enjoying assuming the other identities.

Most of all, he is still remembered as the science-fiction writer who dared to write about sex, and finally pursued his erotic fantasies to their most uninhibited conclusion, in novels such as *The Image of the Beast* and *A Feast Unknown*. I ask him if he believes in any form of literary censorship.

"No. I believe in total access to all types of material. They worry about the very young being damaged, but in the first place, anything that's too adult is not going to interest the young. They don't understand it. They're bored by it. I think there should be nothing left unsaid. I don't see how pornography of any kind could corrupt people; it's a literary thing. I mean, they're just reading it; they're not going to be aroused by something and go out and rape people."

I ask how he can be sure of that.

"I can't be sure, it's just my theory."

But he seems to hold the theory very strongly.

"Yep. But so far there's been no way of establishing whether reading pornography or violence will infect people. So it's *all* theory."

He willingly admits occasions in the past when he made misjudgments, perhaps because of his faith in human nature:

"In 1953, at the Philadelphia science-fiction convention, I gave a speech in which I did some raving and ranting about our sexual inhibitions and taboos. So what's happened? Our sexual attitudes nowadays are much more liberal and permissive. But at the same time, there's been a proportional increase in sexual crimes, and violent crimes. I had assumed, when I made this speech in 1953, that people would become more sexually educated and would know more about avoiding disease and unwanted pregnancies. What's happened? God, is it one out of ten teenagers in this country who has an unwanted pregnancy? It's not just in the cities, either."

He sounds baffled, and disappointed, as if he is unable to understand why some people should not want to educate themselves as he has done, and be liberated in a spirit of moderation.

I ask him what he would have done, had he not chosen to be a writer.

"I would have had to go back to college and get a Ph.D. in anthropology and linguistics. I would have liked to be a linguistics professor. Studying languages themselves, their structure, the phonemics, the comparison of various languages. I would have loved to be able to learn an American Indian language. They're so far out from our occidental viewpoint."

I'm running out of questions, and it's obvious that the interview is somehow winding down. He seems dissatisfied. "I feel not enough has been said," he remarks; but seems unsure what's missing.

I decide to mention Tarzan—who, thus far, hasn't featured in my questions at all. I remind Farmer of what he told me when we first met, about the existence of his myth-figure hero.

"Well, in one sense I do believe he existed, you know, because I started reading the Burroughs books when I was very young, and they became a part of my life. I'm a romantic, in some respects, and I like the idea of the noble savage. Although, actually, Tarzan wasn't a savage, he was really a primitive human being. Anthropologists don't like to use the word 'savage' any more, with respect to preliterate people. Tarzan was raised by the so-called great apes, who were infrahuman. In that respect he was not even a savage. . . . The idea of living off in the wilderness, and making your own laws, is endemic to a lot of Americans. I kind of liked it at the same time that I realized, realistically, it's not feasible. Tarzan was the last of the heroes of the old golden age of mythology. Sometimes I'm not too sure there isn't a Tarzan.

"When I was young I used to play Tarzan a lot. That was my nickname in grade school, because I was always climbing trees. Had a couple of bad falls, too. I lived close to the edge of the wilderness—semiwilderness—and then I used to play deerslayer, used to play Indian, Indian versus pioneer in the eastern forest. That sort of stuff. We used to play John Carter on Mars. . . . I liked to play Tarzan most of all. I was a real tree-climber, in those days. Used to jump from branch to branch—and sometimes miss." He laughs. "I had a bad fall once, where I was paralyzed for a couple of hours. And—" He breaks off suddenly. "I'm sorry, sometimes I get to rambling."

I think it has been the only time, during the interview, when he has forgotten the existence of the tape recorder.

Later, we go out to dinner. Farmer suggests a new restaurant he's been wanting to try, called the Blue Max. He is fascinated by the fighter pilot legends of World War I, and he's heard that this restaurant is full of motifs of that era. Also, he adds, as an afterthought, the food is supposed to be quite good.

When we get there, the place is quite bizarre. It's the Peoria Shriners all over again—oddball images and weird notions, accepted as if they are not at all out-of-the-ordinary. Over the bar hangs a giant, *life-size* replica of a Fokker triplane, painted bright red. Against the walls are stacked piles of sandbags, as if this starkly modern building has been commandeered and turned into a sort of Bauhaus Fuehrer-bunker. There is a garish mural of a burning city—perhaps Dresden?—behind the cash register. While we eat (German cuisine) we sit on chairs whose backs have German military crosses carved into them. Above each table, German military helmets have been adapted as lampshades. And these are not quaint old helmets—the kind with spikes in the top. No, these seem to be Nazi helmets. We sit and eat under Nazi helmets turned into lampshades.

We leave, after our meal. The restaurant has been built so recently that they haven't had time to clean up the site around it. The area is a morass of mud. A churned wasteland. Why, it looks like a real battlefield, as if the crazed imagery is escaping outside and taking over the whole landscape.

Now, maybe life in Peoria is not always as mysterious and deranged as this. Maybe I am overreacting, and it really is a quiet little town, devoid of unusual psychoses. But I think, at this point, it is time to move on, away from scenarists of myth and legend. It is time to head west, to what I can only describe as the relative sanity of California.

(Peoria, May 1979)

Note: Mr. Farmer's additional comments regarding *Venus on the Half Shell* were not taped during our interview. They were added afterward at his request.

BIBLIOGRAPHICAL NOTES

Farmer's controversial and taboo-breaking story "The Lovers" appeared first in 1952. Subsequently it was published in book form (1961) and no longer seems at all shocking, though it remains a masterpiece of detailed biological extrapolation, and is a wonderfully romantic story. Other interrelated tales of alien beings with an active sexuality are collected in *Strange Relations* (1960), featuring recurring Freudian images. *The Alley God* (1962) is a fine collection of longer stories, reflecting some of Farmer's other obsessions. His homage to his heroes is expressed in *Tarzan Alive* (1972) and *Doc Savage; His Apocalyptic Life* (1973); both books begin from the standpoint that the mythic characters really existed. Farmer then goes about settling inconsistencies and implausibilities that were carelessly allowed into print by the characters' "biographers." The result is witty and fun, even for the uninitiated. *The Image of the Beast* (1968) was Farmer's first chance to write a truly uncensored erotic fantasy novel, followed by *A Feast Unknown* (1969), in which Tarzan meets Doc Savage, with explicit sex and violence. The "Riverworld" series, in novel form, began with *To Your Scattered Bodies Go* (1971), and is set in a world where the entire human race has been resurrected along the banks of a vast river. Farmer wastes no opportunity to use a grab-bag of historical figures as continuing characters in this delightful fantasy.

A. E. van Vogt

Sunshine on swarms of gleaming machines. White highways, blue sky; white beaches, blue sea; white buildings; houses scattered up across hazy hills of mauve and brown. Bare feet, blond hair, tanned bodies, faded jeans. Restless motion, teeming life in a fever-dream valley.

Lawn sprinklers casting rainbows; multicolored birds on power lines; lizards basking on the patio. Concrete, steel, and glass, among the bountiful vegetation: evergreens and succulents, jungle foliage nourished by perpetual sun.

Belden Drive is a narrow concrete road which snakes up into the hills. Mounded bushes, shrubs, and cacti surround Mediterranean-style houses at each bend in the street. The air is vibrant. Insects buzz and hum.

A. E. van Vogt's house is a Spanish villa with red-tiled roof and stucco walls. It stands in a niche on the hillside, not very far below the old HOLLYWOOD sign. The veranda overlooks a slope of lush greenery, down to the wide, flat valley of Los Angeles. To my eastern eyes it's a Pacific paradise transformed by wealth and technology into a new-world composite of Life and Future.

I feel van Vogt is oblivious to his surroundings. He is not a Californian; he might as well be living in a log cabin, or a cave.

The bright scenery of the West Coast seems irrelevant to his interests and his work, because its vivid images are trivial compared to the power of his own inner world—the resonant landscapes inside his mind.

Of course, many fantasists pursue their imaginations oblivious to reality around them. But this is especially true of van Vogt, first because he works more intimately with his subconscious than most writers, and second because much of his life has been spent looking inward, studying psychology and human behavior, primarily through Dianetics and hypnotism.

He talks like a theorist. He refers a lot to systems, methods, and other forms of organized thought. His science fiction, also, is concerned with the power of rationality, and disciplines such as general semantics. But really, his talent has nothing to do with science or logic. It's an intuitive, wild talent (even though, admittedly, he expresses it through a superficially systematic, almost mechanical way of writing). Van Vogt is remarkable for his strangeness: he has a compelling presence, an intensity, a slightly mad gleam in his eye, and when he writes he comes up with eerie, powerful journeys into symbolic depths of the psyche. When you open one of his novels, you open the subconscious. He writes dreams.

And by a weird method, he dreams his writing. First, he describes how he originally became a writer, while still very young, in Canada (where he was born in 1912):

"A man called John W. Gallishaw wrote a book called *The Only Two Ways to Write a Short Story*. I borrowed it from the Winnipeg library, and I read it all the way through. It's an incredibly hard book to read; it's so long. It gave all kinds of examples. He had twenty stories in there, which he had numbered and analyzed line by line. He had an idea of writing a story in scenes of about 800 words, and each scene has five steps in it. If all those steps aren't there in their proper way, then there's something wrong with that scene. First, you let the reader know where this is taking place. Then you establish the purpose of the main character or the purpose of that scene. Then you have the interaction of his trying to accomplish that purpose. The fourth step is, make it clear: did he or did he not accomplish that purpose? Then the fifth step is that, in all the early scenes, no matter whether he achieves that purpose or not, things are going to get worse."

Van Vogt adopted this system, and has always used it, making him one of the few successful professional authors ever to have built his career on a popular "how-to" guide. He also learned to write in what Gallishaw called "fictional sentences":

"Every type of story has its own type of fictional sentence. I started by writing 'confession' stories [for women's magazines]. These stories have to have emotion in every sentence. You don't say, 'I lived at 323 Grand Street.' You say something like 'Tears came to my eyes as I thought of my little room at 323 Grand Street.' And the next sentence, and the next sentence. I did that with the very first story that I ever wrote for them, which I called 'I Lived in the Streets,' about a girl who was put out of her room during the Depression. I went to the library every day and wrote one scene. I had just come back from a stint of working for the civil service in Ottawa, on the 1931 census."

It took him nine days of visiting the library, to complete this story, and he sold it for $110. He was soon writing and selling more stories to "Confession" magazines.

"I wrote one story for a contest, and won the $1,000 first prize. It was a 9,000-word story. I would say that that would automatically mean somewhere between 1,000 and 1,200 sentences. It's not impossible to write 1,000 or 1,200 emotional sentences. It's impossible for an unorganized person, but not for somebody who thinks by a system."

The $1,000 first prize was worth a great deal to van Vogt, in the early 1930s—it was equivalent to almost a year's salary in his civil service job. However, he became tired of this genre. He started writing plays for Canadian radio, at ten dollars . . . a time. And then, a couple of years later, almost arbitrarily, he decided to try writing science fiction. His first story sold to *Astounding Science Fiction*, the most prestigious magazine in the field.

Once again, he developed a system:

"In science fiction you have to have a little bit of a 'hang-up' in each sentence. Let's suppose, for example: The hero looks up toward the door." Van Vogt gestures toward the sunlit screen door of his living room, leading out onto the veranda. "He hears a *sound* over there. And *something* comes in. It looks like a man wearing a cloak. You don't know quite know what's going on. Then, you realize this is not a human being. This creature or this being, whoever it is, has a sort of manlike shape. And this creature reaches into what now looks like a *fold of its skin*. It draws out a *gleaming metal object*. It points it at you. Is this a weapon? It looks like a weapon, but you don't know that for sure. It's a *hang-up*, you see. The author furnishes information, but each sentence in itself has a little *hang-up* in it."

As he has been talking, almost hypnotically, he has created such a mood of menace that, for a moment, the California sunshine seems less bright, and van Vogt's little dreamlike description is nibbling at the edges of reality. He would say, perhaps, that this is through the power of his system, but I think it has more to do with the power of his personality and his intuitively accurate choice of words and images. A system is dull and mechanical, without inspiration to fuel it. Van Vogt goes on to describe how he realized his source for this inspiration:

"I didn't notice, right away, what I was doing. In science fiction I was writing for only one cent a word, so because I work slowly I would wake up anxious, thinking, *work out my story*. I'd go back to sleep, wake up anxious, each time thinking about my story. Then in 1943 in Toronto I suddenly realized. It took me all that time to realize what I'd been doing all those years. Had I been Cyril Kornbluth [who died aged thirty-five] I might never have found out how I wrote. It's a good thing my life went past a certain point!

"I took the family alarm clock and went into the spare bedroom that night, and set it for an hour and a half. And thereafter, when I was working on a story, I would waken myself every hour and a half, through the night—force myself to wake up, think of the story, try to solve it, and even as I was thinking about it I would fall back asleep. And in the morning, there would be a solution, for that particular story problem. Now, that's penetrating the subconscious, in my opinion. It's penetrating it in a way that I don't think they'll be able to do any better, thirty centuries from now."

And so van Vogt derived his inspiration through his sleep, filling his science-fiction adventures with fantastic images, symbolic figures, a constant sense of discovery and revelation, and a sense of free, flying motion (aided by those telegraphic 800-word scenes, which enforced a fast pace). Some critics, such as Damon Knight, complained that van Vogt's plots didn't make logical sense, and consequently his books were failures. This seems as foolish as calling a dream a failure because it lacks logical consistency. Dreams are powerful *because* they are so full of change and contradictions, and they violate the laws of everyday life. In any case, despite the critics, most readers were able to forgive the "flaws" of illogicality and enjoy van Vogt's work for its sheer imaginative power—with the result that his early books are still in print, in many countries, thirty years later.

However, he stopped writing science fiction altogether in the 1950s. I ask him exactly why this happened.

"I'm a system-thinker, as I think I told you. I had observed that writers got passé, they became old-fashioned to the readers. Another generation comes up and it's about a ten-year cycle. So at the end of my first ten years in science fiction I thought, Well, the ten-year period is over, and all I can do now, is . . . I'm back in that earlier quaint reality, and there's a new reality coming up, and it'll be as real to the people reading those stories as if God said it Himself; you know, this is the reality of *now*. I thought, What should I do.

"Among other things, I wrote *The Hypnotism Handbook*, for a psychologist. That was in late 1949, though it was not published until 1956. Having written that book, I thought I'd looked into human behavior a little bit, I must have gotten something out of it. Then I began to get letters from L. Ron Hubbard [the science-fiction author who invented Dianetics, a therapy system, and Scientology, officially classified as a religion]. In 1950, shortly after the hypnotism book was published, he began to phone me, long-distance from New Jersey, every morning, and talk for an hour trying to get me interested in Dianetics. . . . That kind of phone-calling, long distance, was completely out of my reality. It was beyond my conception that anybody was phoning that often, and talking that long, from 3,000 miles away.

"He made a statement around the seventeenth morning he called me, that 'We've got all kinds of people who want to send money to somebody out there, and there's nobody to send it to,' and I said, 'Tell them to send it to me and I'll guard it for you!' and I think I got altogether $3400 in the next couple of weeks. It was sent for a course that they were going to give out here. Three days later a letter arrived appointing me the head of the California Dianetics operation.

"The organization spent $500,000 in nine months and went broke, because at that time there were a tremendous number of attacks on Dianetics. We [in California] were the only branch that never did go into bankruptcy, because I don't believe in being involved in bankruptcy. An attorney friend and I went to see all the creditors, and they let us just fold it and pay what we could.

"One of the reasons why the book *Dianetics* impressed me was the fact that it had not one line of mysticism in it that I could detect. I didn't know, at that time, [editor John W.] Campbell had dissuaded Hubbard from putting any into it. You see previously I had met Hubbard in 1945; I had dinner with him and about a dozen other persons, and it became apparent to me that he was *very* mystically oriented. So when there was, later, not a line of that in the book I thought, by God, this has really got to be a good system, because it has already knocked that out of him!"

Dianetics has since been "incorporated into the framework of Scientology, as an earlier phase you have to go through," according to van Vogt, but he remains uninterested in Scientology, because of its mystical/religious aspects. He retains faith in the principles of Dianetics, and is still president of the Californian Association of Dianetic Auditors. He recalls personal experiences using the system:

"My wife [E. Mayne Hull] had been ill, and had had operations about every two years, starting almost within a year of our marriage, in 1939. She made her will at least six times during that period. When I talked to the doctors, every time they said, It looks like cancer. In 1951 there was another doctor that examined her, and said to me, We've got to watch out, that has all the sound of cancer.

"But right in there she got some [Dianetic] auditing, and the problem all faded away just like it never was. She was not sick again, she didn't go to a doctor, until we went to a funeral of a friend who had died of cancer in Phoenix in 1970. On the way back, she said, It's like the end of an era; and she burst into tears. One month later she had blood in her urine and they examined her and this time they said, It *is* cancer.... The point is, it had been put aside somehow by the Dianetic thing. Dianetics is essentially based upon Freudian therapy, but Freud allowed the patient to freely associate, and he never concentrated upon one incident. Dianetics concentrated upon one incident, going through it again and again. When that was done, things seemed to fade away. Certain incidents that my wife ran seemed to be keyed to her health; clearly they were not erased, they were just put back, you might say, into some slot."

Van Vogt recalls his work in Hubbard's Dianetic Research Foundation: "Hubbard, having a naval background, had his staff meetings at seven AM, and I closed that place up at one o'clock at night, when he'd been gone many hours. I went home and went to bed at five-thirty or something like that.

After the organization went broke, Mayne and I decided to

open up our own Dianetics center here in Los Angeles. I partly supported it by putting books together from earlier short stories, because I charged very little at the center—seventy-five dollars for thirty hours of what we called project auditing. In the end I signed off somewhere around 1961."

But van Vogt never stopped thinking about psychology, and inventing his own theories. At one point, he realized that his system of tapping the subconscious, in order to write science fiction, could also be used as a kind of therapy.

"If you take an incident of severe, traumatic emotion, and wake yourself up every hour and a half, and think about it, go through it in your mind, and fall back asleep while you're doing that, it takes about two weeks, for a severe incident, before it fades.

"I have a book here which I ordered from the Department of Health and Welfare—their book on sleep and dreaming—and I read the summarization of all the discoveries that had been made, and it was quite evident, first of all, that my ninety-minute cycle was the correct one. I'd just chosen that automatically; an hour seemed too short. What the brain does, in the first hour and a half, it deals with the previous day: when they wake people up they're dreaming about the previous day. And then in the subsequent ninety-minute periods it's all back history, going into childhood. I would guess that the mind is trying to throw off the shock of the past, and keeps associating from one to the other to the other, and can never dispose of any of it. When it took me two weeks to dispose of a fear incident in my childhood, that seemed a very significant observation and discovery to have made. It faded, and another incident came into view, and I went on and on like that, working with fear incidents.

"The effectiveness of it is not easy to prove, but here's what happened when I was reading up on the background of Naples for a novel I wrote called *The Darkness on Diamondia*. I had a planet many light-years distant, called Diamondia, which had been settled by Italians, and they had sort of rebuilt Italy there. There was a place called New Naples, and they built it right under Vesuvius II, that kind of thing. So I read up on the history of Naples. It's a history of massacres, assassinations, murders, horrible continuous killing. It didn't bother me because I'd been reading before about human nature. But I ran across one incident that bothered me. Two fourteen-year-old boys were turned in as traitors and beheaded. For some reason or other that disturbed me. The next day, I couldn't seem to write, I felt distracted. And the next day, and the next. Two weeks went by, and I thought, my God, this thing is still running around—vivid images, running through my head. And so I thought, Why don't I try the dream therapy on that?

"By this time, I was using an industrial timer and a cassette recorder, not an alarm clock. An alarm clock you have to rewind and reset, whereas this works automatically every hour and a half."

I interrupt to ask him what the tape recorder says, when the timer turns it on.

"First of all it says *Wake up* a few times, and, *Remember, you're doing dream therapy—on this subject!*—because I could wake up with the alarm clock and not know what I was dealing with; completely blank.

"Anyway, so I put the memory of those two executions through my mind, went back to sleep; and again; and by six o'clock the feeling had faded. And it never came back. This was a small example of the effectiveness of the system. It's purely my own system. A complete invention of my own."

I ask him if he ever suggested to the Dianetics or Scientology people that they might be able to use this system.

"No, and I'll tell you why—because I don't see how anybody could charge for it!" He laughs. "It's not for a large organization with overhead expenses. It should be used as a supplement to daytime psychotherapy."

"My own feeling," he goes on, "is that psychiatry's going to have to be saved. I may try to save psychiatry, if you'll pardon the, ah . . . there is an M. D. who writes science fiction occasionally under the name T. J. Bass. He wrote a book called *Half Past Human*. It's loaded with good information. He runs thirty miles every day. He has overage patients. They start, they can barely stagger into the office, age seventy-three, they've heard about him and his system. And then they run the first 150 feet, and lie down, or whatever, and at the end of a certain period of time they're running with him thirty miles a day. I sent out an inquiry to many science-fiction writers asking, had they invented any new sciences of their own. His answer was, 'I think I've got the beginning of the science of immortality.'

"Now, in 1968 I had a beautiful one-year-old dog; she wanted to go out every morning, she'd come in and wake me up at eight o'clock, which was an unheard-of hour for me. I thought, well, now's my time to conduct the experiment I've been planning for fifteen years. The Exercise Experiment. I went out with her on the eighth morning—after you've had somebody wake you up by licking your face with a big wet tongue eight mornings in a row, finally the thought penetrates, all right, the time has come for an experiment. So we went out.

"My theory was that exhaustion is an association with a past illness. Basically it's Freudian-oriented theory. We started to jog. At the end of 150 feet I was absolutely exhausted. Theoretically *I* should have lain down and rested for a while. But the theory said no—the stress of that moment had forced an association with a disturbance from the past. I thought, What can this be, it's got to be some kind of an association from the past, by my theory, forced by the stress into the here-and-now, just as nervousness overtakes the person who's faced with public speaking. So I thought of an incident when I was aged eleven. I had been out with a bunch of kids on a very hot Saturday afternoon and we'd gone some distance. Coming back, I suddenly had a hard time breathing. In fact I couldn't stand up. I sat down beside the road, and just sat there for about an hour, totally exhausted. So I remembered this incident and mentally went through it a few times by the Dianetic scanning method, and the feeling of exhaustion faded! Then 150 or 200 feet later I felt another type of exhaustion, another feeling, and what was this? Well, all my illnesses kept coming into view, and particularly a fall that I had at age two-and-a-half—I was unconscious for three days at two-and-a-half, from falling out of a second-story window. So anyway, I continued to run, and we ran along this street here, Belden Drive, and then down on Beechwood, and the only time we stopped was when the dog stopped and when we came to the foot of the hill leading up to my house. I looked at that hill and I thought, well, let's consider that the human heart should not be put under total stress the first day or the second day, that kind of thing. So I walked up the hill, and I stopped six times on the way up, each time that I felt the exhaustion, and considered what it could be, and dealt with it, counting the pictures past my mind's eye.

"Now, I'm talking about saving psychiatry. See, I don't believe in running thirty miles a day. The mere thought makes me quail. I seem to remember that the world's record for thirty miles is about two hours and three-quarters. I do not propose to get involved in anything like that. It would be more like four and a half hours. Doing that every day sounds totally mad!

"However: if a psychiatrist were to have half a dozen patients, at so much an hour, running with him, and dealing with their cases as they went along, and then at night had them do dream therapy, a combination of these two things, I think that they could get a lot done. Running, if you're up to it, is an *automatic-gain* situation: a person is going to get a little healthier, no matter what's going on in his head. So I believe that that's the direction that psychiatrists should take."

I imagine a team of out-patients jogging around the Hollywood hills, accompanied by their therapist; one by one, the jogging neurotics experience exhaustion and make insightful mental leaps back to significant childhood traumas, which are exorcised in this sudden flash of association. But there seems to be a practical problem, in this scenario of jogging therapy. Isn't it awfully hard to run and talk to your psychiatrist at the same time? And even if you can gasp out your symptoms—what are the rest of the patients doing?

Van Vogt seems slightly irritated by such a mundane objection. "Well, they'd stop for a moment—some of them would keep on running back and forth, while he's talking to one guy. They could just go back and forth, and then everybody moves forward again."

But this conversation seems to be taking us rather a long way from science fiction.

"I met Frederik Pohl in the early 1960s. He said, Why don't you write for *Galaxy* [the magazine that Pohl was then editing] so I wrote, first of all, 'The Expendables,' and then 'The Silkie'; and meanwhile I was working on a book called *The Money Personality*. I had gotten another system going. I had discovered that three men that I had known when I was in my teens had all gotten wealthy in Canada. That seemed incredible to me. So I went over it in my mind: How come *they* made it into wealth, and here I am still working sixteen hours a day?"

Again, I try to get back to science fiction. Does he plan ever to take advantage of living in Los Angeles, and try to write for the movies?

"I operate by systems, and until I have a system for writing screenplays, none will ever turn up from my pen. Many times have I had lunch with a story editor or director, and each time they require an outline [a description of the script that may be written]. An outline I cannot write, but I tried, each time. I would then present this unfinished (as it turned out) outline, which they couldn't make head or tail of, in their world. Then a few years later I would come across this thing, and I'd think, well, I can write a short story around this, which I would then do.

"I don't know what the problem is. You see I work a story out as I go along. . . ."

Couldn't he work an outline out as he goes along?

"No, I don't seem to be able to do that. That's not the way I work. But I joined the Writers' Guild at the beginning of this year. They announced a course, once a month, where some of their great writers of screenplays would explain the writing of these things. I took my retired attorney friend with me and we went and listened, and a couple of thoughts have penetrated, up here." He taps his head. "The beginning of a system. Now, if I ever *get* a system, they'd better *watch out!*"

And the funny thing is, he's probably right; after all, his "systems" enabled him to sell his very first attempt at writing a confession story, and his very first science-fiction story, too. I will not attempt any kind of summing up of the many theories of A. E. van Vogt, beyond noting that, however eccentric he may sound, when he applies his ideas to his own mind, and when he applies his mind to *writing fiction*, the result works.

After the interview, he invites me to a meal down at a restaurant in the valley. He has recently received large royalties from sales of his work in France, where he is an extremely popular writer; I think he feels like sharing a little of the largesse. Also, I sense he does not receive too many visitors these days, and, since the sad death of his wife, the house feels a bit empty. (This interview was prior to Mr. van Vogt's second marriage, later in 1979.)

So we walk out to his car, which is an aging black Cadillac— old enough to possess modestly-sized finns on either side of its trunk. The car's license plate reads NOT A. Van Vogt comments that people stop alongside him in traffic and ask, "Not a *what*?" But of course the cryptic statement refers to his two novels about "non-Aristotelian" (i.e. multivalue) logic—which is another system he advocates.

We drive, extremely cautiously, down the narrow, winding road, in the giant old car. The tentativeness of this foray into the outside world seems to emphasize my impression that he has no special love or need for the California landscape bursting with life all around us.

Over the very pleasant, neutrally American meal, he remarks

that "Were it not for having run into science fiction and gained some consciousness-expansion, I would have ended up a clerk in the Canadian government."

He sounds, as always, logical and matter-of-fact about it, but I know that this impression is misleading—for logic means a different thing to van Vogt from what it means to me, as does reality. Nor does it end here, because, as we will see in the next profile, van Vogt's visions have influenced other writers in the science-fiction field. His strange dreams, themselves a distortion of the world, have been used as a mere starting point for fiction that goes still further into metaphysical realms—and yet, paradoxically, at the same time returns close to everyday life.

(Los Angeles, May 1979)

Note: in describing van Vogt's decision to join Dianetics, I have inserted within the taped monologue three sentences drawn from his own small autobiographical book, *Reflections of A. E. van Vogt* (Fictioneer Books, 1975). The sentences were added for the sake of clarity.

BIBLIOGRAPHICAL NOTES

Van Vogt's first hardcover novel was *Slan* (1946), and probably remains his most popular work, using the classic concept of a mutant superrace which has to exist in hiding, for fear of persecution by dull-witted "normal" people—a situation with which some science-fiction fans identify. Van Vogt says he got the idea from a childhood book, *The Biography of a Grizzly*: "The book starts with a young cub whose mother is killed, and it has to make its way." *The Weapon Makers* (1946) and *The Weapon Shops of Isher* (1951) are both grand galactic adventures, omnipotence fantasies laden with dark resonances from incompletely defined elements of mystery (or "hang-ups," as he would put it). *The World of Null-A* (1948) and *The Pawns of Null-A* (1956, also titled *The Players of Null-A*) return to the theme of a young hero symbolically acquiring "adult" faculties, finally unmasking and overwhelming mysterious father-figures. The books are rich in imagery, as well as packed with action. *Children of Tomorrow* (1970) was van Vogt's first new novel after his return to science fiction. *The Battle of Forever* (1971) is a more successful book, featuring the inevitable superhuman protagonist, who makes an odyssey across a decadent galaxy. *The Anarchistic Colossus* (1977) manages to link Kirlian photography with a kind of mind-control-therapy; more novels (at this time of writing) are forthcoming.

Photo by
"C.C."

Philip K. Dick

The aim of a speculative writer should be to see what other people have not seen. The few writers who manage this offer more than entertainment, more than inventiveness. They give the reader a sense of revelation.

It takes a trace of genius or insanity to see what nobody else has seen, and it takes formidable writing talent to present such visions graphically, in human terms. Philip K. Dick has this talent, and a bit of genius, or craziness, or both. His best books are revelatory almost in a mystical sense.

He remains underrated (especially in his native America) because he is an unpretentious man who has yet to live down a reputation for having produced some undistinguished novels in the 1960s. Certainly at that time he wrote a lot of books very quickly; but even his most superficial work tackled fundamental questions of perception, philosophy, and religion, and in his latest, ambitious books he has become one of the few science-fiction authors whose insight can be called profound. He shows infinite compassion for his characters; their situations may be science-fictional but their problems are real, and Dick's prose painfully, but gently, explores basic questions of life that affect us all. At the same time, he mocks himself with an endearing, quixotic sense of the absurd.

Almost all of his work starts with the basic assumption that there cannot be one, single, objective reality. Everything is a matter of perception. The ground is liable to shift under your feet. A protagonist may find himself living out another person's dream, or he may enter a drug-induced state that actually makes better sense than the real world, or he may cross into a different universe completely. Cosmic Law is subject to sudden revision (by God, or whoever happens to be acting that role) and there are multiple truths.

These surreal ideas, and the hallucinatory quality of his writing, led to Dick being labeled an "acid-head" author. His obsessive anxiety about forces of political oppression resulted in his being dismissed as "paranoid." Recently, references he has made to mystical influences in his life have prompted some contemporaries to refer to him, sadly, as "mentally unbalanced."

When I went to visit him in Santa Ana, just south of the vast sprawl of Los Angeles, I wanted to pin down the truth in these matters. Foolishly, I went looking for objective clarification from a man who does not believe in objectivity. A few hours later I came away feeling as if my mind had been warped. Like a character in one of Dick's paradoxical, unresolved novels, I was left with more questions at the end than I had at the beginning.

Mr. Dick is a dignified, thoughtful, slightly portly figure, with black hair, graying beard, and an informal but distinguished presence. He is erudite, intimidatingly well-read, but has none of the pretensions or detachment of an academic. He lives in a plain, modest apartment with two cats, some slightly run-down contemporary furniture, heaps of reference books, and an expensive stereo system. As I unpack my tape recorder I realize that he has already set up his own; a high-quality Shure microphone is on the black-glass tabletop, and he will be recording me at the same time that I record him. He seems slightly evasive about this, and says casually that he always makes his own tape whenever he is interviewed. I suppose one could regard this as paranoid behavior; I don't, but it does look as if he is intending to check up on me, to see if my tape transcript is accurate—or am *I* being paranoid now? Already, it is hard to define the reality of the situation.

We begin by talking about his life when he first started writing science fiction, as a student at Berkeley also working part-time in a radio-TV retail store.

"I was in a curious position. I had read science fiction since

I was twelve years old, and was really addicted. I just loved it.
I also was reading what the Berkeley intellectual community was
reading. For example, Proust or Joyce. So I occupied two worlds
right there which normally did not intersect. Then, working in the
retail store the people I knew were TV salesmen and repairmen;
they considered me peculiar for reading at *all*. I spent time in all
kinds of different groups; I knew a lot of homosexuals; there was
a whole homosexual community in the Bay Area even then, in
the 1940s. I knew some very fine poets, and I was very proud of
them as my friends; *they* thought of me as strange because I wasn't
gay, and the people in my store thought I was strange because I
knew gay people and read books, and my Communist friends
thought I was odd because I wouldn't join the Communist
Party . . . so being involved in science fiction didn't make all that
much difference. It was a small divergence compared to some of
my other divergences. Henry Miller said in one of his books, other
children threw stones at him when they saw him. I had that same
feeling. I managed to become universally despised wherever I
went. I think that I must have thrived on it, because it kept happening so many times in so many ways.

"I got married when I was nineteen, and it wasn't until a little
later that I really began to write. I got married again when I was
twenty-one. A point came when I began to feel that science fiction
was very important. Van Vogt's *The World of Null-A*—there was
something about that which absolutely fascinated me. It had a
mysterious quality, it alluded to things unseen, there were puzzles
presented which were never adequately explained. I found in it
a numinous quality; I began to get an idea of a mysterious quality
in the universe which could be dealt with in science fiction. I
realize now that what I was sensing was a kind of metaphysical
world, an invisible realm of things half-seen, essentially what
medieval people sensed as the transcendent world, the next world.
I had no religious background. I was raised in a Quaker school—
they're about the only group in the world that I don't have some
grievance against; there's no hassle between me and the Quakers—
but the Quaker thing was just a lifestyle. And in Berkeley there
was no religious spirit at all.

"I don't know if van Vogt would agree that he's essentially
dealing with the supernatural, but that's what was happening in
me. I was beginning to sense that what we perceived was not what
was actually there. I was interested in Jung's idea of projection—
what we experience as external to us may really be projected from

our unconscious, which means of course that each person's world has to be somewhat different from everybody else's, because the contents of each person's unconscious will be to a certain extent unique. I began a series of stories in which people experienced worlds which were a projection of their own psyches. My first published story was a perfect example of this."

For a while Dick attempted to work both inside and outside of the science-fiction field: "I wrote many novels which were not science fiction or fantasy. They all contained the element of the projected personal unconscious, or projected collective unconscious, which made them simply incomprehensible to anyone who read them, because they required the reader to accept my premise that each of us lives in a unique world."

Such books proved difficult to sell. One, *Confessions of a Crap Artist*, was finally brought out in 1975; the rest have never been published. "There are nine or ten manuscripts extant, over at the Fullerton special collections library," he says, apparently without rancor. I ask him if he is really as philosophical about this situation as he seems. "Well, when *Confessions of a Crap Artist* appeared, that took the sting out of it, and I didn't feel so bad. But of course it did take nineteen years to get that published. It's been a long road; but science fiction offered me a route by which I *could* publish the kind of thing that I wanted to write. *Martian Time-Slip* is exactly what I wanted to write. It deals with the premise that was, to me, so important—not just that we each live in a somewhat unique world of our own psychological content, but that the subjective world of one rather powerful person can infringe on the world of another person. If I can make you see the world the way I see it, then you will automatically think the way I think. You will come to the conclusions that I come to. And the greatest power one human being can exert over others is to control their perceptions of reality, and infringe on the integrity and individuality of their world. This is done, for instance, in psychotherapy. I went through attack-therapy in Canada. You get a lot of people all yelling at you, and suddenly the mystery of the Moscow purge trials of the 1930s becomes very clear—what could possibly make a person get up and say in a most sincere manner that he had committed a crime, the penalty for which was execution. Well, the answer lies in the incredible power of a group of human beings to invade a man's world and determine his image of himself so that he can actually believe their view of him. I remember in attack-therapy there was one guy dressed kind of nattily, and he was French. They said, you look like a homosexual. Within half an hour they had him convinced that he was a homosexual. He started crying. I thought, this is very strange, because I know this guy is *not* homosexual. And yet he's crying and admitting to this thing—not to cause the abuse to stop, the screams of these people all yelling at him, *You fairy, you fruit, you homo, admit what you are*. By confessing to it he didn't cause them to stop, he caused them to yell louder and say, *We were right, we were right*. He was simply beginning to agree with them.

"All this can be viewed politically or psychologically. To me it was all viewed dramatically in my writing, as the eerie and uncanny invasion of one person's world by another person's world. If I invade your world you will probably sense something alien, because my world is different from yours. You must, of course, fight it. But often we don't because a lot of it is subtle; we just have intimations that our worlds are being invaded, we don't know where this invasion of our personal integrity is coming from. It comes from authority figures in general.

"The greatest menace of the twentieth century is the totalitarian state. It can take many forms: left-wing fascism, psychological movements, religious movements, drug rehabilitation places, powerful people, manipulative people; or it can be in a relationship with someone who is more powerful than you psychologically. Essentially, I'm pleading the cause of those people who are not strong. If I were strong myself I would probably not feel this as such a menace. I identify with the weak person; this is one reason why my fictional protagonists are essentially anti-heroes. They're almost losers, yet I try to equip them with qualities by which they can survive. At the same time I don't want to see them develop counter-aggressive tactics where they, too, become exploitative and manipulative."

I ask him what his reponse is when people tell him he is being overanxious about authority figures and is simply paranoid. In reply he refers to the harassment he suffered while he was an antiwar activist, culminating in a bizarre break-in at his home which local police in effect refused to investigate. "I was told I was paranoid before my house was hit. Then I remember opening the door, and finding nothing but ruins everywhere, windows and doors smashed in, files blown open, all my papers missing, all my cancelled checks gone, my stereo gone, and I remember thinking, Well, it sure is a hell of a mess, but there goes that 'paranoid' theory.

"Actually I was told by a fairly good analyst that I'm not cold-blooded enough to be paranoid. He said to me, 'You're melo-dramatic and you're full of illusions about life, but you're too sentimental to be paranoid.'

"I took the Minnesota Multiphasic psychological profile test once, and I tested out as paranoid, cyclothymic, neurotic, schiz-ophrenic . . . I was so high on some of the scales that the dot was up in the instructions part. But I also tested out as an incorrigible liar! You see, they'll give you the same question phrased in several different ways. They'll say something like: *There is a divine deity that rules the world.* And I'd say, yeah, there probably is. Later on they'll say: *I don't think there is a divine deity that rules the world.* And I'd say, that's probably correct, I can see a lot of reasons for agreeing with that. And later they'll say: *I'm not sure if there's a divine deity that rules the world.* And I'd say, yeah, that's about right. In every case I was sincere. I think philosoph-ically I fit in with some of the very late pre-Socratic people around the time of Zeno and Diogenes, the Cynics, in the Greek sense, those who live like dogs. I am inevitably persuaded by every argument that is brought to bear. If you were to suggest to me at this moment that we go out for Chinese food I would immediately agree it was the best idea I ever heard; in fact, I would say, You've got to let me pay for it. If you were to say suddenly, Don't you think that Chinese food is overpriced, has *very* little nourishment, you have to go a *long* way to get it, and when you bring it home it's *cold*, I'd say, you're right, I can't abide the stuff. This is a sign of a very weak ego, I guess. However—if my view that each person has his unique world is correct, then if you say Chinese food is good, in your world it's good, and if someone else says it's bad, in his world it's bad. I'm a complete relativist in that for me the answer to the question, Is Chinese food good or bad? is semantically meaningless. Now, this is *my* view. If *your* view is that this view is incorrect, *you* might be right. In which case, I would be willing to agree with you."

He sits back, happy with his exercise at eliminating any foun-dation for an objective structure of values. He has talked easily, engagingly, as if entertained by his own conversation. A lot of what he says sounds playful at the same time that it seems sincere.

I ask how much of his thinking was influenced by LSD ex-periences, and which of his books, if any, are derived from acid trips.

"I wrote *Time Out of Joint* in the 1950s, before I had even heard of LSD. In that book a guy walks up to a lemonade stand in the park, and it turns into a slip of paper marked Soft Drink Stand, and he puts the slip of paper in his pocket. Far-fucking-out, spacey, that's an 'acid experience.' If I didn't know better I'd say that this author had turned on many times, and his universe was coming unglued—he's obviously living in a *fake universe*.

"What I was trying to do in that book was account for the diversity of worlds that people live in. I had not read Heraclitus then, I didn't know his concept of *ideos kosmos*, the private world, versus *koinos kosmos*, which we all share. I didn't know that the pre-Socratics had begun to discern these things.

"There's a scene in the book where the protagonist goes into his bathroom, reaches in the dark for a pull-cord, and suddenly realizes there is no cord, there's a switch on the wall, and he can't remember when he ever had a bathroom where there was a cord hanging down. Now, that actually happened to me, and it was what caused me to write the book. It reminded me of the idea that van Vogt had dealt with, of artifical memory, as occurs in *The World of Null-A* where a person has false memories implanted. A lot of what I wrote, which looks like the result of taking acid, is really the result of taking van Vogt very seriously! I *believed* van Vogt, I mean, *he wrote it*, you know, he was an authority figure. He said, people can be other than whom they remember themselves to be, and I found this fascinating. You have a massive suspension of disbelief on my part."

I ask to what extent he was ever, really, into drugs.

"The only drugs I took regularly were amphetamines, in order to be able to write as much as I had to write to make a living. I was being paid so little per book that I had to turn out a very large number of books. I had an extremely expensive wife and children . . . she would see a new car that she liked the looks of and just go off and buy it. . . . Under California law I was legally bound by her debts and I just wrote like mad. I think I turned out sixteen novels in five years at one point. I did sixty finished pages a day, and the only way I could write that much was to take amphetamines, which were prescribed for me. I finally stopped taking them, and I don't write as much as I used to.

"I used to talk like I was really into acid. But the fact of the matter is that I took it two times, and the second time it was so weak a dose, it may not even have been acid. The first time, though, it was Sandoz acid, a giant capsule I got from the University of California, a friend and I split it, it must have been a whole milligram of it, we bought it for five dollars, and I'll tell ya, I went straight to hell, was what happened. The landscape froze over, there were huge boulders, there was a deep thumping, it was the day of wrath and God was judging me as a sinner. This lasted for thousands of years and didn't get any better, it just got worse and worse. I felt terrible physical pain and all I could talk in was Latin. Most embarrassing, because the girl I was with thought I was doing it to annoy her. I was whining like some poor dog that's been left out in the rain all night and finally the girl said, *Oh, barf*, and walked out of the room in disgust.

"About a month later I got the galley proofs for *The Three Stigmata of Palmer Eldritch* to read over, and I thought, oh dear, I can't read these, they're too scary. That book of course is my classic 'LSD novel' even though all I had had to go on when I wrote it was an article by Aldous Huxley about LSD. But all the horrible things I had written seemed to have come true under acid.

"That was in 1964. I used to beg people not to take acid. There was one girl who came over one night, and I made her an amateur Rorschach ink-blot, and she said, 'I see an evil shape coming to kill me.' I said, 'You'd be a damned fool to take acid.' So she didn't take it then, but she did take it later, and she tried to kill herself and was hospitalized and became chronically psychotic. I saw her in 1970 and her mind was gone, it destroyed her. She said that taking the acid had destroyed her.

"I regarded drugs as dangerous and potentially lethal, but I had a cat's curiosity. It was my interest in the human mind that made me curious about psychotropic drugs. These were essentially religious strivings that were appearing in me. By the time of *Three Stigmata* I had become a convert to the Episcopal Church. . . ."

I interrupt a moment, to ask, why Episcopal?

He adopts the gruff expression that I suspect means he's putting me on—or maybe just the opposite—or maybe he's not actually sure himself. "My wife said if I didn't join the church she'd bust my nose. She says, If we're going to know judges and district attorneys and important people, we have to be Episcopalian."

If this anecdote is told half in fun, it's the last joke of the interview, because at this point he continues in a kind of confessional, which I suspect he planned to make at this time if only to see what reaction he would elicit from me, as a relative stranger.

"I was walking along one day." His tone is sincere, now. "I looked up in the sky and there was this face staring down at me, a giant face with slotted eyes, the face I describe in *Three Stigmata*.

This was 1963. It was an evil, horrible-looking thing. I didn't clearly see it; but it was there. I finally identified it, years later; I was looking through a copy of *Life* magazine and I came across a picture of some French forts from World War I. They were observation cupolas made out of iron, with slots where the soldiers could look out and see the Germans. My father had fought at the second battle of the Marne, he was in the Fifth U.S. Marines, and when I was a little kid he used to show me all his military equipment. He would put on his gas mask and his eyes would disappear, and he would tell me about the battle of the Marne, and the horrors he went through. He told me, a little four-year-old child, about men with their guts blown out, and he showed me his gun and everything, and told me how they fired till their guns were red-hot. He had been under gas attacks, and he told me of the terrible fear as the charcoal in the masks would become saturated with the gas and they would panic and tear their masks off. My father was a big handsome man, a football player, tennis player. I've read what the U.S. Marines did in that war, and those farm boys underwent what Remarque describes in *All Quiet on the Western Front* as unspeakable valor, unspeakable horrors. And there it was in 1963 looking down at me, a goddamned fortification from the Marne. My father may even have drawn a sketch or had photographs of it, for all I know.

"I actually sought refuge in Christianity from what I saw in the sky. Seeing it as an evil deity I wanted the reassurance that there was a benign deity more powerful. My priest actually said that perhaps I could become a Lutheran because I seemed to actually sense the presence of Satan. And this has continued to plague me, as an intimation that the god of this world is evil. The Buddha, seeing the evil of the world, came to the conclusion that there could be no creator god, because if there were, it could not be this way, there could not be so much evil and suffering; I had come to the conclusion that there *was* a deity in this world, and he was evil. I had formulated the problem again and again in books like *Maze of Death* and *Ubik* and *Three Stigmata* and *Eye in the Sky*.

"During World War II, when I was a kid. I remember seeing in a theater a newsreel film of a Japanese soldier who had been hit by a flamethrower by the Americans, and he was burning to death and running, and burning and running, and burning and running, and the audience cheered and laughed and I was dazed with horror at the sight of the man on the screen and at the audience's reaction, and I thought, *something is terribly wrong*. Years later when I was in my thirties and living in the country I had to kill a rat that had gotten into the children's bedroom. Rats are hard to kill. I set a trap for it. In the night it got into the trap, and the next morning, when I got up, it heard me coming, and it screamed. I took the trap out with a pitchfork and sprung the trap and let the rat go out in the pasture, and it came out of the trap and its neck was broken. I took the pitchfork and drove the tines into the rat, and it *still* didn't die. Here was this rat, it had tried only to come in and get food, it was poisoned, its neck was broken, it was stabbed, it was still alive. At that point I simply went crazy with horror. I ran in and filled a tub with water and drowned it. And I buried it and I took the St. Christopher medal that I wore and buried that with the rat. And the soul of that rat I carry on me from then on, as a question and as a problem about the condition of living creatures on this world. I could not exorcise the spirit of that rat which had died so horribly. In my novel, *Flow My Tears, The Policeman Said*, the armed posse is approaching a building where Jason Taverner is shut up in the dark. He hears them and he screams, and that is the rat screaming when it heard me coming. Even in 1974 I was still remembering that rat screaming.

"And then, at the trough of my life, where I saw only inexplicable suffering, there came to me a beatific vision which calmed all my sense of horror and my sense of the transcendent power of evil. My mental anguish was simply removed from me as if by a divine fiat, in an intervention of a psychological-mystical type, which I describe in my new book, *Valis*. Some transcendent divine power which was not evil, but benign, intervened to restore my mind and heal my body and give me a sense of the beauty, the joy, the sanity of the world. And out of this I forged a concept which is relatively simple and possibly unique in theology, and that is, the *irrational* is the primordial stratum of the universe, it comes first in time and is primary in ontology—in levels of essence. And it evolves into rationality. The history of the universe is a movement from irrationality—chaos, cruelty, blindness, pointlessness—to a rational structure which is harmonious, interlinked in a way which is orderly and beautiful. The primordial creative deity was essentially *deranged*, from our standpoint; we are, as humans, an evolution above the primordial deity, we are pygmies but we stand on the shoulders of giants and therefore we see more than they see. We human beings are created and yet we are more rational than the creator himself who spawned us.

"This outlook is based not on faith but on an actual encounter that I had in 1974, when I experienced an invasion of my mind by a transcendentally rational mind, as if I had been insane all my life and suddenly I had become sane. Now, I have actually thought of that as a possibility, that I had been psychotic from 1928, when I was born, until March of 1974. But I don't think that's the case. I may have been somewhat whacked-out and eccentric for years and years, but I know I wasn't all that crazy, because I'd been given Rorschach tests and so on.

"This rational mind was not human. It was more like an artificial intelligence. On Thursdays and Saturdays I would think it was God, on Tuesdays and Wednesdays I would think it was extraterrestrial, sometimes I would think it was the Soviet Union Academy of Sciences trying out their psychotronic microwave telepathic transmitter. I tried every theory, I thought of the Rosicrucians; I thought of Christ. . . . It invaded my mind and assumed control of my motor centers and did my acting and thinking for me. I was a spectator to it. It set about healing me physically and my four-year-old boy, who had an undiagnosed life-threatening birth defect that no one had been aware of. This mind, whose identity was totally obscure to me, was equipped with tremendous technical knowledge—engineering, medical, cosmological, philosophical knowledge. It had memories dating back over two thousand years, it spoke Greek, Hebrew, Sanskrit, there wasn't anything that it didn't seem to know.

"It immediately set about putting my affairs in order. It fired my agent and my publisher. It remargined my typewriter. It was very practical; it decided that the apartment had not been vacuumed recently enough; it decided that I should stop drinking wine because of the sediment—it turned out I had an abundance of uric acid in my system—and it switched me to beer. It made elementary mistakes such as calling the dog 'he' and the cat 'she,' which annoyed my wife; and it kept calling her 'ma'am.'"

At this point I interrupt, just to be sure I'm getting this right: the presence, the voice that he heard in his head, took over control of his body, his speech, and his decisions?

"That's right."

My first impulse is to suspend judgment. My second notion is to look for a second opinion. In March of 1974, Mr. Dick was married: what did his wife think about all of this?

"My wife was impressed," he says, "by the fact that, because of the tremendous pressure this mind put on people in my business, I made quite a lot of money very rapidly. We began to get checks for thousands of dollars—money that was owed me, which the mind was conscious existed in New York but had never been coughed up. And it got me to the doctor, who confirmed its diagnoses of various ailments that I had . . . it did everything but paper the walls of the apartment. It also said it would stay on as my tutelary spirit. I had to look up 'tutelary' to find out what it meant.

"I have almost 500,000 words of notes on all this. I'm quite reticent about it, normally. I've talked to my [Episcopalian] priest about it, and a couple of close friends. I tried to discuss it with Ursual Le Guin, and she just wrote and said, I think you're crazy. She returned the material I had sent her. Of course, when *Valis* comes out, a lot of all this will be in the book. *Valis* is an attempt to formulate my vision in some rational structure which can be conveyed to other people."

I have been listening to all this in a state of confusion. I had come to this apartment for what I assumed was just another in a series of interviews about the business of writing science fiction, and now I find myself caught up in a Dickian reality-warp. I'm listening to what sounds like wild fantasy but is being narrated as fact, with obvious, self-conscious sincerity. I don't know what to believe; my world—my *ideos kosmos*—has been invaded by his, as if I have become a character in one of his novels, and he is Palmer Eldritch, dreaming up a new reality for me to live in.

But I can't live in it, because I can't accept it. I can't suddenly believe that there really are extraterrestrial entities invading the minds of men. I can't believe you can learn secrets of the universe by visiting a science-fiction author in Santa Ana.

And yet he is so plausible! In print it may sound absurd; but sitting listening to his shy, matter-of-fact description of events that are totally real to him, I would like to find a way to accept it all, if only because I find him so immensely likeable, and because I have respect for his intellect generally. As his recent books have shown, he has a practical, lucid insight into the workings of the world. In no way is he a seer or a "psychic" delivering a messianic message or recipe for salavation. He admits readily to his tendency to dramatize life, but basically he is a carefully rational man who questions any concept with persistent logic. He is quite ready to discuss the possibility that his paranormal experience might have been nothing more than one half of his brain talking to the other half; he's reluctant to accept this explanation only because it doesn't adequately explain all the facts of his experience.

These facts are numerous. I can't begin to summarize them. He's had five years to live with the phenomenon of the "presence" that temporarily invaded his mind (and still communicates with him intermittently). He has accumulated notes and records, all kinds of research data, so much of it that, no matter what you ask or what objection you raise, he's already ahead of you, with relentlessly logical deductions, facts of all kinds.

I myself have never seen evidence to make me believe in any psychic phenomena or pseudoscience, from telepathy to UFOs. My faith is that the universe is random and godless. I am the last person to believe that there is a higher intelligence, and that Philip K. Dick has a private connection with it.

I do believe that something remarkable happened to him, if only psychologically; and I do believe that the experience has inspired a rather beautiful vision of the universe (or *koinos kosmos*) and a strange, unique book which may enhance the lives of its readers. This is the minimum with which Dick must be credited. To debate his "mental stability" is missing the point; what matters is the worth of his insight, regardless of its source. There have been men far more deranged than Philip K. Dick who nevertheless produced great art of lasting relevance to the lives of millions of un-deranged people.

Dick remains much the same personality as before his vision. He has not metamorphosed into a religious zealot. His perceptions, and his ironic, skeptical wit, are as sharp as ever.

A couple of days after the interview, I returned for a purely social visit, without tape recorders (so my remaining reportage is from unaided memory). During our conversation I mentioned a whimsical notion I enjoy, that if I'm far away from somewhere, and can't see or touch it, it doesn't really exist.

"Oh, sure," he said, "they only build as much of the world as they need to, to convince you it's real. You see, it's kind of a low-budget operation: those countries you read about, like Japan, or Australia, they don't really exist. There's nothing out there. Unless of course *you* decide to go out there, in which case they have to put it all together, all the scenery, the buildings, and the people, in time for you to see it. They have to work real fast."

At this point, I am treading carefully. 'let's get this straight," I say. "Are you describing, now, a fictional concept, such as might occur in one of your novels? Or is this . . . serious?"

"You mean, do I believe it?" he asked in apparent surprise. "Why, no, of course not. You'd have to be crazy to believe in something like *that!*" And then he laughed.

(Santa Ana, May 1979)

BIBLIOGRAPHICAL NOTES

Philip K. Dick has written such a large number of equally notable novels, it is hard to select the most memorable. His *The Man in the High Castle* (1962) won a Hugo award and is one of his most accessible, least spaced-out books of the 1960s. His "classic acid-head novel," *The Three Stigmata of Palmer Eldritch*, was published in 1964; it is an extremely disturbing book. For light relief I recommend *The Zap Gun* (1967), which is at least half tongue-in-cheek. His short stories can be found in *The Best of Philip K. Dick* (1977), *The Book of Philip K. Dick* (1973) and *The Golden Man* (1980).

Confessions of a Crap Artist (1975) is not science fiction, but gives interesting perspectives on the author, in that to some extent it is autobiographical. *Flow My Tears, the Policeman Said* (1974) deals with some of his earlier multiple-reality obsessions, with far greater maturity, and well-measured prose. *A Scanner Darkly*, his most recent novel to date, is barely science fiction; it is a moving story of the 1960s drug culture, and at the same time is a novel of great wit and acute observation. *Valis* (1980?) is not so much a novel as a revelatory message, becoming fictionalized halfway through, and based on experiences described in my interview with the author.

Photo by
David C. Lustig

Harlan Ellison

The house is full—every niche occupied, all surfaces covered with books, art, ornaments, records, sculpture, curios, awards, objêts, collectibles, knick-knacks, mementos, trophies, toys, gifts, gadgets, treasures, and trivia. Many of the walls are completely hidden behind paintings crowded up against one another—there are even paintings hung on some of the ceilings. And there are 37,000 books, some stacked in drawers because all available shelf space has been engulfed. And there are conversation pieces—a 1940s jukebox; a genuine subway-style candy-vending machine; a photograph of Mars framed in a red neon tube; a complete framed set of Kellogg Pep giveaway buttons. In the master bedroom there is a waterbed atop a platform upholstered in red shag carpet; in the attached bathroom, a Jacuzzi, an art-deco lamp, and ceramic tiles imported from Italy. There's a guest room, a secretary's office (full of unassembled plastic model kits and Japanese monster toys), a living room (with bizarre modern sculpture, giant TV, and two video recorders), and a newly-built library featuring a beige competition-size pool table color-coordinated with the walls, and long shelves of heavy reference tomes, boxed collections of *Esquire* and *Playboy*, and Marvel Comics back issues. Behind one bookcase is a secret soundproof grotto with walls of genuine volcanic rock and a soft floor, like one big custom-fitted, contoured mattress. Upstairs, the writer's work space, featuring a desk on a dais, tiers of filing cabinets, and arrays of awards (seven-and-a-half Hugos, three Nebulas, two Jupiters, one Edgar) along with certificates, signed photographs, plaques, and testimonials. Outside on the roof, past the Paolo Soleri wind chimes and an authentic British dart board, our tour ends amid the Robert Silverbeg memorial cactus garden.

Daily life here is a Los Angelean carnival of people and phone calls, diversions and discussions, women and dinners out, sudden arguments, impulsive decisions, mad errands. While gardeners spray fungicide on the lawn and spread nets over the peach tree, builders and craftsmen debate the architectural complexities involved in the $20,000 kitchen extension, all glass-brick, neon, and stainless-steel, now under construction. Usually there is one long-term house guest (a fellow-writer or protégé) as well as various acquaintances passing through. Ellison trades quips, smokes one of his 400 exotically carved pipes, and plays pool with his full-time assistant, Linda Steele. Then, a conference with lawyers to finalize his metamorphosis into The Kilimanjaro Corporation, for tax purposes. Then a meeting with a designer who has created the new corporation logo. The day, mired in trivia, seems timeless, and yet it devours time. Suddenly it's 5:00 and Ellison is still wrapped in his brown bathrobe with *Don't Bug Me* embroidered on the back of it. They do bug him, though, constantly. They tie up his telephone lines, they jam his mailbox with letters, they accost him, nag him, and pick fights with him, when all he wants is some peace and quiet. Here he is now, at 5:30, still attempting to secure this peace and quiet. He is calling the distributors of a free local newspaper, which is thrown onto the doorsteps of home owners in this area. Ellison hates the newspaper. He becomes enraged. He demands that the free deliveries must stop. He's called them about this before, several times. Once they did stop delivering the paper, but apparently out of spite they then threw hundreds of *rubber bands* onto his driveway instead. Now, the deliveries have started again. It's driving him crazy, he can't stand it; he warns them, he will *sue*, on grounds of invasion of privacy, if the unwanted newspaper deliveries do not cease.

He adjourns for another game of pool. The phone rings. He answers; the calling party immediately hangs up. This happens frequently; it's some kid in San Francisco who likes to bug Ellison. Why? Why do these crazies home in on him? Once, he says, he spotted someone in the distance on the hillside overlooking the back of the house, aiming a *rifle* at him, as he stood in the kitchen. He had to sneak out and circle around behind the guy, to catch him. Then he had to have all his windows specially coated, like mirrors, to be sure that he wouldn't be seen as an indoor target in future. And now here's another phone call—from some weird woman who looked him up in the phone book, has read his stories, and intuitively knows he is mystically inspired—just like her. Perhaps she could meet him . . . ? Politely, he declines, and hangs up on her.

He must answer the doorbell. Tonight's date, a Hollywood-esque creature in thigh-hugging Levis and a red satin blouse, has just arrived in her own Porsche. Ellison receives her, wearing only a towel around his waist. He explains he was on his way to the shower, but first, he has to Xerox one of his own stories in his library. She accompanies him, docilely, and sits watching him, demurely, as he feeds the copying machine. It goes clunk, click; clunk, click. She sits and watches. Clunk, click. A fragment of conversation is exchanged, but most of the time, she sits and watches. Then he adjourns to the delayed shower, but first he must pause in the immaculate kitchen to reposition a couple of ornaments that someone has carelessly shifted out of alignment, and then he turns the knives on the magnetic knife rack so that their blades are all facing the same way, and—what's this? *Ants* have invaded the mansion. He thumbs them methodically, one by one, then stops to polish the white ceramic stove top with a special cleaner, then opens the refrigerator vegetable drawer, which is crammed full of an obscure brand of soft yellow candy that he enjoyed as a child. When he heard the manufacturer was going broke a few years ago he bought up their last stocks, so now, here, in this refrigerator, is the only remaining supply of this candy anywhere in the world. He allows himself to eat one piece. The phone rings. A couple of New York friends are in town . . . meet for dinner? Why not? A foursome . . . he knows the perfect bar-becue restaurant in the valley. . . .

And so on. The question is, when does Harlan Ellison, the writer, find time to do any writing?

Sometimes, he does it in bookstore windows; for Ellison is more than a writer, he is an entertainer. It is as important for him to reach people in person as it is via print. He is aggressive, even hostile—he insults his audience, ridicules their simple ideas and tastes, complains about their intrusiveness. But his life seems intentionally structured so that he is seldom alone, and his hostility is an act of courtship: the more he badmouths his audience, the more they love him for it. I have seen him tell 5,000 science-fiction fans that they are stupid and illiterate; they give him a standing ovation and gather round for autographs. He has been known to treat his house guests as though they are raw recruits and he the drill-sergeant; they shyly ask to stay on for an extra week of basic training. (He knows he has 37,000 books because he once detailed an idle guest to count them for him.) By setting up his typewriter and producing stories in bookstore windows, or in a plastic pyramid at a world science-fiction convention, he has converted even the most solitary act of creativity into a social event—and an exercise in one-upmanship (I'm on this side of the typewriter, and you're not). Onlookers gather, muttering "Who does he think he is?", but they gather, nonetheless, as he knows they will.

The stories themselves cry out for audience response. They are often melodramatic, angry, and controversial in their advocacy of extremism. The writing style is direct, reaching out to accost the reader, and its rhythms are conversational, so that each piece is like a stand-up monologue (indeed, Ellison often reads his work in public). And the stories are frequently prefaced with introductions; after all, any entertainer likes to have the audience warmed up before he starts his act.

Ellison is frank about his need, as a writer, to reach people. "It is very necessary for my work to have an impact. The most senseless cavil that's ever been leveled against me is, 'Oh, you only wrote that to shock.' I say of course, you idiot, of course that's the reason I wrote it. What do you expect me to do, lull you into a false sense of security? I want people's hair to stand on end when they read my work, whether it's a love story, or a gentle childhood story, or a story of drama and violence."

He is sitting behind his desk, on its dais, overlooking the grand panorama of the upper level of his library. I'm on a collapsible wooden chair, to one side of the desk. It's an inferior, slightly uncomfortable position, but it is the closest I could get to spatial equality with my interviewee. The alternative would have been to sit on a contemporary modular couch, fifteen feet distant and one foot lower in altitude.

I ask if it bothers him when people are amused by his acts of writing in public, or when they say, in effect, "Who does he think he is?"

"I think I'm the guy who can write a story that's as good as 'Count the Clock that Tells the Time' while sitting in a goddamn pyramid while thousands of people are trying to break my bones," he snaps. "I think that's who I am, you bet your ass I am, I love pulling off the trick no one else can pull off, I *love* it, man. I mean, my fantasies are not of—of sleeping with the entire Rockette line from Radio City Music Hall, they are—suddenly, while the jazz band is playing, I get up and say to the sax player, can I borrow your ax for a minute? And I begin blowing better than Charlie Parker. Or: there stretches the rope across Niagara Falls, and I say, oh, excuse me for a moment, and walk across it. My fantasies are pulling off the stunt that everyone said couldn't be pulled off. I love it, and I know it pisses people off, because people hate an overachiever, because when they see someone is capable of doing the *grand* thing, they realize how little they have demanded of themselves. I take great pleasure in that, in saying to them, you poor fucking turkey, you could have done it too, all you had to do was *do it*, but you *didn't*. And the stories that I write in those windows are good stories, man, they're not shit, they're good stories. I wrote 'The Diagnosis of Dr. D'arque Angel,' which is one of my best stories, sitting in the window of Words and Music, in London. 'Hitler Painted Roses,' for Christ's sake, which is a *dynamite* story, I did that over the radio, two two-hour sessions, sitting in a radio booth. The story that was in *Heavy Metal* magazine a couple of months ago, 'Flop Sweat,' I wrote that in one afternoon to read on a radio program that night. If people want to laugh, that's fine; let *them* try it and see how easy it is."

Tough talk, frequently backed by tough actions. At age forty-five, Ellison has built a formidable reputation as a fighter, in print and in person. Caution and compromise do not figure in his life-style, and he does not usually allow himself the option of retreat.

"My background is that I come from Painesville, Ohio, which was a very quiet town, but within it I was the object of an awful lot of violence and an awful lot of hatred and bigotry and alienation. I don't take this as a singular state, most people go through a similar thing in one way or another. But there was never a niche for me when I was a kid, so I was never able to get complacent. Early on I learned to take risks, doing the things that a kid does to gain attention, to prove that he's as good as anybody else. And I learned that I can't really be damaged. I can be momentarily hurt, I can feel emotional pain, my heart can be broken, but as

I was saying the other day, real pain only lasts twelve minutes; the rest of the time is spent in justifying it to yourself to make what you went through seem valid and important. So I always took risks, and when I saw how it shook up everybody around me, because I was a kid seeking attention, I would do it all the more. Climbing a sixteen-story building on steamblasters' ropes, bare-handed, just to do it—they called the fire engines. It was always my intention to be noticed. Now, as an adult, that's a very bad thing; seeking attention is a very childish thing. But I still do it. It manifests itself in other ways."

One big risk that he took at the start of his writing career was to join a Brooklyn teenage gang in order to write about gang life and gang warfare. It culminated in a knife-fight in which he was almost killed.

"Joining the gang came naturally to me, because I had ready Hemingway, who wrote 'one should never write what one doesn't know'; so I figured if I wanted to write about juvenile delinquency I must go and do it. These things seem to other people like a death-wish or something, but it's not, it's stretching myself to the absolute limits of my abilities and finding out what new boundaries there are for me. Taking risks is urgently important; I see around me the people who don't take risks, who worship security and comfort, and I see that as a living death. Left to their own devices the human race would settle into a soft Gerald Ford-like hum, a state in which they would just mmmmm along. I think that entropy keeps the society going along the path that it wants to go, and big systems and big units, multinational corporations, armies, and governments, will keep things pretty much in line, and it's only the occasional firebrand or troublemaker who shakes things up enough to get a few people thinking. Those mavericks advance the cause of history. You know that thing from Thoreau that I'm so fond of quoting, 'He serves the State best who opposes the State most.'"

I ask if he is arguing that any kind of radicalism is good, and change is desirable for its own sake.

"There is good change and there is bad change, but I think all change eventually brings about an advancement of one kind or another. Clausewitz said, 'Any movement is better than no move-ment at all.' If you sit still you die, you atrophy, your legs fall off. And besides, I don't think I'm important enough, that any change I made is really going to shake things up. I'm not Ralph Nader, and I'm not Eve Curie, and I'm not Joan of Arc. I'm just a paid liar, and my perceptions of the world seem minuscule by comparison with the work of any of the really, really great writers, like Isaac Bashevis Singer or Tom Disch."

This sudden note of modesty is injected casually, and yet I think it is deliberate. Ellison reminds himself to be humble now and then much as a high-living sinner reminds himself to confess to his priest occasionally. His modesty, when it crops up, is certainly sincere: there truly are writers whose work he admires more than his own, and he is constantly quoting these people—"because they're wiser than I, and they know the way to say things."

In fact his house ("Ellison Wonderland") is named in tribute to one great fantasist, and his corporation is named after a Hemingway short story. Ellison is a fiercely independent individual, and the style and mood of his writing are unique; paradoxically, he is in awe of the words of other writers, to the extent that he embosses their epigrams on bits of Dymo tape and sticks them on walls and work surfaces around his desk. It is as if he needs the wisdom of elder statesmen of literature around him as he works.

So he pays homage to his heroes; but he has only impatient scorn for those who don't dare to be great. As an entertainer, or as an activist, he hates his public to be unresponsive and apathetic. He despises the notion that people might be happier leading lazy, unimaginative lives.

"*Are* they happy? I don't think they are. Anybody who settles for anything less than the moon, anything less than painting the Sistine Chapel ceiling, or voyaging to the center of the Earth, is taking less than what the world holds for them. This thing about ignorance is bliss, and they're happy as drones . . . I don't think so. Circumstances and indoctrination and a lack of self-esteem are the deterrents that keep people from doing whatever that golden thing is within them to do. I've seen the meanest clay do the most remarkable things. Look at the Watts Tower [a huge piece of sculpture built in a back yard in the Watts district of Los Angeles]. Here was an uneducated, illiterate day laborer, Simon Rodia, who built something considered great art, with his own hands. All you need to see is *one* of those, and you say, everybody's got it. I do truly believe that in every human being there is the capacity, from birth, to reach the stars in some way. When we don't we are denying our heritage, what we can be. So I struggle toward that.

"I have been many things in my life. I was not always a writer; I was an extraordinarily fine actor when I was a kid, with an opportunity to go to Broadway. I was a singer, and can still sing, and could have made a living—not a terrific living, but a good living—as a singer. I'm very good with my hands, I was a bricklayer, and that's noble too. There is nothing to which I could have turned my hand, at which I would not have excelled. Because that's what I strive for—excellence. Very early in life when I read Robert Heinlein I got the thread that runs through his stories—the notion of the competent man. I've always held that as my ideal. I've tried to be a very competent man. When I fuck up, which I do regularly, I pillory myself far more than I pillory anyone around me, because I feel I should be above error, above stupid mistakes."

Indeed, one senses that Ellison constantly rates himself, critically, and imagines how others might rate him, in his ability to live up to his ambitions and ethical standards. It's a preoccupation with *looking good*, in two senses: first, as a stylish gadfly with an inimitable image, and second, looking like a good boy who has conscientiously done no wrong. He often makes a point of "doing the right thing" and doing it publicly; he has ostentatiously supported such causes as the antiwar movement of the 1960s, civil rights for Southern blacks, gun control, and, most recently, the Equal Rights Amendment. As guest of honor at the Arizona world science-fiction convention in 1978 he publicized the fact that Arizona had not ratified the Equal Rights Amendment, he advocated that attendees at the convention should camp out rather than spend money on hotel rooms (he himself slept in a van parked outside the hotel and spent no money at all in Arizona, on anything), and he used the convention to campaign for the ERA and raise funds for a local feminist organization. Many science-fiction people hated him for politicizing their field, but they had to admit, here was someone being true to his principles, looking so good, it hurt.

Ellison had no false modesty about the event. "I came back with the sure and certain knowledge that I had done something heroic. I really felt like an honest-to-god hero. I had stood up for my principles, I had done something that I knew in the core of my being was utlimately good for the human race, and I had put my body on the line and nothing had deterred me. The convention was enormously successful, I was enormously successful, and we got $2,000 for the Arizona ERA women, and did a thing that was a *good* thing, it was a *good* thing that we did, and I just burn with pride in it, that I was able to do it. There are so few occasions when one is presented with a clear-cut choice of being courageous or cowardly, and I was courageous. I don't take all the credit—

if it had not been for Linda Steele I probably wouldn't have done it. But she held me to it, frequently, which is why I treasure her friendship, because she is a woman of great conscience, not afraid to say to me, 'you're acting in a cowardly fashion, you're talking the talk and not walking the walk.'"

He adds that ethical questions are a frequent preoccupation, in his life and also in his fiction. "I don't put much stock in morality; it's ethical behavior I care about."

I ask if he has ever been criticized on ethical grounds for a lifestyle that some would call extravagant or self-indulgent.

"Well, I feel I've paid my dues. I came from a poor background. My father died intestate, I paid off his bills, I supported my mother for the last ten or eleven years of her life, so I know what poverty is and I know that it is not necessarily true that poverty is noble and if you live in a garret you will write better than if you live in a nice house. For me, to write well, I must be in an environment that pleases me. I got my home, I got my nest, for myself, and it's filled with my toys and my music and I can come back to it when I need to. The house is an outward manifestation of me, an extension of me. I don't pay much attention to people who say, well, gee, if he was really such a humanitarian he'd be living like Gandhi, or Albert Schweitzer. That's bullshit. I don't live in an exorbitant fashion. I make an awful lot of money but I give a lot of that money to places each year that I think it should go."

Organized charities?

"You never know what you're supporting these days. Everybody is owned by somebody else. I prefer to invest in individuals. Like Dawn Johanson who carved the sculpture, the gargoyle, out in the back yard. I bought it from her and sent her to art school with the money. Octavia Estelle Butler, the novelist whose work I have supported, I encouraged her career and sent her off to Clarion so she's now a successful writer. There are no actual organized causes to which I would subscribe or give large amounts of money; but then I don't want to be rich, I really don't. I used to think $10,000 a year was a lot of money, and that was the pinnacle to which I aspired. I'm alarmed that I make as much money as I make now. They're postulating that I'm going to make $200,000 this year, and I've had to incorporate. I've spent all my life distrusting and fighting against corporations," he smiles, "and now 'I are one.' I personally find it distressing and disturbing."

This from the man building a $20,000 extension to his kitchen.

And yet—the architect of that project is a woman who just finished college, and this is her first project, a unique opportunity to enjoy total creative freedom. The builder runs a small business and is a friend. A young Chicano, newly in business, has been hired for his talent in working in stainless steel. And so on. Ellison's whole house is full of art and artifacts commissioned or bought from artists who could not survive without his kind of rich patronage. Truly, he invests in individuals; he might dislike the label, but he's the image of an enlightened capitalist as a positive social force.

An old-fashioned notion; but in some ways Ellison *is* old-fashioned. His references are often to 1950s culture (the Rockettes, Charlie Parker); he hates fads (he ridicules disco roller-skating and dislikes most modern rock music); he is liberated in the sense of the Playboy Philosophy but staid by the standards of Penthouse Forum. And yet of course he is more fashionably dressed, more aware of contemporary culture than most other science-fiction writers—whom he mocks for their old-fashioned attitudes and resistance to change. It's another paradox, but then, entertainers are seldom easy to sum up in simple terms. The need to be loved by an audience is clear, yet denied, as is the need for drama in daily life, the need to be impressive without seeming to strive for it. At the end of our interview, he sat back and said wearily, disappointedly, "I was hoping I could come up with a terrific revelation which would just wipe you out." He had given his best performance, yet it still wasn't good enough to satisfy his own demanding standards. Like most performers, he finds it unbearable to disappoint himself or his public.

Of course, the rewards for his obsessive efforts are great: he lives well, is a sort of myth-figure to thousands of readers, is revered and admired, and has a unique place in the fields where he has been active—science fiction, TV, movies. His talent and his charm, his vitality and his directness, his integrity and his generosity, all are remarkable, and have rightly won friends and influenced people.

Even when there are bleak moments—when the writing does not go easily, in public or in private, and despite the wealth of names in his huge address book he feels he has few real friends, and it so happens that there is no house guest to talk to, no assistant or handyman around—to give a sense of activity, and not even a girl staying overnight—even then there is some consolation. Because even then, the house is full. Crowded with those 37,000

books, all their titles shouting together off the shelves. Crowded
with all the objêts, many in the form of animals and cartoon
characters and little people. And crowded with art, most of which
depicts human figures and faces. Always, the house is full of
faces, the perpetual audience, looking down from every wall.

(Los Angeles, May 1979)

BIBLIOGRAPHICAL NOTES

Much of Ellison's earlier work was brought back into print in the 1970s,
including *Web of the City* (first published 1958) and *Memos from Purgatory*
(first published 1961). These books are not science fiction; they are good,
hard, documentary fiction—and fact—describing New York teenage gang-
life with authenticity and guts.

Of Ellison's large output of short stories, some of the best are in *Alone
Against Tomorrow* (1971) and *Strange Wine* (1978). The first collection
embodies his recurring themes of rebellion, alienation, and violence, characteristic of the 1960s, when most of the stories were originally published.
The more recent collection shows not so much a mellowing-out as an
increased maturity.

The Glass Teat (1969) is a collection of radical commentaries based
around American television programming. The pieces were originally published in the *Los Angeles Free Press*, and form an angry diary of the times,
notable for its sincerity and idealism, side by side with reduction of complex
issues to simplistic yes/no, good/bad judgments.

Ellison has compiled two landmark collections of new fiction: *Dangerous Visions* (1967) and *Again, Dangerous Visions* (1972). Both feature
copious introductions and explanatory matter by the editor, often as interesting as the stories he presents. *The Last Dangerous Visions* has been
in preparation for ten years; it publication date remains problematical.

Photo by
V. Tony Hauser,
Toronto

Ray Bradbury

Ray Bradbury's stories speak with a unique voice. They can never be confused with the work of any other writer. And Bradbury himself is just as unmistakable: a charismatic individualist with a forceful, effusive manner and a kind of wide-screen, epic dedication to the powers of Creativity, Life, and Art.

He has no patience with commercial writing which is produced soullessly for the mass market:

"It's all crap, it's all crap, and I'm not being virtuous about it; I react in terms of my emotional, needful self, in that if you turn away from what you are, you'll get sick some day. If you go for the market, some day you'll wake up and regret it. I know a lot of screenwriters; they're always doing things for other people, for money, because it's a job. Instead of saying, 'Hey, I really shouldn't be doing this,' they take it, because it's immediate, and because it's a credit. But no one remembers that credit. If you went anywhere in Los Angeles among established writers and said, 'Who wrote the screenplay for *Gone With the Wind*?' they couldn't tell you. Or the screenplay for *North by Northwest*. Or the screenplay for *Psycho*—even I couldn't tell you that, and I've seen the film eight times. These people are at the beck and call of the market; they grow old, and lonely, and envious, and they are not loved, because no one remembers. But in novels and short stories, essays and poetry, you've got a chance of not having, necessarily, such a huge audience, but having a constant group of *lovers*, people who show up in your life on occasion and look at you with such a pure light in their faces and their eyes that there's no denying that love, it's there, you can't fake it. When you're in the street and you see someone you haven't seen in years—that *look!* They see you and, that light, it comes out, saying, My God, *there you are*, Jesus God it's been five years, let me buy you a drink . . . And you go into a bar, and—and that beautiful thing, which friendship gives you, *that's* what we want, hah? That's what we want. And all the rest is crap. It is. That's what we want from life—" He pounds his fist on the glass top of his large, circular coffee table. "—We *want friends*. In a lifetime most people only have one or two decent friends, constant friends. I have five, maybe even six. And a decent marriage, and children, plus the work that you want to do, plus the fans that accumulate around that work—Lord, it's a *complete* life, isn't it—but the screenwriters never have it, and it's terribly sad. Or the Harold Robbinses of the world—I mean, probably a nice gent. But *no one cares*, no one cares that he wrote those books, because they're commercial books, and there's no moment of truth that speaks to the heart. The grandeur and exhilaration of certain days is missing—those gorgeous days when you walk out and it's enough just to be *alive*, the sunlight goes right in your nostrils and out your ears, hah? *That's* the stuff. All the rest—the figuring out of the designs, for how to do a bestseller—what a bore that is. Lord, I'd kill myself, I really would, I couldn't live that way. And I'm not being moralistic. I'm speaking from the secret wellsprings of the nervous system. I can't do those things, not because it's morally wrong and unvirtuous, but because the gut system can't take it, finally, being untrue to the gift of life. If you turn away from natural gifts that God has given you, or the universe has given you, however you want to describe it in your own terms, you're going to grow old too soon. You're going to get sour, get cynical, because you yourself are a sublime cynic for having done what you've done. You're going to die before you die. That's no way to live."

He speaks in a rich, powerful voice—indeed, a hot-gospel voice—as he delivers this inspirational sermon. He may be adopting a slightly more incisive style than usual, for the purposes of this interview, and he may be using a little overstatement to emphasize his outlook; but there can be no doubt of his sincerity. Those passages of ecstatic prose in his fiction, paying homage to the vibrant images of childhood, the glorious fury of flaming rockets, the exquisite mystery of Mars, the all-around wonderfulness of the universe in general—he truly seems to experience life in these terms, uninhibitedly, unreservedly.

Intellectual control and cold, hard reason have a place, too; but they must give way to emotion, during the creative process:

"It takes a day to write a short story. At the end of the day, you say, That seems to work, what parts don't? Well, there's a scene here that's not real, now, what's missing? Okay, the intellect can help you here. Then, the next day, you go back to it, and you explode again, based on what you learned the night before from your intellect. But it's got to be a total explosion, over in a few hours, in order to be honest.

"Intellectualizing is a great danger. It can get in the way of doing anything. Our intellect is there to protect us from destroying ourselves—from falling off cliffs, or from bad relationships—love affairs where we need the brains not to be involved. That's what the intellect is for. But it should not be the center of things. If you try to make your intellect the center of your life you're going to spoil all the fun, hah? You're going to get out of bed with people before you ever get into bed with them. So if that happens—the whole world would die, we'd never have any children!" He laughs. "You'd never start any relationships, you'd be afraid of all friendships, and become paranoid. The intellect can make you paranoid about everything, including creativity, if you're not careful. So why not delay thinking till the act is over? It doesn't hurt anything."

I feel that Bradbury's outlook, and his stories, are unashamedly romantic. But when I use this label, he doesn't seem at all comfortable with it.

"I'm not quite sure I know what it means. If certain things make you laugh or cry, how can you help that? You're only describing a process. I went down to Cape Canaveral for the first time three years ago. I walked into it, and yes, I thought, this is my home town! Here is where I came from, and it's all been built in the last twenty years behind my back. I walk into the Vehicle Assembly Building, which is 400 feet high, and I go up in the elevator and look down—and the tears burst from my eyes. They absolutely *burst* from my eyes! I'm just full of the same awe that I have when I visit Chartres or go into the Notre Dame or St.

Peter's. The size of this cathedral where the rockets take off to go to the moon is so amazing, I don't know how to describe it. On the way out, in tears, I turn to my driver and I say, 'How the hell do I write that down? It was like walking around in Shakespeare's head.' And as soon as I said it I knew that was the metaphor. That night on the train I got out my typewriter and I wrote a seven-page poem, which is in my last book of poetry, about my experience at Canaveral walking around inside Shakespeare's head.

"Now, if that's romantic, I was born with romantic genes. I cry more, I suppose—I'm easy to tears, I'm easy to laughter, I try to go with that and not suppress it. So if that's romantic, well, then, I guess I'm a romantic, but I really don't know what that term means. I've heard it applied to people like Byron, and in many ways he was terribly foolish, especially to give his life away, the way he did, at the end. I hate that, when I see someone needlessly lost to the world. We should have had him for another five years—or how about twenty? I felt he was foolishly romantic, but I don't know his life that completely. I'm a mixture; I don't think George Bernard Shaw was all that much of a romanticist, and yet I'm a huge fan of Shaw's. He's influenced me deeply, along with people like Shakespeare, or Melville. I'm mad for Shaw; I carry him with me everywhere. I reread his prefaces all the time."

Quite apart from what I still feel is a romantic outlook, Bradbury is distinctive as a writer who shows a recurring sense of nostalgia in his work. Many stories look back to bygone times when everything was simpler, and technology had not yet disrupted the basics of small-town life. I ask him if he knows the source of this affection for simplicity.

"I grew up in Waukegan, Illinois, which had a population of around 32,000, and in a town like that you walk everywhere when you're a child. We didn't have a car till I was twelve years old. So I didn't drive in automobiles much until I came west when I was fourteen, to live in Los Angeles. We didn't have a telephone in our family until I was about fifteen, in high school. A lot of things, we didn't have; we were a very poor family. So you start with basics, and you respect them. You respect walking, you respect a small town, you respect the library, where you went for your education—which I started doing when I was nine or ten. I've always been a great swimmer and a great walker, and a bicyclist. I've discovered every time I'm depressed or worried by anything, swimming or walking or bicycling will generally cure it. You get the blood clean and the mind clean, and then you're ready to go back to work again."

He goes on to talk about his early ambitions:

"My interests were diverse. I always wanted to be a cartoonist, and I wanted to have my own comic strip. And I wanted to make films, and be on the stage, and be an architect—I was madly in love with the architecture of the future that I saw in photographs of various world's fairs which preceded my birth. And then, reading Edgar Rice Burroughs when I was ten or eleven, I wanted to write Martian stories. So when I began to write, when I was twelve, that was the first thing I did. I wrote a sequel to an Edgar Rice Burroughs book.

"When I was seventeen years old, in Los Angeles, I used to go to science-fantasy meetings, downtown. We'd go to Clifton's Cafeteria; Forrest Ackerman and his friends would organize the group there every Thursday night, and you could go there and meet Henry Kuttner, and C. L. Moore, and Jack Williamson, and Edmond Hamilton, and Leigh Brackett—my God, how beautiful, I was seventeen years old, I wanted heroes, and they treated me beautifully. They accepted me. I still know practically everyone in the field, at least from the old days. I love them all. Robert Heinlein was my teacher, when I was nineteen . . . but you can't stay with that sort of thing, a family has to grow. Just as you let your children out into the world—I have four daughters—you don't say, 'Here is the boundary, you can't go out there.' So at the age of nineteen I began to grow. By the time I was twenty I was moving into little theater groups and I was beginning to experiment with other fictional forms. I still kept up my contacts with the science-fiction groups, but I mustn't stay in just that.

"When I was around twenty-four, I was trying to sell stories to *Colliers* and *Harper's* and *The Atlantic*, and I wanted to be in *The Best American Short Stories*. But it wasn't happening. I had a friend who knew a psychiatrist. I said, 'Can I borrow your psychiatrist for an afternoon?' One hour cost twenty dollars! That was my salary for the whole week, to go to this guy for an hour. So I went to him and he said, 'Mr. Bradbury, what's your problem?' And I said, 'Well, hell, nothing's happening.' So he said, 'What do you want to happen?' And I said, 'Well, gee, I want to be the greatest writer that ever lived.' And he said, 'That's going to take a little time, then, isn't it?' He said, 'Do you ever read the encyclopedia? Go down to the library and read the lives of Balzac and Du Maupassant and Dickens and Tolstoy, and see how long it took them to become what they became.' So I went and read and discovered that they had to wait, too. And a year later I began to sell to the *American Mercury*, and *Collier's*, and I appeared in *The Best American Short Stories* when I was twenty-six. I still wasn't making any money, but I was getting the recognition that I wanted, the love that I wanted from people I looked up to. The intellectual elite in America was beginning to say, "Hey, you're okay, you're all right, and you're going to make it.' And then my girlfriend Maggie told me the same thing. And then it didn't matter whether the people around me sneered at me. I was willing to wait."

In fact, Bradbury must have received wider critical recognition, during the late 1950s and into the 1960s, than any other science-fiction author. His work used very little technical jargon, which made it easy for "outsiders" to digest, and he acquired a reputation as a stylist, if only because so few science-fiction authors at that time showed any awareness of style at all.

Within the science-fiction field, however, Bradbury has never received as much acclaim, measured (for example) by Hugo or Nebula awards. Doe this irk him?

"That's a very dangerous thing to talk about." He pauses. Up till this moment, he has talked readily, with absolute confidence. Now, he seems ill-at-ease. "I left the family, you see. And that's a danger . . . to them. Because, they haven't got out of the house. It's like when your older brother leaves home suddenly—*how dare he leave me*, hah? *My hero, that I depended on to protect me*. There's some of that feeling. I don't know how to describe it. But once you're out and you look back and they've got their noses pressed against the glass, you want to say, 'Hey, come on, it's not that hard, come on out.' But each of us has a different capacity for foolhardiness at a certain time. It takes a certain amount of— it's not bravery–it's experimentation. Because I'm really, basically, a coward. I'm afraid of heights, I don't fly, I don't drive. So you see I can't really claim to be a brave person. But the part of me that's a writer wanted to experiment out in the bigger world, and I couldn't help myself, I just had to go out there.

"I knew that I had to write a certain way, and take my chances. I sold newspapers on a street corner, for three or four years, from the time I was nineteen till I was twenty-two or twenty-three years old. I made ten dollars a week at it, which was *nothing*, and meant that I couldn't take girls out and give them a halfway decent evening. I could give them a ten-cent malted milk and a cheap movie, and then walk them home. We couldn't take the bus, there was no money left. But, again, this was no virtuous selection on my part. It was pure instinct. I knew exactly how to keep myself well.

"I began to write for *Weird Tales* in my early twenties, sold my short stories there, got twenty or thirty dollars apiece for them. You know everything that's in *The Martian Chronicles*, except two stories, sold for forty, fifty dollars apiece, originally.

"I met Maggie when I was twenty-five. She worked in a bookstore in downtown Los Angeles, and her views were so much like mine—she was interested in books, in language, in literature—and she *wasn't* interested in having a rich boyfriend; which was great, because I wasn't! We got married two years later and in thirty-two years of marriage we have had only one problem with money. One incident, with a play. The rest of of the time we have never discussed it. We knew we didn't have any money in the bank, so why discuss something you don't have, hah? We lived in Venice, California, our little apartment, thirty dollars a month, for a couple of years, and our first children came along, which terrified us because we had no money, and then God began to provide. As soon as the first child arrived my income went up from fifty dollars a week to ninety dollars a week. By the time I was thirty-three I was making $110 a week. And then John Huston came along, and gave me *Moby Dick* [the film for which Bradbury wrote the screenplay] and my income went up precipitously in one year—and then went back down the next year, because I chose not to do any more screenplays for three years after that, it was a conscious choice and an intuitive one, to write more books and establish a reputation. Because, as I said earlier, no one remembers who wrote *Moby Dick* for the screen.

"Los Angeles has been great for me, because it was a collision of Hollywood—motion pictures—and the birthing of certain technologies. I've been madly in love with film since I was three years old. I'm not a pure science-fiction writer, I'm a film maniac at heart, and it infests all of my work. Many of my short stories can be shot right off the page. When I first met Sam Peckinpah, eight or nine years ago, and we started a friendship, and he wanted to do *Something Wicked This Way Comes*, I said, 'How are you going to do it?' And he said, 'I'm going to rip the pages out of your book and stuff them in the camera.' He was absolutely correct. Since I'm a bastard son of Erich von Stroheim out of Lon

Chaney—a child of the cinema—hah!—it's only natural that almost all of my work is photogenic."

Is he happy with the way his stories have been made into movies?

"I was happy with *Fahrenheit 451*. I think it's a beautiful film, with a gorgeous ending. A great ending by Truffaut. *The Illustrated Man* I detested; a horrible film. I now have the rights back, and we'll do it over again, some time, in the next few years. *Moby Dick*—I'm immensely moved by it. I'm very happy with it. I see things I could do now, twenty-five years later, that I understand better, about Shakespeare and the Bible—who, after all, instructed Melville at his activities. Without the Bible and Shakespeare, *Moby Dick* would never have been born. Nevertheless, with all the flaws, and with the problem of Gregory Peck not being quite right as Ahab—I wanted someone like Olivier; it would have been fantastic to see Olivier—all that to one side, I'm still very pleased."

In the past few years Bradbury has turned increasingly toward writing poetry as opposed to short stories. Not all of this poetry has been well-received. I ask him if he suffers from that most irritating criticism—people telling him that his early work was better.

"Oh, yes, and they're—they're *wrong*, of course. Steinbeck had to put up with that. I remember hearing him say this. And it's nonsense. I'm doing work in my poems, now, that I could never have done thirty years ago. And I'm very proud. Some of the poems that have popped out of my head in the last two years are incredible. I don't know where in hell they come from, but— good God, they're *good*! I have written at least three poems that are going to be around seventy years, a hundred years from now. Just three poems, you say? But the reputation of most of the great poets are based on only one or two poems. I mean, when you think of Yeats, you think of *Sailing to Byzantium*, and then I defy you, unless you're a Yeats fiend, to name six other poems.

"To be able to write *one* poem in a lifetime, that you feel is *so good* it's going to be around for a while . . . and I've done that, damn it, I've done it—at least three poems—and a lot of short stories. I did a short story a year ago called *Gotcha*, that is, damn it, boy, that's good. It's terrifying! I read it and I say, oh, yes, that's good. Another thing, called *The Burning Man*, which I did two years ago . . . and then some of my new plays, the new *Fahr-*

enheit 451, a totally original new play based on what my characters are giving me, at the typewriter. I'm not in control of them. They're living their lives all over again, twenty-nine years later, and they're saying good stuff. So long as I can keep the channels open between my subconscious and my outer self, it's going to stay good.

"I don't know how I do anything that I do, in poetry. Again, it's instinctive, from years and years and years of reading Shakespeare, and Pope—I'm a great admirer of Pope—and Dylan Thomas, I don't know what in hell he's saying, a lot of times, but God it sounds good, Jesus, it rings, doesn't it, hah? It's as clear as crystal. And then you look closely and you say, it's crystal—but I don't know how it's cut. But you don't care. Again, it's unconscious, for me. People come up and say, Oh, you did an Alexandrian couplet here. And I say, Oh, did I? I was so dumb, I thought an Alexandrian couplet had to do with Alexander Pope!

"But from reading poetry every day of your life, you pick up rhythms, you pick up beats, you pick up inner rhymes. And then, some day in your forty-fifth year, your subconscious brings you a surprise. You finally do something decent. But it took me thirty, thirty-five years of writing, before I wrote one poem that I liked."

There is no denying this man's energy and his enthusiasm. It's so directly expressed, and so guileless, it makes him a likeable and charming man regardless of whether you identify with his outlook or share his opinions. He projects a mixture of innocence and sincerity; he looks at you directly as he speaks, as if trying to win you over and catalyze you into sharing his enthusiasm. He is a tanned, handsome figure, with white hair and, often, white or light-colored clothing; the first time I ever saw him, at a science-fiction convention, he seemed almost regal, standing in his white suit, surrounded by a mass of scruffy adolescent fans in dowdy T-shirts and jeans. Yet he seemed to empathize with them; despite his healthy ego he is not condescending toward his younger admirers, perhaps because he still feels (and looks) so young at heart himself. In a way he is forever living the fantasies he writes, about the nostalgic moments of childhood. He has a child's sense of wonder and naive, idealistic spirit, as he goes around marveling at the world. He has not become jaded or disillusioned either about science fiction or about its most central subject matter, travel into space.

"We have had this remarkable thing occurring during the last ten years, when the children of the world began to educate the teachers, and said, 'Here is science fiction, read it'; and they read it and they said, 'Hey, it's not bad,' and began to teach it. Only in the last seven or eight years has science fiction gotten respectable.

"Orwell's *1984* came out thirty years ago this summer. Not a mention of space travel in it, as an alternative to Big Brother, a way to get away from him. That proves how myopic the intellectuals of the 1930s and 1940s were about the future. They didn't want to see something as exciting and as soul-opening and as revelatory as space travel. Because we *can* escape, we *can* escape, and escape is very important, very tonic, for the human spirit. We escaped Europe 400 years ago and it was all to the good, and then from what we learned, by escaping, we could come back and say, 'Hey, we're going to refresh you, we got our revolution, now maybe we can all revolt together against certain things.' My point is that intellectual snobbishness permeated everything, including all the novels, *except* in science fiction. It's only in the last ten years we can look back and say, 'Oh, my God, we really were beat up all the time by these people, and it's a miracle we survived.'"

But, I suggest, a lot of the mythic quality of space travel has been lost, now that NASA has made it an everyday reality.

"I believe that any great activity finally bores a lot of people," he replies, "and it's up to us 'romantics'—hm?" (he makes it clear, he still dislikes the term) "to continue the endeavor. Because *my* enthusiasm remains constant. From the time I saw my first space covers on *Science and Invention*, or *Wonder Stories*, when I was eight or nine years old—that stuff is still in me. Carl Sagan, a friend of mine, *he's* a 'romantic,' he loves Edgar Rice Burroughs—I know, he's *told* me. And Bruce Murray, who's another friend of mine, who's become president of Jet Propulsion Laboratories—first time I've ever known someone who became president of anything!—and he's a human being, that's the first thing, and he happens, second, to be the president of a large company that's sending our rockets out to Jupiter and Mars. I don't think it's been demystified. I think a lot of people were not mystified *to begin with*, and that's a shame."

Is Bradbury happy with the growth of science fiction? Does he like modern commerical exploitation of the genre—as in movies like *Star Wars*?

"*Star Wars*—idiotic but beautiful, a gorgeously dumb movie. Like being in love with a really stupid woman." He gives a shout of laughter, delighted by the metaphor. "But you can't keep your hands off her, that's what *Star Wars* is. And then *Close Encounters* comes along, and it's got a brain, so you get to go to bed with a beautiful film. And then something like *Alien* comes along, and it's a horror film in outer space, and it has a gorgeous look to it, a *gorgeous* look. So wherever we can get help we take it, but the dream remains the same: survival in space and moving on out, and caring about the whole history of the human race, with all our stupidities, all the dumb things that we are, the idiotic creatures, fragile, broken creatures. I try to accept that; I say, okay, we are *also* the ghosts of Shakespeare, Plato, Euripedes and Aristotle, Machiavelli and Da Vinci, and a lot of amazing people who cared enough to try and help us. Those are the things that give me hope in the midst of stupidity. So what we are going to try and do is move on out to the moon, get on out to Mars, move on out to Alpha Centauri, and we'll do it in the next 500 years, which is a very short period of time; maybe even sooner, in 200 years. And then, survive forever, that is the great thing. Oh, God, I would love to come back every 100 years and watch us.

"So there it is, there's the essence of optimism—that I believe we'll make it, and we'll be proud, and we'll still be stupid and make all the dumb mistakes, and part of the time we'll hate ourselves; but then the rest of the time we'll celebrate."

(Los Angeles, May 1979)

BIBLIOGRAPHICAL NOTES

Ray Bradbury is probably best known for *The Martian Chronicles* (1950), his enduring collection of stories which use off-the-shelf science-fiction hardware (rocket ships, the planet Mars colonized by man), but explore these ideas in a spirit of fantasy as opposed to predictive reality. Bradbury's vision of the 'lost race' of Martians was powerful enough to eclipse all others and become a tradition, followed in many subsequent science-fiction novels by other writers.

The Illustrated Man (1951) presents fantasy and horror stories linked by the slightly artificial device of embodying key scenes in tattoos on the body of a man who has supposedly journeyed through the various events.

Fahrenehit 451 (1953) is a novel depicting a repressive future where all books must be burned, and firemen start the fires rather than put them out. *The October Country* (1955) is a collection of fantasy and macabre stories. *Something Wicked This Way Comes* (1962) is a novel depicting a peaceful, innocent small town, visited by a sinister carnival which brings pure evil.

Bradbury's recent poetry, much of it dealing with science-fiction themes, appears in a couple of recent collections.

Frank Herbert

I have not read *Dune*.

There it is: my awful confession. I now stand exposed as a poseur, a total fraud; I have written science fiction, I have been a dedicated science-fiction fan, I have taught science fiction at college, I have been a science-fiction editor at two New York publishers, I have run a science-fiction magazine, I have reviewed science fiction, and now I have even interviewed Frank Herbert, while being secretly, unforgiveably ignorant of Herbert's most famous novel—in fact it must be the most widely known science-fiction novel published in America by *any* author in the last fifteen years.

I have read other things that Herbert has written, beginning with his classic *Under Pressure*, back when I was a teenager, and I admire his work. I was a subscriber to *Analog* when that magazine first serialized *Dune*, and I did try to read it even then. I tried again (unsuccessfully) in 1970, when a friend of mine who worked for the UN told me that *Dune* was the most talked-about book among all the anthropologists he knew. I tried even harder, a few years later, when my college science-fiction class voted unanimously to include the book in their reading list.

But these well-intended attempts have been total failures.

Dune—like other massive epics such as *I Will Fear No Evil* and *Dhalgren*—has always defeated me.

I gave it one last try, a week or so before I went to meet Mr. Herbert. (As you might imagine, my conscience was bothering me.) I made myself comfortable, for a long, serious reading stint, with cushions behind me and the book propped up on my knees. I think I fell asleep somewhere around page six.

So, the next day, I read *The Jesus Incident* instead (Herbert's most recent novel at the time of writing—a collaboration with Bill Ransom). I enjoyed that; it was easy; shorter than *Dune* and not at all obsessively detailed.

So much for my personal inadequacies. Now for the short-comings of this interview. I had planned to interview Mr. Herbert at his retreat in Port Townsend, at the northern tip of Washington state. Starting from Los Angeles, I was going to drive all the way up the coast, visiting other authors en route.

But my time on the west coast happened to coincide with the 1979 gasoline crisis. No way could I drive 3,000 miles, round-trip. And my budget wouldn't stretch to a multiple-hop plane ride, with subsequent car rentals in each city. I had to abandon my itinerary.

The only chance I had to meet Frank Herbet was when he came down to Los Angeles, later in the month, for the National Book-sellers Association fair, where he spent four days doing public-relations work and promoting his books. I didn't like trying to fit a civilized conversation into such chaotic, distracting events, but I had no choice.

He suggested we do the interview in his hotel room on Sunday at 8:00 AM, over breakfast. Now, to me, breakfast is a leisurely meal eaten between about 10:30 and 11:30 while sitting half-dressed, reading the morning mail, and making business phone calls to catch editors before they go out for their three-hour lunches. The idea of being awake and alert at 8:00 AM to meet this man (whose famous novel I had never read) did not sound plausible. But I could hardly quibble; Mr. Herbert, obviously, was very busy, and tightly scheduled. Breakfast at eight? Of course!

I remember struggling out of bed at some strange hour; the sunlight seemed to be shining from a peculiar angle, and there were no cars on the freeways. I drove to some weird, futuristic fortress of a hotel, whose towers seemed to have been hewn from gray rock. It had terrifying glass-walled elevators which ran up the outside of the of the building, making you feel as if gravity had suddenly failed, and you were floating uncontrollably into the sky. At 8:00 AM.

Mr. and Mrs. Herbert were bright-eyed and alert, very jolly and charming, in their weird, futuristic, wedge-shaped room (like a pie-slice in the circular gray tower). I set up my microphone on a breakfast trolley. Our conversation was interspersed with long pauses, while Mr. Herbert ate his cantaloupe, drank his tea, and consumed several slices of toast. A difficult context in which to gain intimate insight into the mind and motives of an author (whose most famous novel I had never read).

But, enough excuses. Despite all the peculiar circumstances, I think the interview went extremely well—even if we didn't talk much about That Book.

Frank Herbert has a Santa-Claus beard and a round, cheerful face. As an ex-newspaperman, he seems very much at ease meeting people. This is not to say he is easygoing, however; behind the friendly manner there are walls of privacy, and a strong sense of separate identity; he very much believes in traditional American ideas about self-help, independence, and freedom from most kinds of interference. And he does not suffer those whom he considers to be fools.

"I'm a farm boy. It's very interesting; you can detect self-starting characteristics in this society, of various degrees of strength, and they are strongest among people who have had some kind of rural upbringing at a very impressionable stage. When you come to the time of year when you're making hay, and the hay-baler breaks down, and it's the weekend and the handy little hay-baler repair store is closed, you don't say, 'Well, there'll be no hay this year.' You leap in and repair the thing. You don't even *question* that you can repair it. Obviously you can. My father was a master mechanic; I grew up with a screwdriver in one hand and a pair of pliers in the other—you know, that sort of thing.

"I always had a curiosity about engineering, and no doubt that I could do it. I think that self-limitation is the major limiting factor for most people in the world. People could do far more things than they believe they can. They've been led to believe in these limitations by various factors—the way they're brought up, and their families. If you have a quiescent population, it's much easier to govern; you don't want a lot of people out there doing strange things, producing new things, because new things oftentimes are dangerous to the people in power.

"I have a standard axiom: all governments lie. Don't believe anything they say. And corporations are only kinds of government—do you realize that there are more than twenty multinational corporations in the world right now that have budgets larger than France's budget? Damn few people ever see it in those terms. I'm with John Kenneth Galbraith: I don't believe we have a free market any more. I don't believe we've had it for a long time. The United States is fussing around over an energy shortage; the real problem is that we have developed a very sensitive dependency, and there's no essential need for this, in the structure of our society or in the resources that are available to us. For example, I didn't have to look very far before I found out that the Alien Property Custodian of the United States had confiscated patents and other factors on hydrogenization processes, from the I. G. Farben cartel, during and after World War II, and those hydrogenization processes plus our present state-of-the-art technology in laser furnaces provide the two essential tools which could get the oil out of the shale in Montana and surrounding areas at a competitive price. We could be in full production up there within about three years, with a resource that would last this nation—even with projected increases—approximately 400 years. My best estimate is that, because of our dependency [presumably, on foreign oil sources] if we set up a crash program to do this, we'd have the screws thrown to us. We right now are dependent for most of our oil on shipments from outside our borders. Even if we could get the program through a Congress which contains members who have been bought by this cartel—this monopolistic group—then the second stage, at the barricades, would be to really cut our supply.

"I think the oil companies have correctly projected the political consequences of admitting this. I find myself in a strange position in that I don't believe in socialized industry, nor in managed economies—managed economies always require a compromise. You build a very large bureaucracy to manage it, and the bureaucracy inevitably makes mistakes. Bureaucracies hide their mistakes, because people's careers are tied to those mistakes. Therefore, bureaucracies are a perfect mechanism for perpetuating mistakes. I still think an adjusted capitalist system is best, because it breaks down from its own excesses. When it makes too many mistakes it really falls apart, and you have to readjust the whole thing. In an oversimplified form, this is what I think about it.

"The thing a lot of people don't realize is that a cartel can occur without there being any secret meetings in Amsterdam, Geneva, or any place else. All a cartel needs is a common recognition of common problems and common solutions. The oil cartel has been formed that way and as in most cases of predation, it takes little account of the population on which it is the predator. The extent to which directorships interlock between the oil industry and the automobile industry is a much-overlooked element of the whole problem. I've had some arguments with automotive industry people; they say the public *demands* big gas-guzzling cars. And all the while the industry is spending millions of dollars on advertising, to convince the public that the big gas-guzzler is a sexy machine which they've got to own, otherwise they're nerds. What hypocrisy! The analogue of predation is a good one; the industry has never really seen itself in this light, but it ought to. Because, in a natural system, or in the wild, let's put it that way, because 'natural system' can be a very misleading label. In the wild, when the population on which the predators feed decreases, the predators decrease—or they start feeding on each other! I'm sure the analogy is apt. It already happens: smaller businesses are gobbled up by larger ones."

Heavy stuff, to discuss over an early breakfast. But "discuss" is hardly the word to use, since Herbert is delivering what is basically a lecture. And from his style I would guess he has delivered this lecture many times before. He speaks with righteousness and conviction: the lone individual vs. Big Business, pointing out a few "things a lot of people don't realize." But his monologue carries more authority than similar stories I have heard from other lone voices, because Herbert has had first-hand experience of his subject matter. His years as a journalist brought him into contact with aspects of politics, and his self-sufficient belief in repairing his own hay-baler (so to speak) has led him to make interesting efforts at tackling the energy crisis through research of his own:

"I'm working with John Ottenheimer, who was Frank Lloyd Wright's last personal student. John and I looked at the literature and decided that nobody had ever built a proper wind machine. They were approaching it from what appeared to be the correct direction; but in the last 1,500 years we've discovered quite a bit more about aerodynamics than was available when our present model of wind machine was invented.

"We've made a breakthrough on the relationship of how you put the wind into a wind machine, and how you take the energy out. That's essentially what we've patented. It involves the physical problem that you have of trying to take energy out of a rotating object when the wind going through it will defeat you on the back side, and the turbulence internally will defeat you, too. We have a mechanical system of answering that problem.

"We've built some quite large models. We took a wrecked van—the cab had been badly crushed, but the mechanical parts were in very good condition. We built our model on the truck, because our investigation showed that a wind tunnel does not give you accurate information about a wind machine." Thus, rather than blow wind through the machine, under inadequately controlled conditions, Herbert and his partner decided to move the machine through the wind, in the open air, to test the gadget's efficiency. "We built it on this truck, and the local police calibrated our speedometer for us—with their radar gun!—so that we know when we're going fifty miles an hour. We run it back and forth to get an average of the variations in the ambient air. We built a mechanical dynomometer and bought a digital tachometer, to tell us how fast we're going and how many inch-pounds we're getting from it."

Herbert believes that this kind of jargon shouldn't bother people; he blames poor education, by teachers who don't really understand mathematics, as the cause of public unease when faced with technology. He says he had very little formal training in the sciences himself:

"I was a newspaper reporter, photographer, editor, 'hey-you,' since age seventeen. I picked up a technical knowledge as I went along. You'd be surprised what you learn as a newspaper man.

"You can go knock on the door, and if you're offering something in exchange you'd be surprised at the big names who'd be delighted to have you there—have you as a student, or whatever. Some of the people whom I have worked for, their names would probably surprise you." He says this with some pride and satisfaction.

"My technique was to say, 'You know something that I want to know. I have one talent: I'm good at writing and organizing. If you have any papers you want written, any research you want done, here is your handy lacky. In return, here's what *I* want.' You don't get turned down under those circumstances. You go ask them questions, and they direct your entry into very esoteric subjects."

However, all of this was tangential to his direct amibition:

"I knew when I was still a child in grade school that I wanted to be, quote, an author, unquote. It's what I was going to do. I haven't made comparisons; I've just plunged ahead. I saw that the best way to break into the market was through short stories, and did; I made a name for myself with short stories first, then went to novels because they're more lucrative, and you can do more things with them. But while we were doing all of this we had children to raise. My wife Bev was our main source of income on many occasions; I stayed home and took care of the children and did the cooking and the laundry, and wrote, because the typewriter was at home. She went off to the office, and bought our beans. I find it interesting that our society is becoming more and more acceptant of this; there's still resistance to it—the macho dream still exists. But the macho dream, of course, originated in very primitive times, under extraordinary conditions. Now, we're in a transition period, in more ways than one. The military, as an entity in society as we have known it, is dead, and doesn't yet realize it. It is fast becoming possible for an individual to be as destructively powerful as any military force that can be brought to bear in this world. And there's no way that can be stopped. The computer is going to do no more than accelerate it; and in the United States we are looking at a runaway growth of computers. Right now for $600 I can buy a computer which is more powerful than one I would have had to pay upwards of $200,000 for, in 1962. It is smaller; I can carry it around like a portable typewriter. Most people think of computers as number-crunchers; they've been taught to believe this by people whose interests are clearly in the maintenance of a monopoly. They've maintained their monopoly by making it appear that computers were very difficult to learn to use, and that there was no way of every changing that. Not true! The computer freaks have already changed it.

"Bev and I are putting in a system at our own place, which is being tailored to us. It may very well turn out to be the most powerful word-processor available, because with the mixing of several chips I'm going to be able to do a number of things very rapidly. I'll be able to go right to any place in a long text, and not sit there waiting for a minute or thirty seconds for it to find that place. Floppy-disc, twenty-one million bytes capacity on four drivers, plus very large RAM and ROM. It'll be mainly for word processing, but it will be time-sharing also, and we'll be doing our household books on it. I have an electronics engineer, a brilliant electronics engineer; I told him what I wanted the computer to do, and that's what I'm getting. He's building it for me—even having the boards etched."

Once again, it seems, a question which started out on a personal level has led, through free-association at the breakfast table, into a discussion of political and sociological macrosystems, and now into a jargon-filled area of technology. It's as if this is the conversational zone that Herbert prefers to be in. I'm interested in computers myself so we go further into the technical details of the system which he is having custom-built to his specification. But I realize not everyone will want to know how many bytes of RAM will be available—let alone the ROM!—and there's no avoiding the fact that it makes more sense to talk about the phenomenon which made it possible for Herbert to afford this exotic technology in the first place. I refer, of course, to *Dune*. At the time of our interview, he has been writing the script for the forthcoming film of the book. Did he ever dream, at the beginning, that his novel would be so successful and earn so much money, in its various editions and sequels?

"I simply never considered it. It didn't enter into my considerations. You know, it was turned down by every major publisher. We have some marvelous letters, rejecting it! According to my literary agent, if you include the phone calls where they said there was no sense in submitting the manuscript—'We don't do that sort of thing'—there were twenty-two rejections. Eleven rejections in writing, from major publishers."

I ask him if this tells him anything about the publishing industry. The answer I get is more or less the one I expect, from this individual who distrusts large organizations:

"It was an alarming shock to me, to be in New York City. I was a native western boy, who believed that God must be in New York City." He laughs. "Well, let's say, I thought the best gravitated to New York City. I arrived there one time, with my satchel in my hand, you know, and my turned-up-brim hat, staring at the tall buildings. And I was asked to sit in on an editorial cónference, to decide on the promotion of one of my books. I won't tell you what publishing house, but it was a long time ago. Before Berkley [his current publisher]. We were ten minutes into this conference when I realized that I knew more about the market, and what was really happening out in the marketplace, and more about what should be done to work in that marketplace, than these experts who were sitting around this table. I can still remember the feeling of *betrayal*—a kind of a loss—because I felt suddenly all alone. Here I am in this place, they're supposed to know what they're doing, and they don't! They don't know what they're doing!" He laughs: the laughter turns into diminishing chuckles; finally, it subsides. "So we went our own ways. I just quietly pulled out of all this and went on the lecture circuit, where you really have to be up-front, especially at the university or college level. Boy, do *they* unmask the phonies quickly! So I just did my own, and to hell with New York. They didn't know. Their high-level book tours where you go and meet the critics . . . there is no critic, I believe, myself included, whose taste is the absolute *sine qua non*. They really do not control the market. The market goes on without them, and *Dune* is a perfect example of the truth of that. Do you know that *Dune* was panned by every critic?"

I admit that, actually, I didn't know.

"Not one liked it," says Herbert.

"After a long time, Arthur Clarke sent us a review from India that was good," his wife reminds him.

He nods. "Bev is right. And here and there you might get a little crossroads newspaper in Ohio, with a young reviewer who probably went to the local junior college, and they liked it."

Has Herbert received a satisfying audience response from his readers?

"The feedback has been very rewarding. Because of the kinds of questions I get, I've been able to direct attention straight at what I was doing, and there's no equivocation about it. People say, for example, 'Were you forming a cult?' and I say, for the love of God, no! Quite the opposite—don't follow *me*! Cult leaders have feet of clay, if not worse. They lead 900 people into suicide; they lead their followers into the coliseum where they get to be eaten by lions. What insanity! Really. I have an initial: G.P.M.F.F.—God preserve me from fanatics.

"The bottom line in the *Dune* trilogy is: beware of heroes. Much better to rely on your own judgment, and your own mistakes."

A fitting note to end on. We have finished breakfast; I'm sure Mr. Herbert could talk for at least another hour on aspects of politics, business, and technology, but he has to move on to the book fair, where he will be autographing *Dune* and his other books, and generally oiling the machinery of media-commerce.

As a writer, at least, he has proved that the lone individual can exercise better judgment that those people who are suppose to be experts. Whether this ability really extends into other areas—such as developing alternative energy sources—has yet to be demonstrated as convincingly. In the meantime, it must be immensely satisfying to Frank Herbert that his book has been such an immense success, despite the failings of an unnamed New York publisher and the scorn of all those critics.

(Los Angeles, May 1979)

BIBLIOGRAPHICAL NOTES

Frank Herbert's first novel, *Under Pressure* (also titled *The Dragon in the Sea* and *Twenty-First Century Sub*) was published in 1956. It is a complicated psychological thriller, set in the claustrophobic space of a technologically advanced submarine. The writing is tense and effective. "Dune World" was a serial in *Analog* (1963–1964), later combined with "The Prophet of Dune" and published as *Dune* (1965); it won both the Hugo and Nebula award as best novel. It is an extremely long and detailed study of religion, ecology, interstellar politics, and war. Sequels *Dune Messiah* (1969) and *Children of Dune* (1976) are still not the end of the story.

Some readers (a minority, it seems) prefer Herbert's other work, especially his short fiction in *The Best of Frank Herbert* (1975) and novels such as *The Dosadi Experiment* (1977), which manages to combine a great variety of elements, including many alien species whose life processes are described in detail; the effects of an experiment in overpopulation; advanced psychic powers (including mind-transference in the central characters); and a complex plot.

Kate Wilhelm and Damon Knight

Kate Wilhelm is the only female writer respresented in this book. People have already complained to me about this. They ask me why I didn't interview more women. Am I a closet sexist?

I don't think I am. In various editorial jobs, over the years, I have been able to get a lot of work by women published— including a first novel and a few first stories. It is only as a "profiler" that I have run into difficulties.

The problem is simply that the best-known authors (the ones whom one especially wants to include in a book like this) are almost all men. Even among younger, less-known science-fiction writers, men easily outnumber women. Also, women tend to write fantasy rather than science fiction. As is explained in my introduction, the scope of this book does not encompass writers of fantasy.

I did hope to include a couple more female authors—not out of conscience, or to fill some imaginary quota, but because I admire their work. For instance, I would like to have interviewed Ursula Le Guin. (She had personal reasons for declining my request.)

I balked at interviewing women simply because they were women. This kind of logic seems uncomfortably close to the sins of sexism and racism which it is supposed to be eradicating. To select and study a person's fiction and then interview her, not because of the worth of her work or the fame of her name, but because she just happened to be female . . . surely, this would have been an insult to the writer as well as a dumb way to organize my book.

In the following interview, Kate Wilhelm and Damon Knight (who happen to be married to each other) appear jointly. They (not I) chose to do it that way, partly because of awkward circumstances. The 1979 gasoline shortage prevented me from driving to Oregon to meet them in person, and it seemed unlikely that we would meet elsewhere, during our various travels. To conduct this interview by mail would have been contrary to the basic idea of this book; but Damon Knight had an ingenious answer: if I could send my list of questions, he and Kate Wilhelm would interview *each other*, and then send me the tape.

So this section of the book was, in a way, done for me. I merely compiled the questions and edited the transcript—and there was ironic pleasure in that, because, fifteen years ago, Damon Knight was editing me, when (while working for Berkley Publishing) he bought and slightly rewrote my rather inadequate first novel.

Of course, his involvement with science fiction goes back much further than that. He has been writing it and editing it since the 1930s, when he used to hang out with Frederik Pohl, Donald Wollheim, Cyril Kornbluth, and other New York "Futurians," as they called themselves. Knight has been a strong influence on the science-fiction field; he fathered the Science Fiction Writers of America, a guild, or union, which was intended to make the genre more professionally respectable, with higher literary standards. He initiated writers' conferences, where established authors congregated for a whole week of discussion and analysis of each other's stories; these sessions influenced the thinking of the writers, and, hence, the evolution of science fiction. Knight also established and edited the *Orbit* series of short-story collections, which provided space for new writing of an experimental and nonconformist nature, often by new authors. And he has long been involved in the Clarion writing workshops, for students who have not yet been published, but want to be.

Kate Wilhelm has shared, equally, this involvement in the critical, analytical, educational side of science fiction. She started writing it herself considerably later than her husband, but in no sense has she ever been overshadowed by his reputation. Her work has a unique and obvious sense of identity, and she has written and published much more prolifically in the last ten or fifteen years than has Knight. She is regarded as one of our finer writers of fringe science-fiction; a gentle spirit of humanism and social consciousness flavors almost all her work.

Knight and Wilhelm are an active pair, interested in all aspects of the process of producing good prose. Are they satisfied with the way things have worked out? What were their original ambitions in science fiction?

Knight: "When I was first writing, I just wanted to get published. It was like a twelve-foot wall to get over. And then I wanted to get published more often, and get more money for it, and be popular. After a couple of years of that, I wanted to do something different. I was writing for Horace Gold [then editor of *Galaxy* magazine] and I knew, some way, what kind of thing he would buy from me. I wrote those kinds of things because they were fun, at that time. But I don't think there was any doubt that I was writing for a market—it was Horace Gold. When I started doing other things that were more interesting to me, and more difficult, I lost Horace. That irked me, thought it shouldn't have, because I had stopped writing for him."

Wilhelm: "You expect an editor to tolerate what you do, take whatever you do?"

Knight: "Yeah. When I became an editor myself, my ideal was to be somebody who wouldn't turn down good stuff just because it wasn't the kind of stuff he expected from that writer. But I found out I couldn't do it; you can't keep the shape of the magazine, that way."

Wilhelm: "I think another problem is that we're all tied in on one hand to the commercial world of publishing, where publishers expect a certain return on their investment, and we're also tied in with the concept of all arts being free, including writing. And we're forever battling one side against the other, trying to compromise one against the other."

Knight: "We're so used to that that, it's hard to examine it objectively. We did a workshop with Colombian writers, in Bogota and Medellin last year, sponsored by the U.S. Embassy. The writers we talked to in Colombia were completely uncomprehending when we talked about the balance between art and commerce. Apparently, publishing in South America is mostly through government publishing houses, and you expect to be subsidized and not to have to worry about commercial considerations at all. Maybe that's a better way to do it, but I can't conceive of writing under a system like that. I feel in a sense that you lose feedback— I hate that word—but you lose it in the sense that you don't know if you're just writing elitist, elegant nonsense that happens to be pleasing the person at the government publishing house. I would much rather worry about what some commercial editor will let me get away with, than what some bureaucrat will let me get away with." On the other hand: "In the 1950s I started to try to write novels, and I was discouraged to find that I couldn't write them fast enough to make a living. I wasn't getting paid well enough. You know, on $2,000 a novel, you can't do it. You couldn't do it even then. And I felt disturbed about that, at the time, and resentful. I thought there ought to be some better provision for bright young novelists like myself."

Wilhelm: "How do you feel about grants for writing?"

Knight: "I would have loved to have a grant. If somebody had given me $5,000 and said, 'Write a novel,' that would have suited me right down to the ground. But there were other times, earlier, when a grant wouldn't have done me any damn good at all. If somebody had given me $5,000 then and said, 'Write a novel,' I would have tried, but either I wouldn't have finished it, or I would have produced something unreadable and unpublishable. I was on a committee to choose recipients of some Oregon arts foundation fellowships, last year, and I felt ambivalent about it. I wanted to do it, because I wanted somebody who deserved the money to get it. But I couldn't figure out if I really approved of that or not."

Wilhelm: "I don't know, either, if I approve. I do think it's terribly hard to be a writer with no other income. There's so much pressure to produce saleable work. You don't want to give up your writing, go out, and get a job; but you have to make a living. And that does produce all kinds of pressures. Other pressures of the real world, concerned with the role of housewife, mother, writer, chauffeur, or nurse, are very hard to cope with, too. It's much harder for a woman to be a writer, if she's also married with a family, than it is for a man who can go into his office. The children are trained not to go there; the little children go to their mother with a cut finger or a runny nose."

Knight: "I'd like to say a word about the pressures on men. I think they're nearly as acute, in the case of a guy who's trying to make a living as a writer, and is married and has kids. If he's not bringing in the bread, he feels a terrific impulse to do something else to make money."

Wilhelm: "Oh, yeah. I think it could be even worse, to have that psychological pressure. I can cope better with the physical—the kids knocking at the door—than I could with the psychological, the 'I'm a failure because my family doesn't have this or that.'"

Knight: "I feel a little envious of writers now, in science fiction: it seems to be so much easier for them to make a good living than it was when I was starting. People are getting $15,000 advances for first novels, and that kind of thing. You can live on that. You can do a novel a year, and live quite well. In the 1950s it was no more than $2,000, and you couldn't live on it."

Wilhelm: "My first novel was $1,000."

Knight: "Well, there are still some people getting $1,000 for a novel. But I do think things are much better and easier, now, for writers in this field. On the one hand I'm glad that it's possible for a young writer to devote herself to writing, and make it. On the other hand, I feel, 'Why should these kids get it when I couldn't?' Somebody ought to go back in a time machine and pay *me* $15,000 for a novel, too."

Wilhelm: "I'd be rich today. No I wouldn't—I would have spent it."

Knight: "What made me stop writing for so long was money. I didn't feel I could become a standard, commercial science-fiction novelist, turning out a novel a year with lots of spaceships and aliens in it. Novels were, and are, very hard for me. So I started doing anthologies instead, and I was very successful at it. I was doing three and four a year. One year, I did eight. But I discovered I couldn't do that and write novels too. And I was in a partial or complete writer's block for a long time, becaue I was hung up on the damn novel [*The World and Thorrin*]."

Wilhelm: "I'm glad you finished that novel, because there was a rumor mill going for a couple of years that said, 'Damon Knight has been turned off writing because he married Kate Wilhelm.'"

Knight: "How do you know about these rumors?"

Wilhelm: "People told me."

Knight: "Great to have friends. Anyway, I thought I had to finish that novel before I could write another one, and eventually, by bashing my head against it repeatedly, I got all the way through it. Now I feel I can write anything I want to; the only hitch is that what I seem to want to write is not science fiction. I'm halfway through a long story about a postman in Eugene, Oregon, and I want to write a novel about the people I know here in Eugene. And the kids in Portland turned me on to poetry; I've written twelve poems in fourteen days. I have no idea where I'm going to go with any of this stuff—but luckily, Kate's making a lot of money."

Wilhelm: "I think the whole idea of markets is so depressing, I don't even like to talk about it. Half the stuff I've done . . . I think I had a turning point when I was pregnant [with son Jonathan, now thirteen]. I didn't write for a year, and when I came out of that I had turned my head around, and realized I wanted to do other kinds of things. Since then, half the things I've done have been not science fiction. One of the great myths floating around is that you can't cross categories: if your name is well-known in this field, you can't cross into that field. It *is* a myth, because I've published my science fiction *and* my non-science fiction. So that isn't a hang-up. I don't think you should worry about it. Jim Blish said years ago, 'If it's good, you'll publish it.' And I tend to believe that. I don't worry about markets when I'm writing. I can't seem to keep that in mind. I never think of the reader until I'm through with the writing—which explains why my work so often just misses this market or that market. It falls in between. I very rarely think how the reader will be affected; I think, 'How am I affected?' If it works for me, it will work for somebody else. I suppose that's in the back of my mind, but not consciously."

Knight: "I work entirely differently. I was hung up on technique when I was a kid. I didn't know how to do it. And I think what saved my ass was working for Popular Publications as an assistant editor, where I had to read stories that we had bought and stories that we rejected. I couldn't help seeing the difference between the two, and I think I got an instinctive, deep sense of what will keep people reading. All the time I'm writing I have some idea that if I'm not doing certain things, I'm going to lose my reader. On the one hand this keeps you from being dull, and on the other hand it may make you more aware than you ought to be of the standard demands of the market. You may say to yourself, If there isn't a robot in the story, it will be rejected. And you find yourself throwing in some clunky little robot, just to make sure you don't get your manuscript back. . . . At some point, anybody who wants to become a professional writer has to reach some kind of equilibrium between what interests her as a writer, and what's going to interest somebody else."

Wilhelm: "I think that because you and I have been writing a long time now, and we know there are people out there who will read what we write, we can afford to have more arrogance about what we do. But I feel that I've always had to satisfy my own requirements without wondering if it will satisfy somebody else's. My second novel never sold, because it wasn't quite a mystery and wasn't quite science fiction, it wasn't quite this or that. I could have trained myself early, to think more about the reader and more about the requirements of this market or that, and maybe I could have been much more successful."

Knight: "For each young writer there is some kind of fuzzy barrier you have to get through. You're writing things kind of at random, and striking out in all directions; you never have any idea why some work and some don't. I think we acquire, somehow, usually unconsciously, a sense of what will work in published fiction."

Wilhelm: "Well, I'm still writing things that fall in between. The last two pieces I've done fall in between: neither one is real science fiction, neither one real straight fiction. Neither one fits anybody's idea of a category. But I'm hoping that they will both sell, and be received by people who are willing to read my things that fall in between. . . . As Damon knows, and as I've stated before, I don't like any of my published work. I always see how it failed, how it didn't do what I had hoped it was doing when I was writing it, how it could have worked better if I had had more patience or more skill or more intelligence, or whatever. I think they've all failed in one way or another, and I don't like any of them."

Knight: "I can't imagine living like that."

Wilhelm: "Well, it just means I don't read my own stuff. I read other people's stuff."

Knight: "I can read with pleasure anything I've written since about 1949."

Wilhelm: "I'm very envious of that. I really am my own worst critic. No one has been as harsh on me as I have been on myself. I think my critics, for the most part, are kind." But if a critic or reader complains to her that Kate Wilhelm's writing is 'pointless' or 'self-indulgent?' "Usually I don't say much of anything, because I don't think that's my problem in particular. I think it's the reader's problem, and that reader is reading the wrong thing. That sounds pretty arrogant, but I'm not writing for everybody. If I was, I would be writing *Star Wars*, or dragon stories, or adventure stories of one type or another, and I'm not. The people who do get the point, I think, are the ones I really want to reach. I wish, now and then, that some of the others would either get the point or shut up. I don't know why they keep reading me and complaining. You know, if I've done it to them before, I'm likely to do it to them again, so why don't they read somebody else? I think they're intrigued. Larry Niven reviewed one of my collections, *Somerset Dreams*. He complained, about most of the stories, that he hadn't see any point there. But he also said that they bothered him enormously. He carried away images, and he felt that something was deep in the back of his mind, tugging and bothering him. So I suspect that he got the point more than he was willing to admit, or more than he was able to express. Sometimes that's not bad: sometimes you don't have to be able to say explicitly what a story was about, in order to get something of what the author meant."

Knight: "I think as a general rule, if you hate a story—unless it's because the sentences are clunky—if you hate the story itself, there's something there."

Wilhelm: "This is an area that many people get very defensive about. They feel that, 'If I didn't understand a story, it's because there's nothing in the story to understand, because, obviously, I am a good critic, a good reviewer, a good reader.'"

Knight: "And, 'I've been reading science fiction for twenty years. . . .' Yeah, we get that a lot, from reviewers like Darrell Schweitzer—who is actually not an idiot, he's fairly intelligent, but he's so limited. He assumes automatically that if he can't understand it, there's nothing there to understand. But I've never had any particular problems with not being understood—except once or twice, maybe. One story of mine, "Down There," kind of sank into a vast silence, and I think it's because nobody got the point, except Barry Malzberg."

Wilhelm: "If eight out of ten of your stories got that reception, how would you feel? Eight out of ten of mine seem to."

Knight: "Well, you're a deeper and trickier writer than I am."

Wilhelm: "How would you feel, though? If people didn't get the point you were making?"

Knight: "I'd feel they were all dolts."

Damon Knight and Kate Wilhelm have obviously evolved very differently, as writers:

Knight: "I was trying to write fiction from the time I was, I don't know, fifteen, maybe, and at first I had no idea how you did it. I would start off with the first sentence and just go on from there, with no idea where I was heading. If I did know what I was doing, it always turned out to be not more than 2,000 words long. I had no conception of how you could write anything longer. But by just a fluke, really, just a crazy accident, one of those pieces was published—but not paid for!—by Don Wollheim, in the first issue of *Stirring Science Stories*. I was eighteen. And that gave me a rung to stand on. For a long time, I couldn't do it again, but then I did, and then I did it *again*, and then I got the job at Popular, and that made everything much simpler."

Wilhelm: "I was a housewife with two young children, and I'd been reading an anthology, and I put it down and said to myself, 'I can do that.' And I wrote 'The Mile-Long Spaceship,' and sold it."

Knight: "Then she bought the typewriter she had rented to type that story, and away she went."

Wilhelm: "Actually I shouldn't have been quite so glib in my answer, because I am now aware of something I could have been and wanted to be. I just hadn't thought of it as writing, although as a kid, I did. But I didn't believe people who told me I had talent and could write. I think it was something about the high-school situation that just made me not believe them; I don't know why. So I became a very unhappy housewife. I was a miserable person, I had migraine headaches, I had insomnia, I was not at all content. And I didn't know anything to do. I got busy on all kinds of school work, and oh, social things, volunteer work, this and that, and possibly I would have continued a life like that. Maybe I would have become an alcoholic. I don't know. Maybe I would have suicided out. It's hard to say. I thought writers were gods; I thought they were very, very special people. And I knew I wasn't."

Knight: "I think that's a way that the Clarion workshop, and the Milford conference, are enormously important to writers who have been isolated and have never met another writer. It's a big revelation when you meet one and discover that they put their pants on one leg at a time."

Wilhelm: "That was important to me."

Knight: "And to get the validation, from other people who are professional writers, that you can be one, too."

Wilhelm: "That's one reason I think that if I had had a workshop situation when I was eighteen or nineteen my life would have rearranged itself quite differently. It was ten years after that that

I began to write, and I feel sometimes that I lost ten years of my life. In those ten years, I didn't do anything. I worked. I had children. I gardened. I cooked and did all that, but nothing real. And I feel a little bit deprived: ten years of my life, because I didn't believe my teachers.''

Knight: "I think there's no doubt that workshops do help people. There are so many tiny little things that you find out when you become a professional writer, that nobody has necessarily ever told these kids. You can't supply the mainspring of fiction—you can't pump that into them—but you can teach all kinds of little easy ways of avoiding difficulties.''

Wilhelm: "About the accusation that workshops hurt writers, or might hurt them, I think this falls into the area of, 'Will criticism help people?' Some people are very much hurt by criticism, and they always will be. How they'll cope with bad reviews is a mystery; maybe they can't. Other people will take criticism and milk it dry of everything they can use, and benefit from it. You can't know ahead of time what kind of people you're going to have, especially those who haven't been exposed to a workshop situation. Some of them I think are very badly hurt, and they have no business staying there. But we don't know that until after the fact.''

Knight: "Some of the problems we see at Clarion every year. Some of the people have just enormous writing skills: they can write good dialogue, interesting people, and yet, when you finish the story, there's nothing there. Because there's no plot. It occurred to me it's possible that some writers are concentrating only on technique, and forgetting that you have to have something to write *about* which deeply moves you. So these stories are empty: they're trying to do technique without the substance, and you can't. You get people with highly developed skills in certain areas, and then funny blank spots—like the girl we had a couple of years ago. Beautiful writer, but she had no plots. It was exasperating, for us and for her. She was reduced to tears, and said, 'My problem is I have no problems.'"

Lastly, on the subject of *Orbit*, the series of short-story collections which Knight edited for many years. Why did the series ultimately die?

Knight: "I don't think *Orbit* ever found enough people who could appreciate what the writers were doing. Part of the reason may have been that I wasn't capable of the hype, the ability to promote myself and my work, that—for instance—Harlan Ellison has. His *Dangerous Visions* has been enormously successful, without being, as far as I can see, superior in quality to *Orbit*. And there were chance factors: *Orbit* needed hardcover, paperback, and book-club publication, really, to survive. It never had all three after Berkley dropped the series. Harper & Row, who published the hardcover edition, couldn't find another paperback publisher, and we didn't often get the book club. I was trying to create a renaissance in science fiction; I don't think I succeeded. *Orbit* had some influence, and science fiction is a lot more open now than when I started. I'm not entirely happy with the way the field has gone, though. I think some superb things in *Orbit* were overlooked and, especially in the last five or six years, maybe ten years, a lot of really mediocre stuff has been getting a lot of applause and awards. But I guess I was expecting too much of the people who were going to read those books. It takes a lot of training to write good prose, and it takes a lot of training to be able to read it."

Wilhelm: "I'd think that good prose is so much easier to understand, that people would like it better. But apparently they don't. I read that bestseller, *Coma*, which is the most godawful book. The prose is just terrible. I couldn't even describe how bad it is. Apparently, all they wanted was the story: What Happens Next. I think that's one reason why *Orbit* didn't succeed; people aren't interested in good prose, or beautiful language. I wonder sometimes if it isn't a mistake, to nitpick and go after the prose flaws in students, or even in other writers. Maybe it's beside the point."

Knight: "Well, I'm going to continue to nitpick. I really hate to read something that's full of glaring flaws in every paragraph. I was interested to find out that a lot of science-fiction fans are aware of what I call literary values, but they don't *want* that in science fiction. They don't want prose that demands close attention, they want something they can read carelessly and quickly, for what you call 'the story.' It would actually annoy them if the same story were written very carefully, very well, because it would slow them down, make them pay more attention to the sentences and phrases than they want to."

Wilhelm: "Occasionally I will start a book that's been highly recommended, or that publishers have sent for comments, and I find I can't get past the first page, because the prose is just getting between me and the story or whatever it's about. And I know there are other people who just can't read that stuff; but we're such a tiny minority that it is insignificant."

Knight: "That sounds kind of grim. But I think we're lucky to be able to survive at all. It's continually irritating to read *Publishers Weekly* and see what gigantic advances writers are getting whom we consider to be mediocre on their best days. You can't insulate yourself from that completely. But I think we're sort of living in the cracks—nobody is really paying much attention to us, and we're getting away with it, we're living outside society, like criminals. And I think we're fortunate to be able to do it."

(Eugene, Oregon, July 1979)

BIBLIOGRAPHICAL NOTES

Damon Knight's short fiction achieved more enduring success than his few novels, in the 1950s and early 1960s. The stories are carefully written, with an economy of words, and their themes often are pertinent to human or social concerns. Even the earlier work still reads well today, and does not appear dated. His short-story collections include *Far Out* (1961), *In Deep* (1963), *Off Center* (1965), and *Turning On* (1966).

Because of his reduced output of fiction in the late 1960s and the 1970s, he has become better known as critic and editor. His early critical essays are collected in *In Search of Wonder* (1956). His series of anthologies of new fiction, *Orbit*, began in 1966 (with *Orbit 1*) and continued through to 1979.

Knight's new novel, *The World and Thorrin*, is scheduled for publication during 1980.

Kate Wilhelm's first two novels were collaborations with Theodore L. Thomas: *The Clone* (1965), one of the first science-fiction books to use this concept, and *The Year of the Cloud* (1970), a disaster novel in which the planet is threatened by a change in the viscosity of water. Neither of these novels develops or dramatizes its theme in a particularly unusual or ground-breaking fashion; but by 1976 Wilhelm had progressed considerably toward subtleties of character and prose, and her *Where Late the Sweet Birds Sang*, published in that year, develops the clone concept on a sensitive, human level (this novel won Hugo and Jupiter awards). *The Clewiston Test* (1976) and *Fault Lines* (1977) go further into human affairs, and at the same time further away from science fiction; these novels (and most of her short fiction) are not genre fiction in any sense, and fall somewhere in the main stream.

Her most notable and recent short stories are collected in *The Infinity Box* (1975).

Michael Moorcock

In the science-fiction field, Michael Moorcock is best known for what he did and who he was in the late 1960s.

A fine time it was, then, to be young and in London! Swinging England and so forth—renaissance in the modern arts, recognition of popular culture—pirate-radio ships moored offshore broadcasting high-energy music from the Beatles to Hendrix, mad Carnaby Street fashions—it seemed as if the future had opened up and anything could happen. I moved to the city and met Moorcock in 1964, when he had just taken over as editor of *New Worlds*, the British science-fiction magazine; we ended up working on it together in various roles for many years. It attracted a loose-knit bunch of writers, including Ballard, Aldiss, Sladek, Disch, and Spinrad, who (like Moorcock) were dissatisfied with the old storytelling formulas and the lack of psychological sophistication in science fiction. They shared a radical spirit and set out in various new directions; the result was called by some people the "new wave" in science fiction.

Spearheaded by *New Worlds*, this movement hoped to revitalize science fiction and make it more adventurous, experimental, and relevant to real people in the real world. Moorcock sustained much of the idealistic spirit: he was a charismatic, inspirational editor, iconoclastic and flamboyant—the kind of personality you expect to be expansive and witty, living well and leaving large tips. He encouraged new talent and prompted known authors to contribute to the magazine, despite its low rates of payment. There was a sense of Significance and Destiny about the whole thing.

This much has already been chronicled in various historical overviews and guides such as *The Encyclopedia of Science Fiction*. But these summaries are like history textbooks which record swings in the "mood of the people" without ever mentioning peasants' living conditions or what the upper classes ate for breakfast. The authentic human element is missing.

In truth, behind Moorcock's charismatic act, he was weary and desperate. He enjoyed the obvious rewards of being a central figure in a literary movement; he seemed to like the "messiah" role and the public attention. But the magazine cost him horrendous amounts of money, time, and energy, and it exacerbated domestic strife. In 1967 he bought the title and became publisher as well as editor, despite his total lack of organizational and managerial abilities. Life quickly became a nightmare of missing manuscripts, erratic schedules, and unpaid bills. Before long there were three separate bank accounts, each having been set up because the finances of the last had become so hopelessly tangled that no one could figure them out. Some contributors were paid twice, others never, and there were nightmarish debts to a succession of printers—we moved to a new firm each time credit ran out with the previous one. It was not unusual for the magazine's staff to be found cowering on the floor with the lights out, pretending not to be home, while some creditor rang the bell and called hopefully through the mail slot in the front door—to no avail.

The "offices" of the magazine were in a horribly decrepit London tenement, whose leaky roof and damp foundations created a climate like a moist, alpine cave. It was the sort of building where wallpaper sags off the walls, revealing rich growths of exotic mold. Operating capital—such as it was—came partly from a literary grant of £200 a month bestowed by the Arts Council of Great Britain, and partly from royalties earned by quick fantasy novels which Moorcock wrote himself in a spirit of loathing and despair.

Amazingly, this cottage industry endured for several years. The magazine appeared on a regular, monthly basis, and maintained a national circulation. To those who only saw the ambitious end-product, it seemed a force to be reckoned with—it even ended up fulfilling some of its promise to influence the science-fiction field.

This influence was not generally welcome. There were open confrontations between "new wave" radicals and the science-fiction establishment (this was, after all, the late 1960s). You could feel antagonism in the air, at, for instance, The Globe, a mediocre, obscure pub in Holborn, where diehard British science-fiction fans gathered socially on the first Thursday of each month. Most of them looked like refugees from a pornographic bookstore: rundown, middle-aged men in raincoats, trading tattered copies of prewar pulp magazines and reminiscing about the golden age of "scientifiction"; fat, dowdy college students with pimples amid the fur on their faces, debating monster movies and pop music. It was quite horrible. In this sleazy scene, Moorcock looked somewhat out of place—tall, rotund, long-haired, bearded, dressed dashingly in a pale caramel suit, lavender shirt, paisley tie, and wide-brimmed felt hat. The rest of the staff wore equally colorful clothes (this *was* the late 1960s) and were met with equal hostility. On one occasion some ne'er-do-well hobbling around with his foot in plaster went so far as to beat me about the head with his crutch; but things didn't usually reach that point. There would merely be a succession of sour science-fiction fans, accosting Moorcock rudely and condemning him loudly for having ruined "their" science-fiction magazine by turning it into a cliquish, pseudointellectual thing full of stream of consciousness and poetic self-indulgence. Why, when E. J. Carnell had edited it in the 1950s, there had been all those good stories by writers like John Rackham and James White and E. C. Tubb—stories with a beginning, a middle, and an end (in that order!)—stories you could *understand*.

At this, Moorcock would tear his hair and make throttled, keening noises like a trapped dog, or he'd swear at them and insult them, or he'd threaten violence. None of these tactics ever deflected the single-minded purpose of these aggrieved readers, however. They had inertia on their side.

When the pub closed at eleven and the patrons dispersed, the "new wave" coterie would be left sharing a sullen, moody resentment toward the rest of the science-fiction world for being so conservative and unenterprising. There would be a desperate, drunken drive home, during which Moorcock (who liked being chauffeured) would regard the careening street scenes with serene detachment and sing a few bars of his version of "Yellow Submarine": "We all live in a failing magazine, failing magazine, failing magazine. . . ."

And next day it was back to the world of leaking roofs and unpaid printers—the penniless, despairing crusade in the cause of some strange kind of literary idealism.

Now it's June 1979, 11:30 AM to be exact, and Michael Moorcock is reclining in bed, one naked nipple peeking coyly over the covers. His wife Jill Riches is downstairs working on one of her paintings, but Moorcock (like the late Lyndon Johnson) seems to enjoy receiving guests in informal settings—such as his bedroom—so I set up my tape recorder on his bed and I ask, "Are you ready?"

He winks and pats the pillow beside him. "Any time you are, dearie."

But this is pro-forma bonhomie, of course—merely an indication that one still has a residual sense of the absurd, somehow, somewhere, ten years after those dreadful drunken evenings, when the only way to cope seemed to be by getting misguidedly manic and angry at the whole world.

Ten years have indeed passed. We have lived through that sad decline from the swinging sixties to the senescent seventies—from campus unrest to campus coma, from kaftans to denim, from acid to Seconal. The "new wave" movement lost momentum, at the same time as other radical causes declined during that period. *New Worlds* magazine went from a monthly to a quarterly schedule, and then stopped publication altogether for several lean years. The writers who had worked on it and for it, often without pay, dispersed to pursue their own individual careers, and Moorcock himself was among them.

Life seems a bit saner these days, but duller. The literary status-quo was never seriously threatened by the movement which Moorcock catalyzed. However, he's quick to point out what it did achieve:

"The new wave did change things in Britain, and to some extent in America. We promoted the work of writers like Disch, Sladek, Spinrad, M. John Harrison; we did influence publishers to take risks that they had previously thought would not work. What's gone wrong since then is very simple: most people believe that there's a formula they can follow. So now, instead of getting *Analog* magazine formula stories, you're getting Clarendon—

whatever it is—*Clarion* writing-course formula stories. There are never many original talents; you're going to have run-of-the-mill people who are turned on by other people's ideas, and then attempt to replicate them; and of course these are often the most successful writers, because they're producing a modified form of the stuff which would otherwise be too intense for the mass-market."

Who are these successful, but unoriginal, writers?

"I don't think I'm prepared, in my present attitude of tolerance, to mention Christopher Priest." He smiles cheerfully; then for some reason he fixed on Larry Niven. "I don't think *Niven* can write a paragraph with any inner consistency. The only Larry Niven novel I read all the way through, the characters acted with incredible inconsistency to suit the needs of an obviously patched-together plot, and the level of invention was frankly puerile and derivative. But that doesn't seem to bother his readers, and I don't really care. As with a child toward whom you feel well-disposed, you hope that that child will gradually find something a bit better; but if that child doesn't show any signs of obvious psychotic behavior, and continues to read Larry Niven, or Arthur C. Clarke, or whoever it is, then you think—" He shrugs. "Okay . . .

"Most of these writers are middle-American entertainers, reflecting the ideas of their communities, and it's very hard for me, sitting here in London, to understand that.

"They're not very good, they're popular writers, on the same sort of professional level as your average thriller writer, and you'll find exactly the same elements in Agatha Christie—the middle view, constantly expressed. Middle prejudice. Tubular Bells in print. It doesn't become pernicious because it doesn't really contain enough energy; it's where you get a Heinlein, who produces an energetic lunatic book which lunatics can turn on to, that you've got trouble. Science fiction is not like ordinary literature; it attracts people who will use it—Charles Manson is a very dramatic example—as a means by which to live. But the more authoritative, say, a Heinlein book is, about how to live and how to solve your problems, the more that actually divorces the reader from the reality that he's trying to come to terms with. That kind of science fiction, which pretends to solve problems or offer answers—you might call it Campbellian science fiction—I do find fairly pernicious, because it confuses the young, who, after all, make up the majority of the readers."

So Moorcock's disparagement of "establishment" science-fiction writers is as strong, and as radical, now, as it was in the

1960s. How did the "new wave" really differ from this status quo?

"It was work which stood little chance of being published anywhere other than *New Worlds*. Either its structure was unconventional, or the material might have been idiosyncratic. Most of the writers were using romantic idiom—using symbolism, imagery, and irony. They were courageous stories, written by people who were displaying, often in a confused way, a courageous attempt to grapple with very large issues. If there has to be a typical *New Worlds* writer, that's what that writer tended to possess—a compulsion toward finding out what the dangers were, and confronting certain realities. There were no science-fiction magazines at that time which would publish these stories, and no literary magazines which had any idea what the subject matter was about, in spite of the fact that the subject matter had been around since more or less the turn of the century and many of the forms employed or rediscovered had also been around that long."

Moorcock recalls that the reaction of the British literary establishment against the kind of fiction he wanted to publish was similar to the reaction against William Burroughs's novel *The Naked Lunch*, when that was first published in Britain: "There was a debate, then, which was known as the Ugh! debate, in the *Times Literary Supplement*, in which I took part, and in which Edith Sitwell took part, and said she didn't want her nose nailed to a lavatory seat for the rest of her life—which wasn't long—and Victor Gollancz said he hadn't read the book but he was sure it was absolutely disgusting . . . it was a ridiculous debate. It was similar to people's comments on *Oliver Twist*: 'Mr. Dickens has written this very lovely book of *Pickwick Papers* full of jolly people, and now he is dragging us into the gutters of London.' Indeed, Dickens got exactly the same sort of treatment.

"People will say, obviously, that 'going down a sewer'—a frequently used metaphor!—is a depressing and pessimistic thing to do. But the fact is that somebody has to go down the sewer, to see why it's blocked, or to shoot the rats, or just to catalogue the wild life. And anyway, there wasn't a great deal of obsession in *New Worlds* with what you might call sewers; the obsession was with human beings in situations of stress.

"People tend to think that what we were doing with *New Worlds* was what Harlan Ellison was doing with his collection, *Dangerous Visions*. But we weren't trying to shock anyone; we were assuming that there was a readership for the material we were publishing.

All we ever asked was that the material was as good as it could be within its own terms.

"We were lucky, because the social ambience of the mid-1960s was the best time to be trying these things, because everybody was thinking in those terms, so we were part of our generation in that respect. The current generation is rather more circumspect about everything, and unfortunately—with the exception of the punks, whom I find very agreeable in their attitudes—is getting worried, about whether there's too much atomic energy, and what's going to happen—the lead is poisoning us—all the usual stuff."

I ask if there are any redeeming features in the U.S. publishing scene.

"There are very few redeeming features. The larger the entertainment corporations grow, the less autonomy the individual editors have, the more bureaucratic they become, the less flexibility there is, and the less commercial development they allow themselves, because there isn't anybody prepared to take risks. In other words, the accountants are running it too much and the companies are too big, which produces low morale in editors, lack of faith in their own judgment."

Are they underestimating the audience?

"It's very difficult to underrate a middle-American audience; that's unfortunately what one is up against. . . . One reason there is a strong divergence between British and American science fiction is the writers in America are fighting earlier battles, to win over an extremely prejudiced people of a religious disposition, who will perhaps shift from, say, the Episcoplian church to Dianetics, but are basically a lot of very naive peasants.

"American writers have no tradition—most of them—of that necessary arrogance that the European writer is allowed. If the European writer says 'fuck' in Cologne cathedral, he's not taking a particular risk. If the American writer says 'fuck' in a small town in Arizona, he's liable to get into physical trouble—because he's dealing with ignorant peasants."

As a writer, Moorcock has moved toward work of high literary ambition, away from the quick fantasy novels which he used to produce in quantity for quick money. In fact, it seems that his most indirect, experimental novels have shown a bit too much "literary arrogance" of the type he advocates, for the liking of the "peasant" readership he condemns. Some readers feel Moorcock's work tends to be unnecessarily obscure and elitist, and if it is misunderstood, Moorcock has only himself to blame. Does he have any sympathy with this outlook?

"No. There are 75,000 copies of *The Cornelius Chronicles* sold in America, which is not a huge number, but not a bad number for a book of that kind, and I don't think anyone expected it. Obviously, a number of people are going to get off on it wrong, but I do think those books [the four novels put together in one volume under the *Cornelius Chronicles* title] are more relevant and better understood now than when they first came out, and they will increasingly be better understood and better enjoyed, possibly for the wrong reasons, but that's not my job, all I can do is present what I see as the evidence."

Doesn't he feel any obligation to make himself clearer or more explanatory in his work?

"I did feel—and this was naivete on my part—that all I had to do was present the triggers that people would pull, and their own imagination would do the rest. I'm not sure that this was fair." He thinks about it and seems to become a trifle testy: "But a lot of people *have* enjoyed those books, I mean, I've won a *prize* for one of them, I wouldn't exactly call them failures."

And his current literary ambitions are by no means modest:

"What I'm aiming toward ultimately is to produce something like a Dickens novel, or a particular kind of George Meredith novel, or *War and Peace*, something that combines large issues with specific psychological concerns."

It sounds as if he is looking ahead to a possible future scenario in which he becomes an important British novelist of equal status to, say, Angus Wilson.

"Given that I've had a letter from Angus Wilson only yesterday which says exactly that, obviously there's a possibility of that occurring. I do think I'm doing things which other people haven't been able to do, and I have a range of techniques which most writers would be very glad to have. I've developed these through very hard work, by doing a lot of writing. Therefore if my current project is as successful as I hope it will be, I think that it will be a reasonably important contribution to modern fiction."

If this sounds—dare one say it—a little egocentric, it is because Moorcock's focus on his own work has become frighteningly obsessive, to the point where his monologues on the novel-in-progress are like psychoanalytical confessions, delivered in a rhythm which sedates some listeners while rousing others to dangerous levels of politely stifled angst.

On other topics, Moorcock is much more like the old iconoclast of the 1960s—in fact he revived *New Worlds* magazine in 1978, admittedly in a spirit of target practice rather than with the grandiose original aims of artistic revolution.

The title of his new (non science fiction) novel is *Byzantium Endures*. It does. And so does he.

(London, June 1979)

BIBLIOGRAPHICAL NOTES

Michael Moorcock took over editorship of *New Worlds* magazine in 1964. The previous editor had been E. J. Carnell, who proposed Moorcock to succeed him. Despite resigning from it several times, Moorcock has in fact been associated with *New Worlds* actively or passively ever since, and owns its title.

His "Jerry Cornelius" novels, featuring a continuing "myth figure of the twentieth century," are *The Final Programme* (1968), *A Cure for Cancer* (1971), *The English Assassin* (1972), and *The Condition of Muzak* (1977). *The Cornelius Chronicles*, a one-volume edition of all the novels, was published in America in 1977. In Britain, the novels are published separately. The first of the four remains the easiest to read, and suffers only from the haste in which it was written. The final novel ties the series together and won a British award, the Guardian Prize. John Clute's excellent introduction in *The Cornelius Chronicles* is an aid to interpreting the books, for readers who find them insufficiently comprehensible.

Moorcock's *An Alien Heat* (1972) is probably his most entertaining, witty, and imaginative novel, with wide appeal. Moorcock won a Nebula award for the short-story version of his religious fantasy *Behold the Man* (1969), in which a young Jew goes back in time and becomes Jesus.

*Photo by
Fay Godwin*

J. G. Ballard

Return to Forever. Today I must journey to an enchanted land-scape of mystery and stasis. I must follow a private odyssey to the lagoons where iguanas bask beneath a reborn sun; to beaches of archaeopsychic time, where the solitary figure of an aviator, a refugee from some dislocated future, wanders beside the dark water as if tracing an invisible contour inside his own mind. I am drawn there with a sense of inevitability—to the mud flats, the sand banks, the dunes, the drained lakes—the terrain of primordial resonances and apocalyptic fulfillment.

As if it is keyed to a countdown of cosmic time, my hypothalamus is stirring; my subconscious is throwing up images of that mythic zone—that coded landscape—the landscape of Shepperton, Middlesex.

The Architecture of Entropy. So I get out my bicycle, on a cloudy Sunday morning, and I set off with my satchel containing tape recorder, picnic lunch of bread and cheese, ordnance-survey map, and bicycle-tire puncture-repair outfit. Shepperton is about fifteen miles from the small apartment which I maintain in London. Shepperton, glorified, immortalized in the work of J. G. Ballard, as a nirvana of surreal dreams.

In reality Shepperton consists of a few little streets of nondescript semidetached houses and bungalows, some man-made reservoirs, an airport nearby, and gravel pits where rusty dredging equipment stands mired in oily mud. The visitor who has read Ballard and expects a world of inspirational imagery—of terminal beaches and vermilion sands—will be disappointed.

Only one strange figure fits the fantasies. He is a messiah wandering through his private zone of glittering faceted light and strange symbols of the apocalypse. The Prophet of Shepperton: Ballard himself.

Locus Solus. By bicycle my trip takes a little over an hour, westward to the extreme edge of Greater London. It's flat country. There are interminable streets of two-story houses, here and there a petrol station, or a newsagent with an ice-cream sign outside and kids sitting on the curb looking bored. There is an occasional red double-deck bus, an occasional lorry, then a high-street of more small shops—launderette, Wimpy Bar, electrical supplies, tobacconist, betting shop, post office, chemist—all closed, of course, on Sunday.

Flanked by unsuspecting suburban neighbors, Ballard's house blends in unobtrusively. Its only distinguishing feature (not visible from the street) is a pair of small home-made abstract cement sculptures, standing out in the back garden like enigmatic delegates from a nation peopled by emblems of surrealistic art. They seem to be waiting, watching him as he works in the living room, by the window, seated on an old wooden chair at a 1950s-vintage dining table. Here, looking as if he is camping out in makeshift quarters, he conjures his visions of mythic beauty and strange power—the literary equivalent of paintings by Ernst and Dali.

Surely You Don't Plan to Stay Here, Doctor? In Ballard's early short stories he dwelled on visions of stasis, where time could be perceived as a tangible quantity, suffusing the landscape. In his first four novels, the world was overcome by various natural catastrophes, wiping away civilization and literally turning the clock back. His heroes were solitary figures, courting the apocalypse and ultimately seduced by it. To them, a private, mystical union with a ruined world was more attractive than the pretense of a "normal" lifestyle among organized bands of survivors.

Since the 1960s Ballard's obsessions have broadened to include modern myth-figures (Kennedy, Monroe, Reagan) and a contemporary urban scenario of automobiles, concrete, and perverse eroticism. His fiction has catalogued the sex crimes of technology and has lab-tested the death dreams of fashion models and housewives. His heroes, however, remain as serenely detached as ever, still opting for isolation, much as Ballard himself shuns the social worlds of Central London and chooses to maroon himself in his Shepperton retreat.

The Abandoned City. "I'm completely out of sympathy with the whole antitechnology movement," Ballard tells me. "Everything from the Club of Rome on the one hand to Friends of the Earth on the other—all these doomsayers and echo-watchers—their prescriptions for disaster always strike me as simply wrong, factually, and also appallingly defeatist, expressing some sort of latent sense of failure. I feel very *optimistic* about science and technology. And yet almost my entire fiction has been an illustration of the opposite. I show all these entropic universes with everything running down. I think it has a lot to do with my childhood in Shanghai during the war. Shanghai was a huge, wide open city full of political gangsters, criminals of every conceivable kind, a melting pot for refugees from Europe, and white Russians, refugees from the Russian revolution—it was a city with absolutely no restraints on anything. Gambling, racketeering, prostitution, and everything that comes from the collisions between the very rich—there were thousands of millionaires—and the very poor—no one was ever poorer than the Shanghai proletariat. On top of that, superimpose World War II. I had led a fairly settled childhood as the son of a fairly well-to-do businessman. After Pearl Harbor we were suddenly taken from these huge houses, and suddenly our family was living in a room about half this size"—he gestures at his small Shepperton living room—"for three years, in a camp. And then the war ended and there was another huge jolt. In many ways the period after Hiroshima was more confusing than anything that had happened before; it took so long for the Americans to come in and stabilize things. All that, and those extraordinary inversions taking place all the time...I mean, I remember this little boy, his name was Patrick Mulvaney, he was my best friend, he lived in an apartment block in the French concession, and I remember going there and suddenly finding that the building was totally empty, and wandering around all those empty flats with the furniture still in place, total silence, just the odd window swinging in the wind ... it's difficult to identify exactly the impact of that kind of thing. I mean, all those drained swimming pools that I write about in my fiction were *there*, I remember going around looking at drained swimming pools by the dozen. Or, I used to go down to the waterfront where the great long line of big banks, and hotels, and commercial houses looked out over a wide promenade to the river frontage; one day, you'd see the familiar scene of freighters and small steamers at their moorings, and the next day the damn things would all be sunk—the Japs had sunk them, to form a boom. I remember rowing out to these ships, and walking onto the decks, with water swilling through the staterooms. Given the stability of the society we now live in, this is very difficult to convey. You've got to imagine something like the Watts riots on a kind of continental scale. The Watts riots dislocated the United States, but how long did they last? Two or three days? I lived in Shanghai from my birth in 1930, till I left in 1946—a period covering several wars, including a world war, and all these extraordinary inversions, the transformation of a huge city ... I think all that was fed into my psyche and when I started writing science fiction and looking at the future, the imaginative elements I was trying to extract from any given situation tended to be those that corresponded to the experience that I'd had earlier."

A Language of the Unconscious. Ballard speaks deliberately, forcefully, as if he is putting the key phrases in italics. And he pauses often, to choose the most powerful image or metaphor. Likewise, in his fiction: he is a deliberate, forceful writer, who has never produced an underplayed or unambitious story. His fiction may sometimes seem "obscure," but even if the reader can't see the literal meaning of a piece of Ballard's work, the power of its mood and imagery is always undeniable. He expresses himself via potent, surreal symbols—or metaphors—like recurring dreams. The dunes, crashed cars, enigmatic women, lost astronauts, and abandoned buildings are intended as signposts, keys to the meaning of technology, the structure of the unconscious, and the promise of the Future.

Reality by Inversion; Fulfillment through Oblivion. "Just as, say, reason rationalizes reality for us, so conventional life places its own glaze over everything, a sort of varnish through which the reality is muffled. In Shanghai, what had been a conventional world for me was exposed as no more than a stage set whose cast could disappear overnight; so I saw the fragility of everything, the transience of everything, but also, in a way, the *reality* of everything, as the glaze of conventional life was removed. I think it's the same sort of situation you experience, going around a silent factory—or an abandoned factory. Even a crashed automobile has a reality, and a poignancy, and a *unique identity* that no showroom car ever has.

"In the novel I'm writing at the moment, the United States, 100 years in the future, has been abandoned, and people are returning to it. They find Lincoln sitting in his memorial with sand up to his knees, all this kind of stuff. I think that this presents a sharper image of what the United States is *now*."

Regardless of his reasons for dwelling on scenarios of decay and devastation, Ballard's obsessions have inevitably been labeled "pessimistic," especially since the heroes of books such as *The Drowned World* and *The Crystal World* choose to sacrifice themselves to the catastrophes that have taken over the planet. Ballard responds: "Most of my fiction, whatever its settings may be, is not pessimistic. It's a *fiction of psychological fulfillment*. Most people think that I write a fiction of unhappy endings, but it's not true. The hero of *The Drowned World*, who goes south toward the sun and self-oblivion, is choosing a sensible course of action that will result in absolute psychological fulfillment for himself. In a sense—he has—sort of—hit the jackpot! He has; he's won the psychological sweepstakes. I mean, the book makes no sense, and the hero's behavior is meaningless, if you don't see it that way. It's the same thing in *Crash* [his traumatic novel of perversion, violence, and the automobile]. The whole dynamic of that book, I suppose, leads toward the ultimate car crash, which we all celebrate; something like that. All my fiction describes the merging of the self in the ultimate metaphor, the ultimate image, and that's psychologically fulfilling. It seems to me to be the only recipe for happiness we know."

Inner Space. Ballard started writing in the 1950s, and sold his first stories to the British magazine *New Worlds*. These early stories used some of the jargon of orthodox science fiction, and his early style seemed influenced by the slickness of Americans such as Pohl or Bester. But Ballard never showed any interest in the usual subject matter of science fiction—rockets, aliens, and other planets. Sputnik I had just been launched, opening up the space age, but Ballard ignored outer space and concentrated on what he called "inner space." E. J. Carnell, who edited *New Worlds* in the 1950s, encouraged Ballard to follow his own direction, despite protests from readers who didn't enjoy this kind of innovation. Within a few years it became clear that Ballard was writing stories which were quite different from anything anyone else was doing; they continued to be published in science-fiction magazines simply because that was the only genre with which they had any affinity at all.

An Unexplored Literary Continent. "I went to Canada with the British Air Force in 1953 and was stuck on bases on Moose Jaw, Saskatchewan, and so on, where there was nothing to read, no national newspapers, very few news magazines—*Time* magazine was regarded as wildly highbrow. I discovered that the racks of every bus depot, or in the cafeteria, on the base, were loaded with science-fiction magazines, and their contents were more sophisticated than their covers suggested. So I spent about six months reading science fiction, and then I effectively stopped reading it and started writing it.

"The flight of Sputnik I seemed to confirm all the age-old dreams of science fiction of the 1930s and 1940s, but I was convinced, against all the evidence, that that phase was already *over*, and modern science fiction had exhausted its own material, and had lost that very vitality and relevance to the present day that it had once had.

"I was interested in the visual arts, and pop-art was born in England soon after I started writing. I went to that famous exhibition, "This is Tomorrow," at the Whitechapel Gallery, where Eduardo Paolozzi exhibited, and where Richard Hamilton exhibited I think the *first* pop painting ever, and it struck me then that the very things that these pop-artists found so exciting about science fiction actually belonged to the science fiction of the 1930s and 1940s—not, as should have been the case, to the science fiction of the 1950s. Science fiction had exhausted itself and was now just feeding on itself. When you started reading it, once the first flush of novelty had passed, you then began to see that, Oh, God, here they are permutating another time-travel variation, or whatever; and the whole thing needed loosening up."

I ask Ballard if any science-fiction writers influenced his early work.

"I don't honestly think so. Possibly Bradbury, though I don't know, I haven't read anything of his for twenty years now. I think one influence was Bernard Wolfe's *Limbo 90*, which encouraged me to go ahead, because that had sophistication and irony, and a genuine imaginative and literary dimension explored for its own sake, which was missing in all the others. Bradbury in his way was the genius of science fiction but he was kind of naive, and you don't expect any element of irony and self-consciousness in a naive writer. But *Limbo 90* encouraged me to feel that it was possible . . . within commercial science fiction, which was another important consideration to me; I wanted to write within a form of fiction which was read by a reasonably wide audience.

"I felt that I was moving into a largely unexplored literary continent. Here was a unique literary form that had all sorts of things going for it—its popularity, its reliance on strong story lines, its very traditional short-story form and techniques, much closer to de Maupassant and O'Henry, Chekhov, or the Victorian and Edwardian ghost-story writers—much closer to them than to the elliptical, modern *New Yorker* short stories. It had popular imagery and it was about the real world: the transformation of the present and the future by science and technology was something that would affect everybody, whereas the concerns of so much so-called mainstream novels weren't those that would affect society at large. So almost by definition, science fiction was a popular art form. I thought this was tremendously exciting—but nobody, I felt, then, had really made serious *use* of science fiction. It was like going to an amusement park and finding people toying with aeroplanes and electric light and computers, in a world where aviation and electricity didn't exist. I felt then, and still do feel, that science fiction is a sort of playground, a huge amusement park with all sorts of exciting possibilities that need to be taken out and *applied*, to the real world.

"Also I felt a conscious reaction against what was, in Britain at that time, an extremely sterile literary scene. In the mid– to late 1950s the angry young men appeared on the scene—John

Osborne's *Look Back in Anger*, Amis's *Lucky Jim*, Sillitoe, all the rest . . . I felt they were a totally parochial phenomenon, they didn't shake the literary establishment in any serious way whatever. They were all soon annexed into it. I felt, and still do, that the sort of realist social mainstream novel that's been written in England since World War II needs the shot of adrenalin that can be provided by the kinds of fiction that are bought and sold on the marketplace, just as the cinema can benefit enormously from the shot of adrenalin that, say, the Hollywood thriller has. I've always been a great believer in the strong story. I don't believe in a fiction of nuance."

Image Quanta. In 1964 "The Terminal Beach" was published. This was Ballard's most experimental story thus far, depicting the dreams and memories of a solitary bomber pilot stranded on an abandoned Pacific atoll, formerly an H-bomb test site. This strange, ominous journey through a landscape prefiguring Armageddon was written in disconnected sections—like a movie made up of long, separate shots, some of them flashbacks. It was a transitional story which marked the beginning of a new phase in Ballard's writing. He was to develop its impressionistic form much further, and sever his last links with orthodox science fiction and fantasy.

In June 1966 *New Worlds* published "You:Coma:Marilyn Monroe," the first of what Ballard was to call (with characteristic overstatement) "condensed novels." He had removed all the usual elements of fiction writing—the routines of moving characters around, giving them things to say, developing conflicts and resolving them. All that remained were images, metaphor, landscape, message, and myth-figures—some of them imaginary, others drawn from the powerful contemporary media of advertising, movies, and television.

Ultimately, fifteen of these "condensed novels" were collected in one volume: *Love and Napalm: Export U.S.A.* (British title: *The Atrocity Exhibition*). Almost all of the stories consisted of short sections of text, with bold subheadings (the same format that I have borrowed for this profile). The text sections were slices of spacetime; quanta of experience, coexisting on the page, as memories coexist in one's mind. The overall effect was a montage whose parts interlocked; an overall statement derived from many different perspectives.

Dislocation. "In the early 1960s I felt I'd done enough extrapolative fiction set in abandoned Londons of the future or strange research establishments out in the desert. The future had *arrived* by the mid–1960s, so it seemed to me that the main subject matter for the science fiction writer was the present day. And I think I was right. We were *in* tomorrow, and I felt that I had to write about it, and it seemed to me there was no other way of doing it than the way I used in the *Atrocity Exhibition* stories. I couldn't have handled all that material, the subject matter of those pieces, otherwise.

"They were very much a product of all those dislocations and communication overlays that ran through everything from 1965 to 1970. We've moved from a period of high excitement to a period of low excitement, and it's very hard for people who are younger to realize just how flat life is today, and how pedestrian are people's concerns. Leading politicians, trade-union leaders . . . in the British general election, for example, you'd expect there'd be some appeal to the imagination, even if only on the level of Kennedy, and yet all they're talking about is getting inflation down from seventeen percent to twelve percent. It's like going to a shareholders' meeting of some large insurance company and listening to a lot of accountants quibbling over decimal points. Everything is far flatter now; the 1970s have been enormously flat; the technique of the *Atrocity Exhibition* stories seems too crowded, in a sense, for the present day. I think if the 1960s had continued and not turned into the 1970s, the stories wouldn't seem so strange.

"Also, one reason why those stories may now seem to be an experiment that hasn't worked is that we're now so mentally lazy. I think if Borges were published for the first time now, people would say it's far too literary and too complicated. It's a good thing he established his reputation in the late 1960s when people were still prepared to make a bit of an effort. People are amazingly lazy now; it's difficult to imagine a film like *Star Wars* being the success in the 1960s that it has been in the 1970s. I think critical judgments were sharper then."

Disaster Area. In Britain and other European countries, especially Germany and France, Ballard has a wide readership, a loyal following, and a strong reputation. Almost all of his novels and story collections remain in print in paperback. He has found much less success in America—ironically, since a lot of the images and obsessions in his work are drawn from the American scene. I ask him if he knows why his work is not well-received by the American audience.

"It's mysterious, I can't really say; you know the American scene better than I do. I think it's easy for an English writer like myself, who doesn't really know the American publishers and readers, to overestimate the literary interests of a huge market like that. I think the readership of fiction generally, in the United States, is far less sensitive and open than one realizes, over here. This sounds bitchy, and I certainly don't intend it to be; but I read American novelists who have a high literary reputation—let's say, that school of writers like Roth and Vonnegut. The *New York Review of Books* goes overboard on them, *Time* magazine brackets them with Hemingway and Faulkner. But they're middlebrow writers who don't stretch their readers' imaginations in any way whatever. They're serious writers in the sense that somebody like Daphne duMaurier is serious. Or those writers of the 1930s, like A. J. Cronin. It seems to me it is possible for a writer here to overestimate the literary capacity of the American market."

Beach Head. Still Ballard's new work continues to appear in America, through important hardcover publishers. And he continues to write ambitious, powerful novels. It is more than twenty-five years since his fiction first appeared in print, but, if anything, there is more energy in his work today than there was then. His three children are now away at university; Ballard (a single parent) is left with considerable time in which to write. He seems happy to be alone out there in his Shepperton retreat. He is amiable, slightly shy (despite his uncompromisingly stated opinions), and not especially sociable: "I'm not a gregarious character. I go in to London on average once a week, I suppose; most of my friends are in London."

He claims that, in his eyes, Shepperton really is a world of beaches and lagoons, an inspirational landscape of mystery. Indeed, this is how he describes it in his novel of metamorphosis and messianism, *The Unlimited Dream Company*. To me, Shepperton will always be a rather grubby little suburb surrounded by a derelict wasteland of mud and refuse. But then, Ballard is a visionary. His style can be imitated, his obsessions can be mocked, but his imagination and insight are unique. His surreal, vibrant images of apocalyptic fulfillment endure—as an enrichment of life, and as a strange kind of prophecy.

(London, September 1979)

BIBLIOGRAPHICAL NOTES

The Best Science Fiction of J. G. Ballard (1977) is the ideal introduction to his short stories, covering the period from when he started writing to when he commenced producing "condensed novels." This volume features short but useful introductions by the author, and the selection of stories is his own choice. There are numerous other collections of his early short fiction. His most recent collection, *Low-Flying Aircraft* (1976), includes more experimental work. *The Atrocity Exhibition* (1970), (U.S. title: *Love and Napalm: Export U.S.A.*) includes all his "condensed" work.

Of his first four novels, *The Drowned World* (1962) and *The Crystal World* (1966) are undisputed classics and show unique vision. One could argue however that the ideal length for these books would have been 40,000 words rather than 60,000; indeed, Ballard seems most comfortable writing to this sort of length, since his obsessions are more with landscape than with ordinary human relationships.

Crash (1973) was his first novel in eight years, and a radical departure. Where the early books are set in distant landscapes of surreal beauty, *Crash* is neurotic, ugly, and as close to home as a TV news bulletin. It is however a masterpiece of horror. *High-Rise* (1975) is equally contemporary, but much more entertaining, with moments of fine ironic comedy, and *The Unlimited Dream Company* (1979) is an upbeat fantasy of life-force and fulfillment, expressed in characteristically surreal images.

E. C. Tubb

Let us now take a brief rest from discussing image and nuance and symbolism and all that. Let's put the "new wave" to one side, for a moment, along with social relevance, profound statements, insightful observation, and all the baggage of so-called "major novels" (an increasingly meaningless phrase). Let's get back to basics, down on skid row in the good old science-fiction ghetto. Let's talk about the fundamental traditions: action and adventure.

After all, Flash Gordon lives—as Perry Rhodan, or even as Luke Skywalker. A lot of books of pure entertainment are still being written, without any pretensions or ambition. A strong plot, flaming rockets, galactic warfare, a beautiful woman, a desperate hero—that's what the most basic science fiction is all about. And most of us can yield to the romance of it all, even now, if we let ourselves.

The authors of these stirring stories of quest and combat remain largely anonymous. Not for them, critical acclaim and Hugo awards. In fact, this kind of writer is likely to be scornful and cynical about tokens of literary prestige.

My book would not be complete if I failed to include the viewpoint of one such author. His name is not famous. He has written no bestsellers or "classics" of the genre. But his no-bullshit, down-to-earth outlook is a fine antidote to the extravagant rhetoric of our prophets and poseurs. And his expertise as a prolific storyteller is beyond question.

His name is E. C. Tubb. In the thirty years he has been writing (almost always part time) he has produced hundreds of short stories, and 102 novels ("Not a lot," he says with a shrug). Much of Tubb's work has been published under other names; he has been everyone from Charles Grey to Volsted Gridban (that's right, Volsted Gridban). Most recently, under his real name, in Britain and America, he has published a series of adventures of Dumarest of Terra: a tall, lean hero with brooding eyes and a blaster at his hip, searching for the mythical lost home-world of the human race. There have been twenty-one Dumarest novels so far, and the hero's quest is still by no means over.

To Tubb, writing science fiction is not some intense creative experience, or a dedication to Art. It is simply a matter of doing your job, as a skilled storyteller, as well as you can. He is suspicious of writers who claim anything more than this. In his own inimitable words: "There are three grades of author. There's the bestseller, who writes one book and lives on the proceeds. There's the hack [a category in which Tubb includes himself] who has to write like a job, and cannot afford to write only one book. And then you get the 'artistic' sod, who has to live in a cottage in Scotland for three years, and he produces one book about an owl, which nobody buys . . . but he writes for *himself*. You'd think you couldn't afford to live like that, but they always seem to have friends who lend them cottages, and wives who work, and knit them garments. God knows what they use to write on—toilet paper that comes from the local library? Or sugar bags on the train? And then when the book comes out, they always launch it with a literary dinner, and all the critics laud it, you know. They had a thing on TV about a bloke like that, and I reckoned he had written one word a day. Even I can do better than *that*."

Tubb used to work successfully as a salesman, and he still talks with a salesman's rapid, fluent spiel. But he becomes self-conscious and modest when he's asked to talk about himself. In fact he had never been interviewed until, one summer evening, I set up my tape recorder in his family home in southwest London.

He began by telling me that he thought the interview was a misguided idea, because it couldn't possibly be relevant for readers to know the details of an author's life:

"I've always sent back forms from these people who want to

know the date of your brith, grandparents' marital status, everything about you. I think it's a lot of nonsense. Who the hell cares? If an author ran a brothel in Istanbul when he was fourteen, does that improve his writing? It doesn't, does it. There's a curiosity about how old the man is; does that help you, when you read a real good sword-and-sorcery novel, to know he's a doddering old octagenarian, sniffing at little girls? But to be serious—I started writing science fiction just previous to the war, sold the first story in 1950, and went on from there. I started writing, as most authors do, first through love, and then through money; and I'm afraid, like the majority of authors, the love starts vanishing and the money stays."

I interrupt to ask him if he's sure he means the *majority* of authors.

"The way they talk, it must do. You can get any bunch of authors together and what are they talking about? They're not talking about improving their work, they're talking about how high an advance they can screw out of the publisher. They're working, fair enough; the only trouble is, like politicians, they tend to inflate their own value, and then start saying, 'I wouldn't write a word unless I got X income for it.' Why the hell publishers ride along with this is a mystery to me. How can one man get, say, $1,000, and some one else get $100,000? His book is not 100 times better. It can't be. In fact some of your bestsellers are a damned sight worse. So when authors start believing they are wonderful, because they're paid so much, they're living in a fool's paradise. In the science-fiction field, reputations are easy to come by. Someone writes a book and there seems to be a conspiracy to say how good this book is. No one ever stops to read what the man's written. I mean *read* it. They're looking at the name. Heinlein is a perfect example. I mention that man because I think he's done himself a tremendous disservice. This may sound sour-grapish but I liked Heinlein—lik*ed* him. I well remember reading *Stranger in a Strange Land* and telling myself all the way through, Heinlein wrote this, it has to be good, there's going to be a great reward for wading through this Christ-legend crap . . . and unfortunately, there wasn't. I don't think Heinlein is to blame for this. I think there's too many plaudits—and the trouble is, he might believe them—that *Stranger in a Strange Land*, or the ones that came after it, are good. They're not good. He's lost all critical faculties if he thinks they're good. I suppose another case is Samuel Delany, with his *Dhalgren*, which is a monument of unreadability.

It does seem that whenever you read the books that have been chosen for the Nebula awards, you can only explain this choice by knowing how the choice was made, which is by twelve people in a smoke-filled room saying, 'Ah, to hell with Sam, he's no good, but nobody hates Harry, so we'll give it to Harry.'"

Does Tubb really feel the award system is as corrupt as that?

"Corrupt in the sense that it's not honest. It cannot be honest. No one can read everything that's going, and make an unbiased vote on it. I well remember when I was a member of the Science Fiction Writers of America [the organization which votes the awards], I was getting voting forms through the post at a time which was later than the date when I was supposed to return them. They'd taken six weeks on a boat, getting to me. So I couldn't even vote, which was a convenient way of making sure that I didn't. Now, I'm not saying that this was deliberate. But there was such a thing as air mail, and still is, I believe.

"I feel that the Nebulas have been tremendously inflated as regards importance, and they *are* important in that every publisher plasters 'Nebula Award Winner' on the cover. I think it's detrimental, because we're all writing in a small field, and we were all at one time honest enough to admit that half of what we turned out was sheer crap for the market. That was the money aspect, though you could even like doing that. In the early days the pay was so low it was ludicrous, but this is where you cut your teeth. A lot of young authors, now, never knew this. They've come into a market that's paid higher from the beginning. And whether this is good or bad, I don't know, but if you start by getting a wad of cash for your first book, you're very slow in taking less for the next one. And this makes the advance a status symbol. How good is he? Well, what money did he get?"

In case this diatribe might make it seem that E. C. Tubb is embittered or envious, I must say that I don't think that's so. His complaints are delivered in a wry, offhand style, with a shrug and a grin. When he mentions the success of some well-known author, he usually adds "and good luck to him!" on the principle that there's nothing wrong with getting what you can. Tubb himself seems to live comfortably off his writing and his other work; there's an air of middle-class prosperity about his home, with its new decor and furnishings, a video recorder sitting beneath the color TV, wall-to-wall carpets throughout.

Of course, it wasn't always this easy.

"I started selling printing machines at the same time I started writing. I did it on and off for the next seventeen years. They ended up bribing me to become manager; it nearly drove me mad. Then I did demonstrating; reached my peak selling knives and kitchen equipment. Did quite well at that. I've found it a great asset to be working as well as writing. I'm not a 100 percent full-time writer. You get stale, and it's blasted boring, living in one room with a world of your imagination, and a typewriter. The job you can leave any time, because you've got another source of income. As for the writing you can say, 'Not today'; really, that's the only way to stay sane.

"I've always been somewhat numbed to realize that I am an author. I suppose it's a feeling of inferiority that could stem from never having had a proper education. Not only was I trying to learn English, and how to spell, but also trying learning how to write. I left elementary school at age fourteen and went out and got a job. I gave my parents all my money, whatever it was, twelve shillings a week, and they gave me back two, for fares, and this went on until the war came and stirred everything up. I'd always been an avid reader of science fiction. We read it for escape, because life was very depressed before the war. I feel that this separates people of my generation from young science-fiction people, because the incentive to read it was different. It was a golden age inasmuch as for a few coppers you could escape into worlds of fantasy which were unobtainable anywhere else.

"Just after the war, the army had gone, I was freshly married . . . it's always funny to talk this way, because people think you're exagerrating. Even my children do. They say, 'How did you start?' Well, we started in one room, no larger than this, about ten by eight. We had a baby in one corner, in a cot, and a sink in one corner, and a gas stove in the other, and a double bed, and that was home. This was so common; but you talk to people now and they'll say, 'You can't have lived like that, the council [local British government] wouldn't have allowed it.' It's like saying, 'You couldn't have worked for such little money—you'd have got more on social security [British welfare handouts].' They don't realize, there wasn't any social security then, no easy handouts. I don't think there's any intrinsic virtue in pain at all, and I don't think there's any virtue in doing without. But I do feel there is character-forming. It's like being thrown in the deep end: you hate it, but by Christ you learn to swim. If there is nothing for you except what you're going to get, you get it. So, you counterbalance the misery against the development of guts, if you like.

"In the early days, when I was selling to magazines, I was an extremely prolific author. I didn't exactly write the entire contents of one magazine, but I came damn near it. Ted Carnell was short of material so he put two or three of mine in one issue, and invented a few names for me, among them Charles Grey. With three magazines running at the same time, and me producing far more than three stories a month, Ted got in the habit of using noms-de-plume. When I became editor of *Authentic* [a now-defunct British magazine] it wouldn't do for an editor to keep printing his own stuff, so I still had to use noms-de-plume. I practically wrote it from cover to cover, one issue, not because of love of money, but—I never would have believed this, before I'd done the job—you were getting rubbish in, and you had a deadline to meet, so you thought, 'I've got to do something to fill out this 2,000 word gap,' so you wrote one. We were paying pretty low, and I could always sell myself cheaper to make the budget go further. I was doing the book reviews and the articles for free, as well as anything else.

"The next thing that happened to me was that I went on to writing cheap paperback books. Got robbed, but, it's all education. In the early 1950s I met a friendly fellow who came along to the pub, and he was a reader for Curtis Warren. He said, 'You write the story, and I'll put it in as mine, and that way it's certain to sell.' Now, it's the oldest con job out; he took all the money, I only got paid for one book out of the three. He still owes me fifty-four pounds, wherever he is. Not fifty-four pounds for each novel—for the pair! I suppose it was about four weeks' work. Anyway, that was my first education—trust no one!

"Later on, they wanted a complementary name to Vargo Statten [a pseudonym used for years by the late British writer John Russell Fearn] so they invented Volsted Gridban, which was me. Oh, I was doing westerns and God knows what—one of my prime books was about the Foreign Legion. I knew absolutely nothing about it; all I'd read was *Beau Geste*. So all I knew was 'Mon Capitain.' It was all done under phony names. I even did one detective novel, which was a very poor, third-rate Chandler. I'd written the story, and I liked it; but there was no way anyone could have committed the crime. I had to throw half of it away and invent a character halfway through who was the villain. Until I did that, *no one* could have done the murder—they were all accounted for. So I realized that plots are my weakness. And that is the trouble, plots *are* my weakness. I start writing the story and then have to plot it as I go along, which means an awful lot of rewriting. If I take six weeks to do a book, I think that's an awful long time. Mind you, of course, I don't do a book every six weeks; there's gaps in between.

"At the moment, I'm working. I've got an ordinary job, which I suppose I'll get somewhat tired of. I'm doing it because I'll get so fed up I'll *want* to write a book. I've done this before; I think there were two years when I didn't write a word.

"I'm married, I've got two daughters, five grandchildren, but I don't think anyone's interested, frankly. There's no reason whatsoever why I should not be open about biographical detail, it's simply that I think it's so uninteresting, to me, it must be boring as hell to other people. You feel inadequate when you've done nothing special. I'll always remember the most off-putting moment, when I met John W. Campbell at a convention. He looked me in the eye—and I'd sold to this man, though I didn't expect him to remember me—and he says, 'Tubb,' he says, 'tell me something about yourself.' And I shriveled. How the hell can you answer a question like that, and be honest? They must ask questions like that deliberately. They can't possibly be interested. They can't be. For one thing, I've done all the things that authors are supposed to do. I did all this scad of different jobs—in those days, you did a lot of jobs because you didn't stay in one very long. Unless you were a good boy, you got sacked. I was an errand boy, delivered a handkerchief at the front door, by the time I got back I was sacked—because you never deliver a handkerchief at the front door, you should go around to the tradesman's entrance. That actually happened to me. Then I washed up and worked in hotels, I was a short-order cook—literally!—I was, for all of ten days. I got the push. But still, that's not the point, you write all this down and people will think, 'No, I can't believe this, it's a cliché, it's too much of a pattern.' So I'm very reluctant to talk about it. I'm trying to think of some other things . . . well, whatever I say, you've got to lie, so why bother. Authors are professional liars; anything you read about an author is bound to be a bit of a lie, after all. He's going to gloss himself up, he's going to polish things. Like: 'I married a beautiful White Russian countess, that was my first wife, I was sixteen and she was twenty-one, and she promised me an estate in Estonia...that poor woman, never shall I forget, the red smear under the bus.' And then the balalaikas play, and they say, 'Ah, that man's lived, hasn't he! That man's lived!'"

(London, July 1979)

BIBLIOGRAPHICAL NOTES

E. C. Tubb has written so many adventure novels, under so many names, it's hard to provide a concise guide. Of the twenty-one 'Dumarest' books so far published, *Winds of Gath* (1967) was the first. The series uses as its backdrop a galactic empire which has fallen into decay, ruled by zombie-humans linked telepathically to a computer. Dumarest is on a dedicated quest to rediscover lost Planet Earth.

The Space-Born (1956) is one of Tubb's own favorite books. Set on a multigeneration interstellar spaceship, it suggests that the population of such a closed, artifical environment could be limited by "death control" as opposed to birth control—a concept which Tubb feels is original and has been overlooked.

Another earlier, popular novel is *Alien Dust* (1955), a strong, dramatic tale of interplanetary exploration. It still reads well, more than twenty years later, even though science has invalidated some of its assumptions about space travel.

Ian Watson

Horrors of academia! Erudite dissertations, formal analyses, footnotes, digressions, contentious debate, qualified conclusions, all that pedantry and "scholarship" which so often says nothing *tangible*, and says it in elaborate, mannered language whose bulk—like soft white bread—yields no real nourishment when it is digested.

Whenever I find myself on the streets of Oxford or Cambridge, the academic horrors close in. Those fine old stone buildings, so dignified, so historic, so much a part of our British cultural heritage, tell you right from the start that whoever lives here has to be taken extremely seriously. Here reposes the leaden legacy of formal education, higher learning—not that preprogrammed, simplistic, homogenized stuff they hand out at provincial universities; this is authentic, the real thing, complete with tweed jackets and briar pipes. Why, walking toward me down this quaint sidewalk of weathered flagstones, there *is* someone in a tweed jacket, smoking a briar pipe. I've only been in this university town for one minute, and already I've sighted a bona-fide academic. An M.A., I'll bet. And there goes another, riding a bicycle. They all ride bicycles, don't they? Wonderful British eccentrics. And they punt down the river, watch rugby football (winter) and cricket (summer), share a drop of sherry now and then, or some port—all those clichés are *true*, acted out with complete deadpan seriousness.

Of course, I am a little bit biased. I dropped out of Cambridge, myself; no, that's an understatement. Cambridge drove me to alcoholic depression, suicidal despair. I ran screaming. Of course, that was years ago . . . the old university towns must have loosened up a bit since then . . . I mean, when I left my college, they were planning to go coeducational (starting with thirty female students, as a daring "experiment"). And these days, I understand, you don't even have to wear your gown when you eat dinner in the college cafeteria! Oxford and Cambridge, without a doubt, are creaking into, if not the present day, at least the recent past.

So what is Ian Watson doing, living in Oxford? Is he of the academic ilk, this bright new science-fiction writer who is the only British newcomer to make a real impact on the American field in the 1970s? Well, Watson did graduate from Oxford, and he does have a kind of academic seriousness. Not stuffy, though. Brusque and engaging, at the same time. And inside the quaint little stone terrace house where he lives with his wife, Judy, and five-year-old daughter, everything is contemporary and brightly modern.

The one trait that Watson shares most obviously with academia, or has learned from it, is a tendency to think and argue in theoretical terms. He seems happiest when playing with conceptual abstractions. Though this can be a weakness (a writer of abstractions is never powerful when describing character) it is also Watson's strength. His rather detached perspective has enabled him to write a succession of novels which are quite remarkable in the originality of their ideas. Reading Watson's fiction, you get the impression that you couldn't have a more intellectually stimulating experience if you ran into some wild-eyed university theorist—a younger Fred Hoyle, perhaps—debating reality and the universe over tea and biscuits at the college buttery.

Who is Ian Watson?

"I was brought up on Tyneside. I did actually want to be a scientist at one time; I studied three science subjects up to 0 level. But I didn't do all that blindingly well, so I ended up taking Latin, History, and English. I got a scholarship to Oxford when I was sixteen, to read English Language and Literature, and then, inevitably, I did research—because I got a first. Anybody who got a first did research. It was on nineteenth-century literature.

"By then I did have the idea that I was going to be a writer. But about what I would write, I did not know. I'd been reading science fiction a long time. I got corrupted early; possibly the Eagle comic switched me on to it in 1953. I hadn't thought about becoming a science-fiction writer; I loved it, but literature was something else, rather holy, and I was very holier-than-thou about it, and coming to Oxford doesn't really help that. I was lying around in the meadows reading the rather precious romantic aesthetes of the late nineteenth century, and I wanted to write prose like that myself. I did start writing precious little scraps, when I was at Oxford, and by the time I finished my research degree I had managed to turn out two short novels, in rather highfalutin prose. They were based on contemporary reality. The first one I sent to Calder [a British hardcover publisher]. They expressed interest, but, finally turned it down.

"I got a job at the University of East Africa in 1965, which was the sort of thing you did when you'd finished your research degree in Oxford—get into the Commonwealth teaching circuit. I was married, then; got married when I was a student. We went off to Tanzania and I taught Jane Austen and James Joyce, and it was a very boring and hot experience. I did get some political enlightenment; I was at the same time busily reading whatever science fiction I could pick up.

"What made me realize that science fiction was what I ought to be writing was when I got out to Japan. I had applied for a job in the Cameroons through the British Council; they said, 'We don't think you should go there. We'd like a person with severe brain damage to go *there*. We think you'd be happier if you went to, for instance, Tokyo. You'd go mad if you went to the Cameroons.' So they gave me this job in Tokyo, teaching English Literature and composition.

"Being in Japan made me realize I ought to be writing science fiction, because it's the ultimate twenty-first century environment. There were all the fun and gimmicks—super opulence—and a completely zany intersection of traditional culture and futuristic whatnot. But it was a disaster area, they were pushing up these skyscrapers, and the place was rocking with earthquakes, cracks were running down the walls of the new buildings, which are not earthquake-proof. The bombardment of technology, applied to an awful lot of people's daily lives—for instance, taxis with coin-in-the-slot TV. I watched the Watts riots as I drove through Tokyo. Then, all the monster films, and gimmickry, balloons floating overhead—the sheer fun of it coupled with the sheer death of it, the slow poison of the air. I saw that, in these circumstances, writing a precious, decadent novel was really not on.

"Some of the Japanese material is in *The Jonah Kit* [Watson's second published novel]. *The Embedding* [his first] contains a little bit of Tanzania, but most of it's set in Brazil. I like to feel my way into other cultures which I haven't even been to, because if you can't imagine another place on this planet, how can you imagine other planets?"

Before he wrote the novels, Watson produced his first short stories while he was still living in Japan. The only science-fiction magazine he was familiar with was the British *New Worlds*, so that's where he sent his work, and that's where he was first published, together with his wife, who is a talented graphic artist. However, he makes it clear that he didn't have much enthusiasm for the "new wave" in science fiction, which *New Worlds* was pushing in the late 1960s:

"I thought it was dreadfully pretentious. We used to read the magazine in intense annoyance and fury—Look at all this pretentious rubbish! We can do better than this! We *will* do better than this! In that sense, I'm a sort of non–new wave writer. A reactionary. A lot of the new wave seemed awfully self-congratulatory and self-satisfied. Of course, when I sold a story to the magazine we thought—well, there might be something in it after all. . . .

"As I zipped in from Japan, the United Kingdom looked like the nineteenth century, equipped with motor cars, seen through a sheet of glass six feet thick, slow and half-dead.

"By the time I wrote *The Embedding* I was in a state of pure fury. The monthly *New Worlds* had packed up [Michael Moorcock was editing only an occasional book-format story collection under the old title, at infrequent intervals]. I'd get a scribble from Moorcock, about six months late, saying, "Sorry, can't use your story, try next time.' Meaning, try in six months, by the time he'd produced his next issue full of his friends. I wrote *The Embedding* in a white-hot fit; the original version was in a semiembedded style, as a sort of deliberate slap in the face to any readership. I sent it to Gollancz and they said, In here is a fascinating story, if it can only be written in plain English."

The Embedding was an unusual novel, imperfectly structured but full of imagination. Though Watson was an unknown, obscure British author, the book gradually acquired a following in America. I ask Watson if he knows exactly how it happened, without any promotion or advertising to pave the way.

"I'm not absolutely certain. I guess it got good reviews; in *Locus*, Michael Bishop reviewed it, and it got a good review in the *New York Times*, from Gerald Jonas. I didn't know enough then to realize that this was actually a bit of a miracle. The book also caught on in France; it won the Prix Apollo there, and the French have been very appreciative ever since. I'm rather amazed, in retrospect, because I didn't think anyone would pay much attention to the book.

"I've got a very close relationship with Gollancz, especially John and Sheila Bush [John Bush is the managing director of Gollancz]. They dissect my books as they come in, and order very necessary rewrites. With all of the books I've done so far, I've had to rewrite them after submission. Usually John and Sheila are pretty right, and keep on turning the screw—not that I'm lazy, I do actually rewrite the things over and over again. The books are written about five times. But you know, I try to put in too much that's inexplicable, and it doesn't just fall out onto the typewriter first-go. I usually have dinner with the Bushes and crack a bottle, and then they get going, and they really *read* those books—two or three times over—and they've got sheets of notes. My sternest critics are not the critics, it's the publisher. But they're right, all the time."

I ask what Watson's own tastes are, as a reader.

"Philip Dick, I love—the middle period, where reality is very distorted. Frank Herbert fascinates me, because of the kinds of themes he is exploring. The fact that he very often does this in a slapdash cowboys-and-Indians way doesn't appall me as much as it ought to, because I'm more interested in the structure of the things he's exploring. They do interest me considerably, though at the same time I can see the obsessiveness, the bad politics, the flaws.

"I'm interested in Piers Anthony. Now, he's another appalling writer, who deals with very interesting themes. He turns out a trilogy a week, as far as I can see, and continually I read them, conscious of the appalling flaws, but really rather interested."

Who does Watson dislike?

He finds it hard to come up with a name, right away. "I like an awful lot of science fiction," he explains. Then: "I find Heinlein totally unreadable. New and old, they're all awful, they mean nothing to me, nothing whatever."

Watson talks rapidly, and his movements, too, are quick. There is an obvious air of intellectual agility about him. He tackles every question with a brusque, cooperative spirit; I imagine that I could ask anything, no matter how personal, and he'd respond in the same cool, civilized fashion, without obviously taking offense. On the other hand, this same coolness discourages me from becoming too personal. I feel as if it would be out of place—like bringing slander into a debating chamber. Improper. Bad form. Also, unproductive. Easier to talk about Watson's work, rather than his self—especially since many of the ideas he has used in his fiction are ideas which he sincerely believes. His fifth novel is a case in point:

"*Miracle Visitors* was a novel about what UFOs might be. There is a UFO phenomenon; it seems evasive in the sense that it affects people yet refuses them any kind of hard or concrete proof, and it also appears to leave physical traces, echoes on radar screens, and things like that, yet at the same time it appears to be a psychic or psychological phenomenon, so it's somehow intermediate between reality and consciousness. And that's the way I'm trying to analyze it. The idea that I put forward in *Miracle Visitors* is one that I think is right . . . a plausible, nonloony one, nevertheless far out . . . but a lot of modern physics is far-out, as well. It's possible that the Jungian explanation [for UFOs] is one which he himself was pussyfooting about—wasn't willing to go the whole hog. It's an okay explanation, collective archetypal imagery presenting itself to people, yet I think you've got to go one stage further and say that imagery is projecting itself onto reality, in an evasive self-removing fashion. UFOs don't contain extraterrestrial beings, as far as I'm concerned. They *simulate* extraterrestrial beings, which play the same kind of role as fairies did, in fairy appearances and other anomalous sightings. I've tried to construct a general theory which also keys into the main preoccupation in my books, which is the intersection of reality and consciousness: To what extent is consciousness constructed by the reality of the universe?

"I'm attempting to alter the states of mind of my readers, to make them more conscious of the operating programs that are running their brains—the sort of thing that John Lilly refers to as 'metaprogramming.' I'm interested in ways of examining the structure of your thinking, and trying to present narratives that make people think a bit about the pattern and style of their thoughts, and what alternative thought-structures they could enter into. This is what I say science fiction ought to be about, presenting you with an alternative-reality paradigm, a different way of conceptualizing reality and the universe.

"In orthodox science fiction, you tend to get the objective correlatives of alienness, without any of the psychological alienness underneath—because you've got blundering nitwit heroes rampaging through the environment, most of the time. What I really want to do is investigate alien thought-structures. This is implicit in science fiction as soon as you start dealing with the concept of alien beings. My fault is that I would tend to write philosophical, abstract books. I have to keep my old failings under control—aesthetic frivolity, and decadent prose, and overelaboration.

"By working within the science-fiction genre, which has a strong adventure element in it, I *am* keeping myself under control, and perhaps putting over a more articulate message than I would otherwise."

(Oxford, July 1979)

BIBLIOGRAPHICAL NOTES

The main themes in Watson's first published science-fiction novel, *The Embedding* (1973), are anthropology and experimental psychology's effects on the people whom it studies, and reality as a function of one's mental vocabulary. The book suggests that an isolated group of children, educated to think differently, would inhabit a reality different from ours, with different natural laws. This type of concept recurs in Watson's later books, such as *The Jonah Kit* (1975) and *The Martian Inca* (1977), both of which deal with the notion of different or higher realities, possibly accessible via drugs or communication theory.

Watson's most recent novel, at this time, is *God's World*. He also has one early work which he has been unable to publish in English, thus far. In French it has appeared as *Orgasm Machine*; in English, it is to be titled *The Woman Factory*. Cowritten with his wife Judy, it is a science-fictional satire portraying rebellion by women against a future totalitarian regime imposed by men. The book's sexual content has been a barrier to its publication.

Photo by Nelson Redland

John Brunner

Many of John Brunner's near-future novels are set in America. They have an American tone, they describe crises in urban life, and they explore the future of high-level technological society.

Paradoxically, Brunner is British, and lives in a quiet, old-fashioned village in the southwest corner of England, surrounded by acres of farm land. When he takes the dogs out for a walk, or goes shopping, he greets other village residents in the street by name. No crises, here—the nearest thing to excitement is the annual folk-music festival created by his wife, Marjorie. It's a peaceful, genteel retreat.

True, Brunner makes visits to America, and is by no means out of touch with London. But it does seem that he prefers his home life to be well insulated from the subject matter which he repeatedly writes about, and which he holds at arm's length.

This distance is one way of maintaining control, or detachment. It's very different from the style of, say, Harlan Ellison, who dislikes being cut off from the action, and has lived in real life the impassioned radical philosophy of his fiction. Likewise, Ellison's writing is often dramatic, attacking social problems via aggressive activism; in Brunner's work, the style is measured and disciplined, and the same social problems are likely to be dealt with via discussion and diplomacy, rather than by wading in and knocking heads together. Brunner almost seems to suggest that our problems wouldn't exist to begin with, if we would just live more rationally and behave in a civilized fashion.

"I do like to think of myself as a balanced person," he says. "When I was a kid, I used to be the sort who was baited, in order to see me fly into a rage. But I decided that was extremely bad, on all counts. So I gave it up. Over the course of the years, as I've become more secure in my view of myself, I've been able to take a more balanced and less passionate view of the world."

He is talking, quietly, in the rather elegant living room of his fine old house (which, he says modestly, "used to be the servants' quarters of the mansion next door"). There are large, modern abstract paintings on the pastel-colored walls, a grand piano in the corner, comfortable arm chairs. A Siamese cat wanders across the flower-patterned carpet. Classical music plays on the radio in the next room. I am struck by a sudden fantasy: *The door bursts open. Three militant American ghetto blacks hurl themselves inside, toting rifles, gas masks, and grenades. Their clothes are torn and bloodied. They look mean and desperate. One of them levels his gun at Brunner: "Get 'em up, honky! We come for our share! You ain't gonna exploit us brothers no more, baby!"*

John Brunner (I imagine) is unperturbed. "I do understand the cultural deprivations which have driven you to this state of desperation. But surely you can see, violence isn't necessarily the best way of achieving equality. My wife and I have always supported civil rights. In fact we instituted the Martin Luther King Memorial Prize. So why not put down those guns, and have dinner with us, and perhaps we can find somewhere for you to stay overnight. How's that?"

At which point—perhaps—the urban guerillas exclaim: "Hey, right on, man! That's cool! You're okay, baby!" and, once again, compromise triumphs over unreason.

Such civilized surroundings, coupled with such a moderate-liberal master of the house, tempt me to indulge in such subversive fantasies.

In truth, John Brunner deserves to be taken a little more seriously than this. He really did create the Martin Luther King Memorial Prize, which is given each year to a literary work furthering interracial understanding, and he is sincerely dismayed by prejudices of all kinds. "I do find it a little alarming," he remarks, with characteristic mildness, "that people are prepared to dislike other people whom they have never met, on the basis of what they've read in the right-wing press. There's an amazing amount of color prejudice, even here in the village, which never surfaces if you have a colored person around. That is something of a disappointment to me, I must say."

As a science-fiction author, John Brunner originally built his reputation writing space adventures in which there was no social comment or relevance at all. The turning point didn't really come until the time of his most ambitious novel, *Stand on Zanzibar*, in 1968.

"I felt I'd gone as far as I could on the standard path I'd been pursuing," he recalls. "I'd been writing mainly bread-and-butter stuff for Ace Books. Ace was very literally my bread and butter. When I first started selling to them, they were putting out something in the order of sixty science-fiction titles a year, and I owe a tremendous debt to their system of launching a new writer on the back of an established one [in the Ace Doubles series, each of which contained two novels in one volume].

"These straightforward adventure stories were punctuated with more ambitious undertakings, at intervals, usually, of a year or so. I suppose the two best examples of this are *The Squares of the City*, which is based on a chess game, and *The Whole Man (also titled Telepathist)* in which I came up with the notion of a society where telepaths were functional members rather than outcasts, or 'Slans,' or whatever. But I felt that I'd pushed my craft ability as far as I could get it, by setting myself these irregular exercises, and I really did need a major challenge in order to find out just how much I had learned during my apprentice days.

"My then London literary agent got me a commission from Penguin Books, to write two novels, for a guaranteed advance royalty of £1,500, paid by quarterly installments. This, of course, was munificent by the standards of those days, so I thought, Now is my chance to write as well as I know how. I turned in suggestions for three books, they chose the two I wanted, and I spent 1966 writing them. The first was *Quicksand*, and the second was *Stand on Zanzibar*. They turned them both down—in the former case, after sitting on the damn thing for longer than it had taken me to produce it."

Eventually, of course, a different British publisher took the novel, and in America, it won the Hugo Award as best novel of 1968. Brunner says that "I got a lot of very favorable reviews, not only in the science-fiction press, but also in the general press—

which I suppose I'd better not quote, although some of them are among my most treasured possessions. When it turned out that I'd got the Hugo, I was just flabbergasted; it looks as though I must have touched an awful lot of raw nerves in that book. Its conception began with this question: Suppose, in a grossly over-populated world where people have reluctantly come to accept the necessity for eugenic legislation, somebody comes along with a means for optimizing the embryo? I realized that in order to make this future world convincing, I was going to have to do something radically different from anything I'd done before. Then I realized I didn't have to invent my technique, I could steal it wholesale, from John Dos Passos's *U.S.A.*"

I ask if he had a problem, thinking of a follow-up for *Stand on Zanzibar*.

"I did have a problem, and that's why *The Jagged Orbit*, my next major work, is not as good. I wrote it too soon afterwards, and I kept finding myself asking myself, "Am I doing it because the book is calling for it, or am I doing it because it worked in *Stand on Zanzibar*?' So I think of *The Jagged Orbit* as being a flawed book."

Next came what is probably Brunner's grimmest piece of prophecy, *The Sheep Look Up*. Again, it was a book of considerable social relevance. "I wanted to tackle a major book of this kind about once every two years," he says. "I certainly can't do it more often. Letting my life lie fallow is a necessary prerequisite. I have written a number of books subsequently which I would still class as entertainment, minor things like *Total Eclipse*, but I've never been driven back to the wild and woolly space-opera stuff, which may be spectacular, like *Star Wars*, but ultimately becomes a bit hollow.

"Since *The Sheep Look Up*, I've done only one really sub-stantial novel, and that's *The Shockwave Rider*, which I based on some themes that I drew from Alvin Toffler's *Future Shock*. That remained, for five years, the last science-fiction novel that I had actually wrapped and mailed. I went through an extremely bad period just after moving out here to Somerset, when I developed blood-pressure headaches. It turned out I suffered from acute hy-pertension, and they put me on a drug which wiped a year out of my life. It did very seriously affect me: I was losing my temper for no apparent reason, sleeping badly, my digestion was shot to hell, and my power of creativity was just wiped out. I had no imagination. So a long time went by between science-fiction novels.

"I decided to write something totally different, as a challenge: a novel about a steamboat race on the Mississippi. I spent a long while doing my research. I wound up with 1,200 pages of typescript, and the book not nearly finished. I'd fallen into the trap which many science-fiction writers fall into when they tackle a historical novel for the first time. I got too fascinated by my background material, and it kept getting in the way of the story. Some time, I am going to have to go back and scrap everything that doesn't actually move the story along, and I'm going to hate every minute of it."

This, then, is the explanation for John Brunner's declining output of science-fiction novels in the past five or six years. He also seems slightly ambivalent about writing science fiction in the future.

"It was my preferred entertainment when I was a kid, so when I set out to become a writer, it was perfectly natural that I should write the sort of stories that I used to enjoy reading. I had rather a lonely childhood; my parents moved a great deal, particularly during the war. I never really had the chance to make close friendships, and of course I spent eight years of my childhood in boys-only boarding schools, which are scarcely an education for the real world. When I dropped out of school at age seventeen I envisaged a certain range of ambitions: I wanted to make my living as a writer, I wanted to win a Hugo, have a nice home, be happily married, all the usual things. Twenty years went by and I suddenly realized that I had achieved all the ambitions that I was capable of visualizing when I was seventeen. There I was, approaching middle age, doomed to have to create a whole new set for myself. I'm not quite certain that I've made up my mind about everything that I want to do with the rest of my life. I'm still casting around for something which will concentrate my faculties. I suspect this happens to many people who reach that age which, in the wild state, would correspond to one becoming a tribal elder."

Does he have any idea what he might have done instead of writing, if the childhood ambitions had been thwarted?

"When I was a kid I remember being told that there was absolutely no hope for me to make my living as a writer, so I used to box clever and tell people I'd like to go into broadcasting. As a matter of fact, I think I might have liked to do that. I think I might have made rather a good news reader."

It's important to him, to have an audience?

"If I can, I do like to influence people, without preaching at them."

Has he taken this to its logical conclusion, by getting involved in real-life politics?

"I've never actually been involved with a political machine, apart from working in the Campaign for Nuclear Disarmament, which was a very ad hoc organization. I've never belonged to a formal political party; if you had to classify me, you'd have to put me in some vague area like 'fellow-traveling idealistic anarchist.' Somebody who believes that the world could be rather better than it is, and is looking for a way to do something about it. The trouble is, I haven't yet found a political group which convinced me of the total rightness of its ideology.

"I find it very possible to join groups which *don't* have a fixed program. I belong, for example, to the Society of Authors, and the Writers' Guild, and other professional organizations. I recently applied for membership of the Folklore Society, I'm a life member of the Herb Society—the number of membership cards I carry around is almost ridiculous. But I'm afraid I'm not terribly active in any of them until something comes along which looks like a one-off project, which I think is going to engage my attention long enough for me not to get disillusioned with it. There's one such coming up in the county at the moment. We're on the steering committee for a countrywide arts festival that's going to be held in 1981. This is exactly the kind of thing that I do enjoy, and usually the kind of people I meet in operations like that seem to be the kind I can get on with very well. And of course I'm publicity officer for our village folk festival, which is Marjorie's brainchild. We've just had our third, and this year we had over 100 performers, and several times that number came to the village. Everyone was very pleased. It went down extremely well. It looks as though we've established that as a permanent feature of the village calendar, and I get quite a charge out of that."

Brunner also enjoys some frankly domestic pursuits:

"I have a favorite hobby, which is gradually taking over from all my others. I've discovered I can cook. It dawned on me that it was really rather unfair to make Marjorie worry about what we were going to have for dinner, every day of the week. So now, as a matter of routine, I have her to dinner one evening a week, either on her own or with friends. She can do whatever she likes with the extra time—watch television, play the piano, read, do the gardening, whatever. I thoroughly enjoy it. In cookery there is no editorial interference, you get immediate audience response, and there is no tedious rewriting or revising if you get it wrong— it's done once and for all. So it suits me."

And so, again, we are a long way from future visions of urban crisis, and dark warnings of ecological doom. John Brunner's village life really is a world apart from the scenarios and messages of his fiction. Yet to him this is not necessarily a paradox or a contradiction.

"I long ago realized that I could reach far more people by writing something, than by walking down the street with a banner," he explains. "On top of that, writing about the future, I have a vested interest in there being a future for me to write about. I don't want us all to go *smash* in a nuclear war, and I don't want us all to have to suffer through the kind of revolution which leaves the gutters running with blood. I want nice, comfortable progress—toward a better future than the one we are currently lined up for. This causes my revolutionary friends to dismiss me as halfhearted, and it causes my conservative friends to regard me as a Red of the deepest dye. So," he sums up, with a satisfied smile, "I suppose I must be somewhere around the right area."

(Somerset, July 1979)

BIBLIOGRAPHICAL NOTES

Through the second half of the 1950s and into the 1960s John Brunner published a great number of competently written, American-style science-fiction adventures, mostly set in space, or involving space travel. Many of these novels appeared in the back-to-back Ace Double format, paired with novels by other writers.

The Squares of the City (1965) and *The Whole Man* (also titled *Telepathist*) (1964) demonstrated that Brunner harbored ambitions to grow as a writer, beyond the usual restrictions of simple adventure fiction. The latter book attempts a psychological portrait of a malformed human being with telepathic powers; the former is a symbolic chess game. *Stand on Zanzibar* (1968) was a vast novel of the near future, styled after *U.S.A.* by John Dos Passos; it is a scrapbook of future scenes and images, described in various styles and formats. More recently, *The Sheep Look Up* (1972) is a gloomy examination of ecological doom, coupled with a deep suspicion of the motives of politicians and other figures of power.

Gregory Benford

Many science-fiction writers seem to be misfits. It's dangerous to generalize, but a lot of the authors in this book have mentioned, for instance, how much they felt alienated as children, estranged from other kids or from their family backgrounds. Writing science fiction was a way to create a private refuge, within which there was a sense of freedom, power, and possibilities.

Some people get the same experience from reading science fiction. I'm not talking about people who casually pick up a science-fiction title every month or two; I mean the ones who feel a real *need* for the stuff. You'll see them in any specialist bookshop, scanning titles with obsessive intensity. Through science fiction they are able to go beyond boring and, perhaps, disappointing everyday life, to explore a world of other worlds.

Picture the dedicated science-fiction writer, then, as a slightly introverted, quirky individualist, with vivid imagination and, often, a set of vehement opinions. And picture the diehard reader as an obsessive dreamer, a manic social outcast. And now imagine about fifty of these writers and 4,000 of these readers, all milling around together inside a giant hotel for four days and nights, with few restrictions on behavior, and plentiful supplies of liquor. Now you have some idea of what a science-fiction convention is all about; in particular, the 1979 world convention.

Usually the annual world convention is held in America, but in 1979 the venue was Brighton, England. I went there; I saw and at times felt part of that strange crowd, thronging hallways, jamming elevators, watching nonstop movies, listening to panelists from Arthur C. Clarke to Fritz Leiber, buying books, going to room parties, browsing through a science-fiction art gallery, witnessing the ceremony surrounding the year's Hugo awards, and watching the costume parade. It was like being among a minority group who suddenly feels it's safe to come out of the closet—or, rather, suddenly find that their communal closet has expanded to the size of a hotel, where you're allowed to play together as you will.

For me, the convention also provided a chance to catch up with the last of my subjects for this book. The sensory overload of thousands of people, and parties and special events, tended to make coherent thought difficult at times, but I managed to talk with Robert Silverberg, whom I had missed while I was in his home state of California, and Gregory Benford, whom I had not met before.

Benford is an American physicist. He doesn't fit the science-fiction writer stereotype; few scientists write science fiction, and of those who try it, hardly any seem to care very much about the finer qualities of the writing itself. But Gregory Benford cares—so much so, that he is actually going back to his first few published novels, and reworking them. He freely admits shortcomings of his prose; he is conscientiously trying to transcend himself.

Benford is neatly bearded, short-haired, and California-tanned. He looks lean and physically fit; he seems equally vigorous, mentally. His conversation can be almost hyperactive, touching not only on the sciences but also making frequent literary and social and historical references. When I first started talking to him he came out with a string of witty one-liners and pointed put-downs aimed at areas of the science-fiction field which, one might say, are a little short on finesse or creativity.

Then the tape recorder is turned on, and suddenly Benford's satirical humor evaporates, to be replaced by a more balanced, mellow, and tolerant view of his science-fiction contemporaries. As he says himself, scientists don't just think twice before speaking for the record, they think three times.

The interview takes place in a plush hotel suite rented by

Berkley Publishing for the duration of the science-fiction convention at Brighton. Framed by heavy velvet drapes, a big bay window faces south, overlooking beach and sea. Golden sunlight gleams on the waves. The old, elegant room provides a serenely Edwardian setting.

Benford stretches out full-length on a velvet-upholstered sofa, and I wonder if he might actually fall asleep—we're all suffering from hungover Sunday-afternoon convention torpor. But when I play back the tape later, I realize that my fears were misdirected; while my own voice sounds like that of someone in a deep hypnotic trance, Benford, sustained by his mysterious reserves of mental energy, sounds no more out of it than, say, a victim of mild jet-lag.

He tells me he started writing science-fiction stories in 1964, "As a recreation during graduate school, at the University of California at San Diego, because the pressure of work was so intense. I started out in solid-state physics, and got my doctorate in that area, but have since moved over into plasma physics and into relativistic astrophysics—extragalactic radio sources and pulsar radiation theory, and also laboratory stuff. I'm head of a small laboratory group. Somewhat diversified.

"I'm in England on a research sabbatical. I'm working on stability and dynamics of the immense streams of relativistic particles, which come out of distant galaxies—the biggest things in the universe. A hundred times bigger than a galaxy. Huge streams of particles. They're probably ejected from black holes, and I've been investigating their stability and what you can learn about how they were made.

"I'm a fairly visual thinker. In doing science, I think in terms of pictures of things happening, and then do the mathematics. I spend most of my time doing mathematics. In writing I tend to think in pictures, also. Paintings influence me a great deal, and I tend to use ocean images, because I grew up near the ocean and it has a lot of ramifications for me. I go surfing and diving a lot. The analogy between space, as an ocean, and the voyages of exploration which inaugurated modern times, is not lost on me, just as it is not lost on Arthur Clarke, who has the same obsessions.

"The thing that has interested me most in the last decade has been trying to learn how to write well; that is, stylistic concerns. I've never had a course in English Literature beyond high school; I took my college courses by examination because I could save money that way. I just read a bunch of Hawthorne, and so on, and took an examination in it. But now I go around and ask people, who should I read next?

"My secret vice is that there are all kinds of science fiction which I've been unable to read. I find many great works—certainly things like Edgar Rice Burroughs and E. E. Smith—completely unreadable. Also the Asimov *Foundation* series; I couldn't read those even when I was a teenager. They just didn't seem true or real; my memory is of saying, This is *obviously* not the way things would be.

"I'm either in favor of deliberately mannered, usually stylistically mannered, stories that are trying to make a point through that method; or else realistic narratives, so you get the feeling that this is actually the way it might happen, as contrasted with stories where you think, This is not the way it would happen. Those stories are actually fiction based on other fiction, not fiction based on life. Fiction written by somebody who has read hundreds of issues of *Astounding* magazine, and not much else.

"Most science fiction I find unreadable. But most *fiction* I find unreadable. I probably attempt more science fiction that I don't finish, than I attempt mainstream fiction that I don't finish, because I usually have a better guide in mainstream fiction. If you read the best novels of Faulkner there's a pretty damn good chance you're going to be reading something good. That's not true of a lot of reasonably well-known science-fiction writers. I suspect that this field probably has standards which oscillate because of economic reasons, more than anything else. The standards right now are not as high as they could be."

I ask if he gets impatient with readers who seem satisfied with the status quo, and uninterested in experiments in science fiction.

"'Impatient' would imply I was trying to get something out of the reader that he didn't want to give," Benford replies, carefully. "In which case the answer is 'no.' I realize the limitations. I just don't speak to him. I'm sure that to him I am a cipher, and to me he is a cipher. We're just looking for different things. I do feel that the science-fiction audience could try to grow a bit, but the problem is that the audience is always changing. People really do pass through, get what they want, find the kick isn't so great any more, and go on to watching *Starsky and Hutch* in the evenings. The audience does change, and is pretty young. Nothing has proved better than the last five years of media hype that the basic science-fiction audience remains the seventeen-year-old who is encountering things for the first time. I think you just have to accept that fact, until the world changes and there are more people who will read science fiction. The prescription for changing the world, I don't know; but one thing certainly would be to write more intelligent novels which are basically science fiction but can do something that will entice the ordinary intelligent reader who has never read any science fiction. I have always felt that that was the case, and I also felt that I was not the sort of writer to do that, because I didn't know how. But the book I've just written may do that, if it's successful. It's called *Timescape* and it's basically a novel about how science is done. It may be that that's interesting enough for a non–science-fiction reader.

"I, like many others, have written the exploration-of-space-motif novel, and I haven't always done it from a very original point of view. I would like, myself, to write fiction that reflects more of my own experience. J. G. Ballard's line about the problem with science fiction being that it's not a literature won from experience, means something to me; to me, you get a sure grip on things if you can write from direct experience.

"It slowly dawned on me that the life of the scientist, and science itself, is an area simply lying there waiting to be written about, and nobody does it. There are C. P. Snow novels, and a few memoirs like *The Double Helix*, and autobiographies. But the people who are active in science, who have a career in it, don't ever write fiction about it because they're so far from the habit of mind of couching things in fiction. And so I'm a very odd person, not because I'm particularly able, but because I've got this funny background. I'm actually from the South, grew up among uneducated, near-illiterate people—most of my relatives are fishermen or farmers. Because of my father's military career, I lived in a rash of foreign countries, so I'm basically an outsider wherever I go. And it slowly dawned on me that the landscape of science is maybe what interests people a great deal in science fiction. They get a partial flavor of it; the wonders and so forth are graphically developed, and the scientist is frequently a hero, but the depictions of the scientists are not very real and, unfortunately, the science has got mingled in with melodrama and sentimentality so much that they're inextricably wedded, particularly in the minds of the authors, and maybe in the minds of the public. So you get the good coupled with the bad, and the bad eventually drives out people who want to read better writing, and it drags in people who are not interested in the science. That's a possibility, anyway. I don't know if it's true. And I don't mean, by this, to say that all science fiction is shit; I'm just trying to analyze what is bad about a lot of science fiction.

"Science fiction is prone simply to allow you to hold up totems for real things, without looking at them very carefully. As a science-fiction writer you can carry around a briefcase full of these totems, which you hold up—'Galactic Empire,' or whatever. And of course there are some new-wavy ones, like 'Kafkaesque Horror at Technology' and 'Unforeseen Side-Effects.' And you still get the science-fiction story which starts out on page one with the guy taking out the garbage and ends up with him having understood the secret of the universe—and *done* something about it—by page 192. And I don't mean the star-spanning sagas, either.

"When Heinlein did that kind of thing, he at least gave you a series of close looks at things. He didn't just pull out totems—props—every ten pages. There was some thinking going on. I've written a book which is pretty much a Heinlein book, called *Jupiter Project* in its first printed version. I'm rewriting it and may retitle it. It is a conscious attempt to write a close-focus book about a seventeen-year-old in a research satellite around Jupiter. It does have many of the Heinlein sort of attitudes in it, because in fact I had a number of those attitudes myself. I was, after all, the son of a military officer, an army officer who fought in the Battle of the Bulge and was on MacArthur's general staff. (That was why I was living in Japan, which is one of the reasons I have oriental influences in my fiction.) I rather drifted away from some of those attitudes, while still seeing some of their virtues. I wrote that book as an homage to my earlier self. It may not be that way by the time I get through with rewriting it."

Does Benford have the real-life confidence in technology that is so much a part of Heinlein-type fiction?

"I think technology can solve most of the problems we confront. But of course fifty years from now, we'll have different problems. I think we could solve our problems more easily through strength of character; but that's always been a commodity in extremely short supply. For example, the U. S. energy problem could be solved by a truly intelligent conservation program, which should simply require that we change our lives a bit, usually for the better, in the sense of health. For that matter, many social issues could be solved by simple rational planning—I don't mean top-down planning, but by using the adroitness and competitive spirit of the small scale. In that sense, I'm sort of an unvarnished capitalist, not because I believe in the ownership of things, but because I believe small units are useful. You could as easily call me an anarchist. I think, for example, that the drug problem could be solved simply by legalizing it and licensing it, prostitution ditto, and these are not new solutions. The fact that, when applied, they seem to work, apparently has no influence on whether or not they will be adopted elsewhere, and that's what I mean by stick-in-the-mud–ism as being one of the big problems for the human race. But often our problems have been solved essentially by expansion; it's the one thing we've shown we're actually good at. I would suggest that, until somebody can demonstrate another path, we should keep pushing that strong suit—not stupidly, of course.

"There's a feeling I've gotten from a number of critics that the belief in expansion is itself a juvenile bias, which wanes as you adopt wife, children, mortgage, and so forth. But I think that's nonsense. The people who discovered the new world were not sixteen years old, and neither was Darwin or any of the other people who really struck out into new territory. There's that great spirit, which perhaps runs counter to the current fashion of European world-weariness. World-weariness is not a hell of a lot of help, unless you are trying to fight obvious overexcesses. If it leads you simply to give up on problems, it's no damn use.

"The obvious error in science-fiction stories which purport to solve problems is that often the solutions aren't solutions. The most common thing that goes wrong is that they start out with a problem that is immense or is so basic, that of course you can't solve it. So you put in a technical fix, and just kill somebody at the end . . . and that's not a solution, that's just a stopping point. But there's another thing, in that problem-solving stories often mislead you about the nature of science. Because science doesn't fundamentally solve problems, ever. It erects the best possible model at the moment. All people, science-fiction writers included, tend to want certainties, or they like problems to be nailed down, forever. But the habit of mind that the scientist should have is that you *know* you haven't got the full answer, you *know* your model is wrong in some regard. It would be unthinkable that we now had, say, an understanding of all the basic laws of physics. That habit of mind—of partial solutions, and remaining somewhat skeptical even of highly-valued theories—doesn't come through in science fiction, because everybody's trying to put the lid on problems, and tie it all up neatly at the end.

"In real life, for instance, the whole problem of energy sources is going to be solved by little two, three, and five percent solutions, not by some big new piece of technology that does everything. In fact we got into this crisis by believing that we had one big new piece of technology that would do everything, namely the technology of extracting oil. We abandoned windmills and coal, which we really need now."

Most of Benford's conversation—at least, during this interview—deals with things that can be examined, discussed, and evaluated in an objective style, as if in a laboratory experiment. He seems uncomfortable (at least, under these particular circumstances) whenever the topic has a more personal basis, or deals with people as opposed to systems. I'm always willing to talk about whatever the person I am interviewing wants to talk about, because, after all, his choice of subject says as much about him as the actual comments he makes. And so we're left with a picture of Gregory Benford as a rather serious person who seems driven, as if by conscience, to pursue his science-fiction writing not only as a part-time recreation, but as a literary endeavor. He seems quite dedicated.

However, he digresses into one anecdote which hints at a whole other side to the serious scientist:

"I read in a book about a year ago a story about the science-fiction crowd in New York in the 1940s. It seems Donald Wollheim [for a long-time editor at Ace Books, and now publisher and editor of DAW Books] had a parlor trick of pressing a pen flashlight up his nose and then turning it on: *click*. And a couple of months ago I had a dream in which I was in a crowded room, like a convention room-party, but there were no lights on. There was a pressing of bodies. I remember it being rather sticky, and people exhaling in my face, and very dim light, and then a figure appeared in front of me and began to say in a kind of New York drawl, 'The world of tomorrow...' *click* '...today!' and the light came glowing out of the flesh of this face. It was a very graphic dream. I don't quite know what it means, but I think it reflects my sort of plus-and-minus balance about the science-fiction heritage."

(Brighton, August 1979)

BIBLIOGRAPHICAL NOTES

Because Gregory Benford is first of all a full-time physicist, who writes science fiction only part time, his output has not been considerable. Also, it seems pointless to say too much about his earlier books, since he has plans to rewrite them, and until then they lie in a state of limbo, awaiting facelifts.

He undoubtedly feels that his new novel, *Timescape*, is his most important work, and the sizeable royalty advance paid for this book by its publishers seems to indicate they share Benford's opinion. By the time these words are in print, *Timescape* should have been published.

In the Ocean of Night (1977) is a novel built out of interconnected stories, describing a near-future Earth society making contact, tentatively, with an alien race. Benford takes considerable trouble to describe everyday events in detail, and he shows real-life workings of the space program; the result is conscientiously realistic. *If The Stars Are Gods* (1977) was a collaboration, written with Gordon Eklund; the short story of the same title was published three years earlier and won a Nebula award in 1975. *The Stars in Shroud* (1978) is one of Benford's most popular novels prior to *Timescape*.

Photo by
Melissa M. Hall

Robert Silverberg

In the early 1970s Robert Silverberg made his departure from the
world of science fiction. He said there was no future in writing
for readers who constantly maligned and misinterpreted his work.
The creative process was itself becoming painful, pointless, and
unrewarding. He was wealthy enough to stop writing indefinitely,
and he intended to do exactly that.

This news didn't go down too well. Science-fiction devotees
disliked being told, in effect, that they suffered from myopic taste
and retarded critical faculties. Nor did they warm to Silverberg's
personal manner. He is a very private man, who never seems to
lose his cool. He makes no secret of being wealthy, and seems
almost smug about his lifestyle.

And he has an air of suave boredom, like an intellectual who
is constantly being forced to suffer fools. I don't think this impression is deliberate, but it's indelible—no matter where he goes,
Silverberg appears as a sophisticate doing his polite best to get
along with the proletariat. I think it would be the same whether
he was visiting skid row or a reception at the White House.

But his disenchantment with science fiction was not a matter
of snobbism or affectation. He was quite sincere.

"My whole life had been spent in the science-fiction world," he says, "first as a reader in my boyhood, then as a mass-production writer, and then as quite a serious writer. I had operated on what ultimately seemed to be a fallacious theory: that as you grew, and deepened, and enchanced your craft and your art and all of that, you'd have someone appreciating what you were doing. There would be a reward—and I don't mean a monetary reward—for merit. Well, of course, there is, in a way, in that the things that people say about my books now are not the things they were saying twenty years ago. But foolishly I expected the whole audience to rush around saying, Here it is, finally, he's got it all together and he's doing the thing we want! Well, it wasn't the thing they wanted. They wanted more of the same old thing. Brian Aldiss has been through all of this, and Moorcock, and Ellison. We build a fantasy of louder applause for more difficult work, and that's preposterous, it just doesn't happen.

"I was at first bewildered by the response I was getting from the audience. There are passages in *Dying Inside* or in *Nightwings* which I think are sheer ecstatic song, but people would come up to me and say, Why do you write such depressing books? Something was wrong, either with my perceptions or with their degree of literary response. I still don't know which it was, but I no longer care. I've come to see my response to all of that as my own folly.

"I was doing battle, in my own anthologies, in my critical writing—such little of it as there was—and in talks at conventions, trying to shake them up, trying to say: Look, E. E. Smith was a sweet old man, but there is more to science fiction than E. E. Smith. Well, I've lost that urge. It's hopeless. There's no point in pushing against the impossible; everybody's following his own path, and the path of those who are content to read *The Lensman* is not my path. Perhaps they'll wander on to it some day, but it won't be because I've seized them by the hand and dragged them onto it."

And so Silverberg is now more indifferent toward his audience than actively angry. His feelings of disenchantment seem less intense.

"I've suppressed them, let's say. I still have grave doubts about the viability of science fiction as serious literature. To pick three names that come to mind instantly, I don't see Ballard, Aldiss, or Disch as great commercial successes, at least in the United States; they seem to be struggling along. I admire those particular writers. I also feel kinship with them. We were all trying to use the material of science fiction and carry it closer to literacy. I don't see any reason why that should succeed; it seems almost folly to think that it should, since science fiction is basically a mass-market category of entertainment and we were trying to make something elitist. When you take an elitist approach, you're going to get a smaller audience. So some of my feeling toward my field remains a bit uncertain. But during the four years that I was not a writer, and stressed that fact, many of the reasons for my having stopped writing—political reasons, personal reasons—evaporated, leaving me in a curious position where I was simply not writing because I was not writing. In the spring of 1978, at the Nebula Awards banquet in San Francisco, all the New York editors were in town, wheeling and dealing with other writers, which made me feel a bit posthumous; and some large personal expenses had suddenly arisen; and then, simultaneous with all of this, I had a book idea that seemed quite irresistible. Also, I felt a certain curiosity. As we got into the world of very large royalty advances for science-fiction writers, I wondered what I was worth on the current market. The only way I could answer that question was to test the waters. So, very suddenly, between one afternoon and evening, I conceived this book—*Lord Valentine's Castle*—and overcame my very firm resolve never to write again."

The book sold to a hardcover publisher for a lot of money— a sum large enough to arouse some envy in Silverberg's colleagues. But: "It didn't really change my financial condition in any important way. It all passed through my hands immediately, to settle my large personal expense. I was well-off before it, I'm well-off after it, nothing much different. I don't have a yacht. But it was a heavy symbolic thing and it drew some heavy symbolic results. I *wanted* it to be a heavy symbolic thing—all those books that I wrote in my most fertile period, I wrote for almost nothing. *Nightwings* I got $2,500 for, and so on. So when I came back, having worked my way through all that load of resentments and angers and political statements, I wanted a giant advance as a kind of lubrication, a purge, a release from that feeling that I'd been grossly underpaid. I wanted to be grossly *overpaid* for once.

"My approach, in *Lord Valentine's Castle*, is definitely not that of my books of the late 1960s and early 1970s. It's a far more accessible, cheerful, and open book, partly because I'm a far more accessible, open, and cheerful person now than I was during the period of those rather dark books, but also because I had reached the end of the plank, with *Dying Inside* and *The Book of Skulls* and *Born with the Dead*. I couldn't go any further in that direction except into silence or into real confrontation with the audience.

"What comes next, after *Lord Valentine*, is probably a year or two of silence and recuperation, and then either a few short stories or a novel which I suspect will be closer to the *Dying Inside* texture. I doubt that it will have the emotional intensity and, if you will, downbeat tone of that period; I hope not, because I hope to be in a different state of life myself. But I think I will return to fairly serious and intense fiction after a couple of years, and just ignore the consequences. That will be a whole new phase, of just not caring how the books are received."

We're talking in Silverberg's hotel room at the 1979 world science-fiction convention. He's sitting on one unmade bed; I'm perched on the other. An awkward setting for a serious tête-a-tête, especially since I had been feeling ambivalent and uneasy about the interview beforehand. Silverberg has published such thorough, comprehensive statements of his outlook on science fiction, it seemed to me he would have hardly anything left to say on the subject, and I might end up searching desperately for topics to talk about. Also, I interpreted his cool, controlled manner to mean that he would be generally difficult to talk to.

But once we get started, I realize how misleading his manner is, because his replies to my questions are open, spontaneous, and not at all condescending. Oh, maybe there is a touch of elitist spirit—he talks, at times, from an implied position of literary dignity and status, which he must feel he has earned, through his work. After all, he's done a lot: not only has he written ambitious, serious novels, but he has also produced a vast earlier output of entertainment fiction, and a number of significant nonfiction books, too. I ask him about those early days of prolific writing, when, as he puts it, a novel would roll out in two or three weeks, and he worked solidly, every day, as if on a one-man production line. Presumably it didn't seem strange to him that he had the facility to work like this; it seemed strange, rather, that other people couldn't.

"Exactly. And then, later, of course, I wondered how I *had* done it, when I looked back at some of those books I'd written in two weeks. But part of it is just concentration. *Lord Valentine*, which is three times as long as most of my other novels, took about five months for the first draft. I worked daily, five days a week, with some of that old dedication to getting some of the job done every day, without allowing myself any kind of scrutiny, self-examination, self-pity, or distraction. I think if I had wanted to, I could have written it in half the time, just by driving myself harder. But God knows I didn't want to, and I wasn't going to try. All that's over."

Silverberg says that part of the change in his outlook is due to his having moved from New York to California. "I've been there about a decade now. Just living in the open air, in a society which regards itself as capable of pulling itself together, has made a great change in me, coming from New York, which regarded itself as a collapsing society. It's very difficult to live in a collapsing society without feeling you're collapsing, yourself. To go out on a January day and run around on the beach under a golden sun makes a very great change in your outlook on the universe.

"I only get, I believe, one life. So I want it to be a rewarding life, an interesting life. I've always organized my life so that, basically, I do what I need to do. That's not quite the same thing as saying that I do what I want; there is a shade of difference there. But that's true freedom, to me: to be able to do what I need to do.

"I was terribly shy and insecure, when I was a boy; I was younger than everybody else around; and smaller, for a long time; and brighter, which doesn't help you in the society of your friends. I simply survived all of that, and that in itself builds confidence. And even while that was going on, I always did have some sort of knack for getting where I wanted to go, somehow, not even by always the most direct or even the most honorable route. But I always got there. I've now had four decades of watching that happen to me, and I begin to feel that perhaps this is the way my life *is*. I do understand, by the way, the perils of hubris, and I always qualify my smugness internally; I just don't feel the need to say to everybody else, Yes, I know that this may be all conditional on getting through tomorrow. But it's been pretty good so far. I've fulfilled nearly all of my early ambitions, I guess. At the age of sixteen or seventeen I thought it would be a wonderful thing to be a famous science-fiction writer; certainly that happened to me, though I felt a certain embarrassment about the fact that I hadn't—at least up to the age of thirty—written very much science fiction that I, as a sixteen-year-old fan, would have wanted to read. Well, I took care of that later on. I also wanted to live the kind of free life that would allow me to taste everything; I've realized that, too. It's very odd to be living all of your own adolescent fantasies. I had a feeling through most of my twenties that I was cheating—that I was escaping all of the traumas of life—that I had just picked up the silver spoon and was running to the finish line, to mangle a couple of metaphors. I lost that feeling as a result of three very bad events of the 1960s, at the time my New York house was wrecked by a fire. But I regard that as essential—I hated to go through all that stuff, but it was essential in becoming who I am now.

"The most terrible things could happen tomorrow, and I do fear that. The great earthquake, the plane crash in my back yard, all that stuff. But you don't let that operate your life. There's nothing you can do about it. There's no point in wasting your spirit fighting the impossible.

"So it's been a very good life; I couldn't have done a better job if I'd written the script myself. I'm a confident man, now, because everything has worked out."

He says this in his soft, matter-of-fact voice, not at all assertive or full of bravado, just spelling out the truth as he sees it. Does he realize the extent to which his quietly satisfied manner disconcerts and/or antagonizes people?

He shrugs. "I draw a lot of curious emotions from people. I am in some ways a very open man, and in some ways a very aloof and self-contained man. That, and the money, and . . . it's a kind of smugness, I guess, that I must project, when I say that I'm content with who I am and what I'm doing. That must upset people.

"I suppose I'm a materialist; but money to me is freedom, and freedom is essential. Money allows me to say that I will now devote my life to being me, rather than putting on my shoes and tie, and going to an office every day."

We've talked a lot about how Silverberg and his work are perceived by the science-fiction field. But how is the current state of science fiction perceived by Robert Silverberg?

"Science fiction seems to be in spectacular commercial health. I suppose that's only to be applauded. It's certainly a great deal easier for young writers now, than it was in my time. Nobody was courting me and begging me to write novels for $10,000 or $15,000, when I was twenty-one. I was courted by editors considerably back then, because I was so dependable; if they said, 'Give me a story by next Tuesday,' I would. But they would only pay me fifty dollars for it.

"I think the bigger the science-fiction world is, and the more booming it is, the more room for diversity there is within it. In the 'new wave' period—the revolutionary period of 1969 or so—all sorts of wonderful, crazy things were going on. I don't see much of that happening now; we've settled into a more conservative but not necessarily deplorable period where the fireworks have been fired, and now we're still operating under their glare, in a quieter way. We're integrating all of those explosions, coming up with a synthesis—watch those metaphors go rolling by!—and I have a feeling that this is a better time for science fiction than even the late–1960s period when I was doing most of my best work, and when everybody else was turning into something strange and wonderful overnight. It's a more settled time, now, and I'm rather a sedate man in some ways. I don't like all those explosions, constantly. I don't like surprises. I like wonders, I like a certain amount of excitement, but, moderation, moderation even in excess."

Does he feel a long way away, now, from those intense books he wrote, which were so misunderstood by the science-fiction audience?

"I can never approach a book of my own from the outside, the way the rest of the world can. But when I picked up a copy of the British edition of *Dying Inside* downstairs, a little while ago [in the booksellers' hall at the convention] this time, I was approaching it from the outside. I read a little of it and I thought, Well, this is very fine indeed; and, This is quite painful in its accuracy. And I felt an odd moment of guilt—I almost wish this were not going on tape!—at having written a book like that and having just walked away from that gift, and not returned ever to that level. But, of course, it wasn't proper to return, then. When it is, I hope I will."

(Brighton, August 1979)

BIBLIOGRAPHICAL NOTES

Robert Silverberg has written more than 70 novels, 60 non-fiction books, and 200 short stories, under his own name and pseudonyms. His early, prolific output of science fiction tended to be predictable and lacking in originality, but in the late 1960s he began to write much more thoughtful novels, with themes that tackled larger questions of life and human psychology. *Thorns* (1967) deals with a kind of psychic vampirism, and is a stylized study of alienation. *Nightwings* (1969) portrays the conquest of Earth in a lyrical form. *Tower of Glass* (1970) describes a new Tower of Babel and deals with a struggle by androids to be recognized as human. *The Book of Skulls* (1972) is barely science fiction; closer, if anything, to fantasy. It is a character study of four young Americans traveling in search of an immortality myth. *Dying Inside* (1972) is an intense, dark study of a telepath losing his psychic abilities; this novel marked the end of Silverberg's "serious phase" in science fiction. *Lord Valentine's Castle*, which marks the beginning of a new (as-yet uncategorizable) phase, is due to be published during 1980.

Photo by Geoff Goode

Brian W. Aldiss

This is the man who once locked me in a wardrobe because I wrote a bad review of one of his books. Was he overreacting to negative criticism? Not really. The fact is, many offensive, twenty-year-old self-styled critics (as I then was) deserve to be locked in wardrobes. It's a pity there are so few writers with the wit and initiative to take this kind of prompt corrective action.

I'm not attempting to embarrass Brian Aldiss with this anecdote. It would be hard to embarrass a man whose spontaneous nature has provoked so many unusual scenes. Why, just this year, at the world science-fiction convention, I seem to remember a rather exclusive cocktail party in a hotel suite; Aldiss was standing on a coffee table, screaming, and a rather aggressive American named Pournelle was threatening to—

But, I am straying away from the point. The point about Brian Aldiss is that, though he is in every sense a gentleman, one should not be fooled by his respectable British manner. He is also an impulsive character, an iconoclast who has the energy and the initative to go ahead and *do it*—make the grand gesture—even if he risks looking foolish afterwards. His impulsive spirit has led him into more important situations than the odd social fracas. It prompted him, for instance, to go out and get government funding for *New Worlds* magazine (in the astonishing form of an Arts Council grant). And it has led him to write unpredictable, unconventional books, marking a zig-zag career which by American standards would seem to be commercial suicide. Yet, in the end, somehow, even Aldisss' most whimsical work sells, and he has the satisfaction of staying true to his spontaneous nature, without ever having had to compromise.

He is probably our most all-around literate science-fiction author, measured by his command of language and his critical faculties. He has written a literary history of imaginative fiction (*Billion-Year Spree*); he used to copublish a small critical review long before science-fiction criticism was taken seriously by the rest of the world; and for many years he was a regular critic for the Oxford Mail. Moreover, Aldiss is unique in that he moves just as easily in higher levels of the literary establishment as he does among fellow science-fiction writers. He is not a literary snob, however. Quite the opposite:

'Having seen what are supposedly the big fish in the big pond, at a Booker Prize dinner, I thought what an awful giveaway mainstream literature was. I felt, then, very intensely, the virtues of the science-fiction field. The Booker Prize is the most prestigious prize for literature in Britain. The year that I went to the award dinner, it was won by Iris Murdoch for *The Sea, The Sea*. There were a lot of tables, about ten people to a table. At my table, of the six books that were runners-up, I think I'd read one, someone else had read two, and nobody else had ready any of them. There was such an air of weariness and uninterest in what went on, and I thought the speeches were very poor. The reservations of the judges, concerning the winners, I felt were an awful let-down—enthusiasm is a valuable quality. You couldn't help comparing it with the Hugo awards, which maybe you've always looked down on simply because they're part of the science-fiction family, or whatever you call it—the tribe. But if you go to the Hugo ceremony, everyone's read the novels, and they're saying, you know, my *God*, if X doesn't win this year, I'll *shoot* myself. The partisanship is tremendous. It may be misdirected, but it's *there*, and I did feel, after the Booker Prize, that we in science fiction really have the edge in a lot of ways. Come on, I mean, take the world convention at Brighton; how many people were there, 4,000? Where else would you find such an event? The enthusiasm is quite extraordinary. One of the BBC people filming the convention said to me, 'I can't remember when I went to an event where there were more intelligent and interesting people that I want to talk to.' Well, he wouldn't have found them at the Booker Prize dinner. I have to say it. You know, I was one of the 'don't knock mainstream' brigade for a very long time. I don't say I've changed my tune, but—well, maybe I *have* changed my tune."

Indeed, Aldiss seems a little mellower these days than he used to be. Ten years ago, he was extremely critical of what he saw as the many flaws in conventional science fiction, and he was solidly behind the radical spirit that fueled the "new wave" in general and *New Worlds* magazine in particular.

"I think it had a benevolent effect," he says. "I believe that what *New Worlds* did was not create a new audience—the audience was there; but you gave them something to focus on. Heaven help us, but we could liken this to Hugo Gernsback! When he started that first science-fiction magazine in 1926 he found there was an audience; it was there, it just needed something to focus on. And I think that's what we found, in the 1960s."

As Aldiss sees it, science fiction is no longer such a closed and separate genre. It has benefitted from outside influences. He now feels that some "mainstream" literature could be revitalized by the reverse of this process:

"I can't see why, shall we say, someone as gifted as Iris Murdoch doesn't give a wider background to her books, instead of these country-house dramas.* I would think that they would benefit enormously from the sort of backgrounds which we take for granted in science fiction. I do know the lady, and she's very pleasant, very intelligent, but I mean that's what one *feels*, that's where your loyalty to science fiction resides."

Aldiss is talking to me in my flat in London, on one of his fairly frequent visits to the city. It's much closer to being an informal conversation than an interview; he's in his usual convivial humor and obviously prefers an informal chat to a carefully worded, structured, question-and-answer session. He asks me about the other people I have interviewed, and we talk about the strange sense of community that there is among science-fiction writers and fans—what Algis Budrys refers to as the "brotherhood." I mention the spontaneous hospitality extended to me by some of the writers whom I had never even met before.

* See Appendix, last page

Here again, Aldiss delights in making comparisons with the world of serious literature. "Let's say you were doing a book of profiles of modern English writers," he says. "It wouldn't be quite the same, would it? I mean—shacking up with Beryl Bainbridge? It's a different kettle of fish! But I can tell you I know mainstream writers who would be better for the sort of understanding that exists among science-fiction people. J. G. Farrell—another Booker Prize winner, by the way. I met him once or twice. I used to go and lobby in the House of Commons, for the P.L.R. [Public Lending Rights, a proposal to pay authors a small royalty rate whenever their books are taken out of public libraries]. Farrell was there, such an intelligent but lonely man, he didn't know any writers, didn't feel anything in common with them. I think it would be hard for a science-fiction writer to be in that position. I mean, wherever you go—if you wound up in Tokyo, instead of landing in skid row, you'd look up the nearest science-fiction fan, and you'd be all right. The devil taking care of his own."

All this talk of unity and brotherhood warms the soul, but of course, the fact is, there have been obvious differences of outlook and method between Aldiss and, say, most American science-fiction writers. The insults and invective have long since died down, it's true; but some of the differences remain, as Aldiss himself agrees:

"I believe that in science fiction as we've seen it over the last three or four decades, there are two methods of writing, which struggle for supremacy. One always wins, and that is the heritage of the pulp magazines, where what you really have is *plot*—you've got a guy in trouble and he's got to get out of it. This is the formula. It requires a narrative hook at the beginning, and lots of excitement, and finally a startling conclusion. I believe the other way to approach a story, or a novel, is to think of some scenes that are going to be telling something that the reader will remember; and you've got to have people who are in some way memorable. No, 'memorable' is an easy word. Let's say, people whom you readily distinguish. This is rather more tricky, actually, than thinking of a plot, but I believe that if you have creditable characters and powerful scenes, the plot springs from that, while remaining subordinate to it. This is the difference. I prefer the second method; it's the method I work on. Now and then I have thought of a plot and have used it, but I don't think the results have been as good."

I ask Aldiss which authors, in the science-fiction field, he feels particularly close to.

"I think there are a lot of people for whom I feel—is 'comradeship' the word? Maybe it is. At the end of a long campaign you get to know your friends and the enemies, not that it's quite the end of the campaign, yet, by any manner of means. But let me list them. I suppose of course I have to start with Jimmy Ballard and Mike Moorcock; that's obviously the case. I always liked what Jimmy did, and we both started in the same little hole, in *New Worlds* when it was edited by Carnell. You could always *read* his stories, unlike some of the other stories in there.

"Further afield—well, the people that I got together in *Hell's Cartographers* [a collection edited by Aldiss, of essays by writers about their own work] were people that I had some feeling for. It was obviously a book that was never going to make money, so they were going to have to 'cooperate or else,' as van Vogt once said." Aldiss laughs happily. "So, Fred Pohl—I've known Fred for a long time—and Bob Silverberg, Damon Knight. Having behaved rather badly in Damon Knight's house, I feel an affection for him. And Alfie Bester. Those were people, I wanted to hear what they had to say. Fred Pohl, I think, takes the sort of view of science fiction that I do—he uses the freedom that success has given him to travel around a lot. He's interested in other parts of the world, as I am, and that seems to be such an obvious trait for a science-fiction writer to have. My God, you're interested in Martians, surely you're much more interested in the Malays? But my experience is that people don't feel like that, there's a lot of American writers who have never left the States, or they've just had a day-trip to Tijuana. Same sort of thing with British writers.

"One of the things I like about Ballard is that he can conjure up foreign backgrounds. This is, of course, a result of his experience in the Far East, and it stood him in good stead. One of the things I first liked about science fiction was that it did give me strange backgrounds; for instance, in the early work of Ray Bradbury. But after a time I realized he was really talking about things in his own backyard, and the novelty wears off. The same with Clifford Simak: I thought Simak's backgrounds were fantastic. But then it seemed to me that they were all the same and were actually his back yard, or front porch."

Aldiss himself started writing in the 1950s. Did he have specific ambitions, back then?

He thinks about it, but can't seem to decide. "Whatever I say is loaded and probably doesn't represent the truth anyway," he says. "I really can't remember; I think I was full of modesty and full of ambition at the same time. I'd wanted to be a poet, but then I'd started reading modern poetry, and decided, right, well, that was out. You know I was so lucky, that *Faber* [a British hardcover publisher] wrote to *me*, and asked me to write my first novel—extraordinary!—but perhaps that's why I've been so wayward ever since. Actually I would have liked to have written social comedy, and perhaps if Kingsley Amis hadn't been around just a few years earlier, I would have done that. My first book, *The Brightfount Diaries*, was social comedy; it had appeared in chunks in a periodical, and Faber wrote to me and said, 'Would you like to put these things together and make a book?' And within the next six weeks, six other publishers wrote to me with the same request. Amazing! Then after the first book, Faber said, 'What are you going to do for an encore?' and I said, 'Well, I also write science-fiction stories.' 'Oh, *good*!' they said, "*We're* science-fiction fans.' And that was true: Sir Geoffrey Faber, Ann Faber, Charles Montieth." Aldiss shakes his head and laughs at how easy it seems, in retrospect.

I ask him if he's happy, overall, about the way his career worked out.

He immediately looks evasive. "Beware the furies," he says. "I'm still working on my career. I think I've been very fortunate. I always have a sense of having escaped slavery. I spent ten years working in bookshops, before I could afford the price of petrol to drive away from that depressed area. Even before that, I had escaped from my father's loathsome gents' outfitters establishment, and I had escaped with one bound from my uncles' architecture firm. There was little that I was qualified to do, I wasn't even very good at digging roads. But I'd always had the urge to write, and I've been able to do it, now, securely, for, oh, however long it is. Twenty-five years? Twenty-one years? Been jolly lucky. And you know, I still enjoy it."

At the same time, of course, Aldiss has had his problems, especially in America, where some of his work has not sold well, and he remains vastly underrated.

"Well, it's true I've had troubles," he agrees, "but that's something to do with my rather cavalier attitude, I think. I've felt like this mainly with *The Malacia Tapestry*; before that, I felt it was all someone else's fault, and that's never a good thing to feel. If you're in there pitching, then it's your fault, ultimately, if things don't go well. I felt *The Malacia Tapestry* was a good book. It was published first of all in hardcover by Harper & Row. It didn't sell very well and no one would buy the paperback rights, until Ace Books picked it up, very cheaply. Well, it's done quite well through Ace, but there was a certain sense of déjà vu in being published by them again, where I'd begun twenty years before, and for about the same size of royalty advance, to be candid. You know, it's time to think again, when that happens. So in a certain sense I suppose I am, in rather a lazy way, reforming myself now. I've got a rather ambitious scheme on, for quite a hefty novel called *Heliconia*. I think that will be good, and this time I'm going to get a commitment from a publisher, get it laid on the production line, as it were, ahead of time. You have to work with the publishing system, not against it. In Britain I think it's still, rather pleasurably, a cottage industry. In the States publishing is mechanized. The message has got through to me, I think.

"Another problem has been that my science fiction is never involved with high technology. And that's something of the difference between the United States and Britain. Science fiction in America is much more involved with high technology, that's where the cutting edge is, and it's natural that that sort of fiction is always in demand, there, and always in supply. That I think is a positive point; the negative side is that the media have a great grip in the States, and so you get hogwash like *Star Trek*, with its bright—well, it's *not* very bright, actually—this tinsel view of the future, and the galaxy, which has to be optimistic. I did once manage to see an episode all the way through, and at the end Captain Kirk says to the—the chap with the ears—'Well, this proves that the galaxy's too small for white men and green men to fight one another,' and Spock nods and says, 'That's right,' and they clap each other on the shoulder, and up comes the music. Well, what Spock should have said was, 'Why the fuck shouldn't white men and green men fight together? Of course there's plenty of room.' Liberal platitudes do distress me. And yet I remember having this argument with some quite high-powered chaps, and they said, 'That's a very subversive point of view, you may think these are platitudes, but they actually do a lot of good.' But I still think that science fiction *should* be subversive, it shouldn't be in the game of consolations, it should shake people up, I suppose because that's what it did to me when I started reading it, and that was valuable. It should question things. I have to say, I owe a lot to John W. Campbell and his damned editorials in *Analog*. I *believe* that you should challenge everything, you know? Occasionally, in my more manic moods, I still carry that early Campbell banner: Science fiction should tell you things you don't want to know."

Does Aldiss feel that the American publishing scene is growing still more media-dominated, with little room for offbeat material?

"I think it's difficult to say whether it's getting worse. It seems worse, but perhaps if you came into it now you wouldn't see it that way. It's like everything else, when you've known it for some while, it seems worse. *London* seems to me worse than it was in the 1960s, but if I was discovering it now, I'd think it was a glorious place. All I can say is that I have produced some eccentric books, and somehow or other they have been published here and in the States—even my new collection of essays, *This World and Nearer Ones*, is going to be at least marginally published by St. Martin's Press. So, there's room for hope.

"You know, I have faith in doing what you think is best. Go down with all guns firing—maybe you won't go down at all. Also we have the very good example of John Wyndham. Whenever it was, 1952? Suddenly on the way to Damascus he saw the light and stopped being John Beynon Harris, a hack writing for American magazines, and decided that he would become John Wyndham, and write in an English style. It was actually rather a teacosy style, I know. But it was just amazing, the success he had with *The Day of the Triffids*. I knew him a bit, he used to come to the early meetings of the science-fiction luncheon club, in the days when I didn't dare to say a word to anyone. He was very popular. He would always rise and make the same speech, which was, 'Why do they call it science fiction? It's such a *nasty* name.' It was quite a long speech, and he would never suggest an alternative. He was a sort of instinctive writer, but he did convince everyone, I think, that you *could* write science fiction in an English idiom— whatever the hell that means, I'm not quite sure. It means, actually, rather a dated idiom, I think. The Wells tradition? Yes, but I believe that the ideas Wells had were important, whereas Wyndham's ideas weren't important. But his example was quite important."

Is Aldiss in favor of recent trends such as teaching science fiction in schools and colleges?

"What education should do, to my mind, is inculcate imagination, without which we all die. And imagination is something that you get pouring out of your ears if you read science fiction. It hits you, at the age of what—fifteen? Twelve? Eighteen? It blows your mind. If you aren't taught it, you'll still read it anyway, so it seems to me quite a good thing that it's on the curriculum.

"The bad side of this, I suppose, is obvious to everyone: you get a lot of academics who teach it and don't care about it. But why should they care about it in the way that you and I care about it? They haven't got that sort of commitment. I met someone who was to have taught a course on Dryden, but no one had enlisted in the Dryden course, so she was teaching Heinlein and van Vogt, poor lady. Well, I'm not sure whether I would want to read a lot of van Vogt *or* a lot of Dryden, but I can see the impulse that lies behind that sort of mischief.

"I can also see another mischief, in that it's led some science-fiction writers to tramp off on the university beat, giving lectures, and eventually writing . . . this is a fascinating phenomenon, you know, science fiction can do anything. To its detriment. We now have the science-fiction college-campus novel. The John Barths of our field. Someone like *Delaney*, you know. Very interesting!" There is a slightly wicked gleam in Aldiss's eye. "But I don't see that it does much *harm*, you know. If you look at it with wider perspective, you see that this is inevitably part of a process: Eventually I suppose science fiction will fossilize the way the modern novel has fossilized. At the same time, we're very aware about this business of fossilization, and formularization. Certainly when *New Worlds* appeared, with one bound, we were free, as it were. But I can also remember when this seemed to happen with the publication of *Fantasy and Science Fiction*, and *Galaxy*."

When Aldiss writes, does he have any specific idea of the audience he is writing for?

"I do recall thinking, when I began, that I would like to write for everyone, and not a narrow audience. It struck me, for instance, that half the population of these isles was female, and it would be rather nice, wouldn't it, if more women read science fiction. That was not actually a target, but it was an area in which I thought. I remember when I wrote *Non-Stop* [his first novel, retitled *Starship* in America] I was rather uncertain of my audience. I put in—whatever you call them—human touches, which I felt were often lacking in the science fiction of the time. And I wasn't sure how well they would go down, because I wasn't sure whether anyone but the science-fiction audience would read the damn book. You know I'm getting to that John Fowles stage where I'd like to rewrite *Non-Stop* with a preface that would be longer than the novel." He laughs. "But I think in a way it's an exemplar for much of my fiction since. The idea of people imprisoned by circumstances—in that case, a giant spaceship—has been one of my themes. I can't think why, really, because I don't regard myself as imprisoned by circumstances, but I think I did as a child, and you know you always draw on that reservoir of experience."

What has Aldiss been doing recently?

"I was Chairman of the Society of Authors, the year before last, and that actually occupied my whole year. I didn't do anything else except write *Pile*, which is an epic poem I wrote in a week. I was so involved with the Society of Authors, getting them unionized and doing various other good or bad things, that I was offered a place on the Literature Advisory Panel at the Arts Council of Great Britain. I decided that things couldn't be any worse, so I might as well do it. Now I'm coming to the end of my stint with them, and I'm rather disillusioned. There's nothing much you can do; you mainly seem to be okaying grants to a lot of people who don't work. They *don't work very hard*; you know, that's the damned answer, never mind whether they're good or not. And I don't much approve of that. Also I don't like the way in which there are assumptions at the Arts Council about everyone there being, if not able, prepared to distinguish between what is good and valuable and what isn't. That gets very boring. I tried to get an Arts Council grant for the world convention, you see; I thought that might be an interesting exercise. There were going to be 4,000 avid readers down there at Brighton—why not? Why not put some money up front, to be repaid later if the thing made a profit? I thought it would be a token of something or other, God knows what, or why one should care. And of course they wouldn't do it, the Arts Council said the machinery didn't exist. There were various difficulties; I don't know what the underlying assumptions were, but I didn't care for them, anyhow.

"My next novel to be published is in fact a contemporary novel, set in that somewhat mythical year, 1978, and it's due out early in 1980. It's very ambitious, it's called *Life in the West*, and I regard it as taking my science fiction a stage further. It's my Iris Murdoch, in a way, if you like. I put into an ordinary novel, or attempted to, the perspectives that I use in my science fiction, talking about today and seeing it as a period rather late on in the Byzantine II history of the West. I regard that as rather important—

you always do, when the things are in the works, you know. Terribly important. I shall be sad when, eventually, it appears and floats off into the haze of all the other books.

"I fancy people will find it pretentious. I'm rather concerned with this whole business of pretentiousness; I actually hate pretentiousness in others, and think it's a good subject for comedy. But I also think that because I'm so interested in it, I must be rather pretentious myself. I mean if you're interested in a subject, and knock it, that must mean you have an element of it in you.

"You can evade pretentiousness by using metaphor, in fiction. A lot of science fiction is metaphor: you can put up a grand picture, as it were, without being pretentious. You give the reader a chance to interpret the picture in his own way. That's one thing I like about science fiction, and perhaps it's what I *don't* like about the ordinary novel, which is pinned to realism, and therefore lacks the metaphorical quality that good science fiction has.

"You know, despite all its failures, science fiction is not myopic. It does try to see things in a wide-screen way. That's what you like about it. Christ, where else do you go? Perhaps that's why I seem mellower, these days. I have seen that there are other literary places to go. But I no longer think that they're much better."

(London, September 1979)

BIBLIOGRAPHICAL NOTES

Brian Aldiss's first science-fiction novel was *Non-Stop* (*Starship* in its American edition), originally published in England in 1958. It was an attempt to humanize the classic science-fiction idea, previously used by Heinlein et al., of a whole society enclosed in a vast spaceship on a voyage which will last many generations. *Non-Stop* is a book of vivid imagery and great compassion, though clearly an early work. *The Long Afternoon of Earth* (titled *Hothouse* in Britain) is a fantasy of the far future, with mankind reduced to primitivism, among giant vegetation. Built from interconnected short stories, the book won a Hugo award in 1962. *The Dark Light Years* (1964) describes mankind coming to terms with friendly aliens who are to us disgusting; a book for coprophiliacs. *Greybeard* (1964) is an underrated study of a world in which there are no more children. As the old folk die, so does the human race. *Report on Probability A* (1968) was Aldiss's first truly experimental story, or short novel, maddening or amusing, as you will, using surreal slow-motion prose whose vast detail produces a cumulative sense of disorientation. *Barefoot in the Head* (1969) is a sequence of stories set in a future Britain decimated by hallucinogenic weapons; the prose is correspondingly lyrical and awry. *Frankenstein Unbound* (1973) is a time-travel fantasy starring Mary Shelley. *The Malacia Tapestry* (1976) is a love story set in a mysterious, eternal, future city.

Self-Profile

Charles Platt is author of fifteen fiction and nonfiction books. He started writing full time after he dropped out of Cambridge University, where he had studied economics for a couple of semesters. He moved to London from the small, dull, British town where he had spent most of his childhood, began working for *New Worlds* magazine, and also played keyboards in various obscure rock groups for a couple of years.

He designed, production-managed, and edited *New Worlds* at various times, from 1965 through 1970. During this period he also wrote his first two novels: *Garbage World*, a slapstick science-fiction satire, and *The City Dwellers*, a neurotic view of future trends in British urban life.

Platt left England during 1970 and resettled in New York City. Here he wrote some undistinguished novels in order to finance an itinerant lifestyle, traveling all over America. Then in 1972 he was appointed consulting editor, specializing in science fiction, at Avon Books in New York. He compiled their "rediscovery" list of science-fiction classics, and persuaded them to publish a couple of new issues of *New Worlds* in book form. He resigned when Avon refused to buy Philip K. Dick's *Flow My Tears, The Policeman Said* because they disliked its title.

Platt spent some time writing outside of science fiction, producing a versatile assortment of books from *Outdoor Survival* (a guide for young people) to *Sweet Evil* (a fantasy of Mansonesque decadence). He was New York columnist for the *Los Angeles Free Press*, taught evening classes at two New York colleges, and even worked briefly as a magician.

He returned to the science-fiction field with *Twilight of the City*, a realistic view of the near future, very loosely based on his earlier *The City Dwellers*. It remains his most substantial work of fiction, notable for using economic theory as a way of building the future scenario.

Platt's greatest influences have been Alfred Bester, the great innovator of the 1950s, and J. G. Ballard, great innovator of the 1960s. Platt remains interested in most forms of experimentation in literature, and continues to play an active role in *New Worlds* magazine—in 1979 he financed, edited, and designed one issue himself and organized distribution of this and many back issues. He feels *New Worlds* is still the only truly radical, skeptical voice within the science-fiction field.

Platt maintains a small, modest apartment in London's Notting Hill area, a hippie haven during the late 1960s, now infiltrated by the upper-middle-classes. He also has a small, quaint apartment in Manhattan's West Village area. He travels between these beachheads by Laker Skytrain, while it lasts.

His recreations include urban bicycle riding, hobby-electronics, graphic design, and pursuit of those few decadent novelties which don't cost too much. He is 35, and divorced.

Platt's science-fiction criticism and commentaries have been published by *Harper's, Time Out, The Los Angeles Free Press, New Worlds, Ariel, Ad Astra, Gregg Press, Unearth, The Village Voice*, and small magazines such as *Foundation* and *Science Fiction Review*.

Appendix: Right of Reply

Inevitably, some of the people I have written about were critical of the way in which I described them. I have heeded quite a few of their comments, and have made small changes in the profiles, to correct factual inaccuracies or inaccurate preceptions. But in other instances I was not persuaded to change what I had written; instead, I prefer to give my interviewees "right of reply" here.

Robert Sheckley pointed out that the photograph of him used in this book, showing him with a moustache, is not of the *new* Sheckley, who is clean-shaven.

Edward Bryant, though basically pleased with his profile, complained that it made him sound a totally pathetic poverty case on the edge of starvation. "I shouldn't be surprised if good-hearted people start sending me canned goods after they read the piece," he commented. "A shame it'll be published in the fall of 1980 rather than now, when I could use the food."

Samuel Delany objected to my referring to his "academic habits of analyzing prose and speech." He pointed out that he has spent a total of only three-and-a-half terms, as teacher and student, in any academic surroundings. However, my own feeling is that one can exhibit academic habits without necessarily having put in a lot of time at college.

Barry Malzberg said, of his profile, "I don't like it particularly, but it's a fair representation. I don't like the self-importance (self-mockery is my *shtick*) . . . but then, I don't like my career."

Both Harlan Ellison and his assistant, Linda Steele, berated me at considerable length for my usage of the word "girl" in his profile, instead of the word "woman." The usage was, however, conscious and intentional in this instance.

Ian Watson argued rather forcibly that it was unfair to characterize him as an Oxford academic, because he hates Oxford and has now moved to a small village in a totally different part of the country.

John Brunner, responding to my slightly irreverent fantasy about him confronted by urban black militants, pointed out: "How many people do you know who've been invited to the Sunday Afternoon Blackening at the National Black Theatre in Harlem . . . or taken home for a soul-food supper in the Ninth Ward of New Orleans? Thought I might just mention that!"

Lastly, Brian Aldiss wanted to insert an apology for what might seem to have been an implied criticism of Iris Murdoch, whom he mentioned a couple of times during his interview. No criticism was, in fact, intended.